JAVA and the AS/400

Practical Examples Using VisualAge for Java

Daniel Darnell

A division of
DUKE COMMUNICATIONS INTERNATIONAL
221 East 29th Street • Loveland, Colorado 80538
(800) 621-1544 • (970) 663-4700 • www.29thstreetpress.com

Library of Congress Cataloging-in-Publication Data

Darnell, Daniel, 1968-
    Java and the AS/400 : practical examples using VisualAge for
Java / by Daniel Darnell.
    p. cm.
    Includes index.
    ISBN 1-58304-033-1 (pbk.)
    1. IBM AS/400 (Computer)—Programming. 2. Java (Computer program
language) 3. VisualAge. I. Title.
    QA76.8.I25919 D37 1999
    005.2'762—dc21
                                    99-6633
                                     CIP

Published by 29th Street Press
DUKE COMMUNICATIONS INTERNATIONAL
Loveland, Colorado

Copyright © 1999 by Daniel Darnell

This book was printed and bound in Canada.

ISBN 1-58304-033-1

2001 2000 1999 WL 10 9 8 7 6 5 4 3 2 1

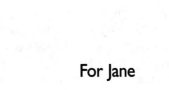

For Jane

ACKNOWLEDGEMENTS

Heartfelt thanks to my wife Jane and my daughter Emily for persevering during the months that I spent working almost every night and weekend to write and revise this book.

Thanks also to the folks at 29th Street Press: Editors Marion Agnew and Trish Faubion for their expert work creating a polished book from my manuscript; Angie Anderson for the production work; John Morris-Reihl who designed the cover, CD-ROM, and Web site; Tricia McConnell for approaching me with the idea for this book and encouraging me every step of the way.

Thanks to George Voutinas and Larry Schweyer at IBM for providing valuable feedback as a part of their technical edit. Thanks to Paul Conte for contributing his ideas to my original outline and for writing the Foreword. Thanks also to Dale Agger, Lori Piotrowski, and everyone at *NEWS/400* magazine.

I am grateful for the support that I have received from colleagues and from my employer. In particular, I want to thank Walt Rector, Larry Benning, Lynn Grotewold, Todd Mason, John Ellis, and Jerry Coston.

TABLE OF CONTENTS AT A GLANCE

Table of Contents

FOREWORD

Daniel Darnell will be familiar to readers of *NEWS/400* magazine and the
AS/400 e-Developer newsletter from his many Java contributions that have
appeared in those publications. Expanding his efforts, Daniel has put together
a book that aims right at the AS/400 programmer who needs to learn how to
develop Java applications for the AS/400. The book starts with a simple "Hello,
AS/400 Java World," in which Daniel explains how to create and run a Java
program using SEU and AS/400 commands. By the end of the first chapter,
you will have experienced Java programming on the AS/400. From here Daniel
hits about every important tool or technique a Java developer needs to get
AS/400-related applications running.

This book targets an AS/400 high-level language (HLL) programmer who
has learned the basics of Java programming but needs to know how to use
these to work with DB2/400 database files and other AS/400 resources.
Although Java is a platform-independent language, many aspects of developing
and deploying an application require some system-specific guidance. For
example, every platform has a slightly different way to set up the necessary
processes for Java's Remote Method Invocation (RMI). In addition, the AS/400
Toolbox for Java provides access to important AS/400-specific resources, such
as calling HLL programs. Finally, many AS/400 programmers will select
VisualAge for Java Enterprise Edition because of its specific AS/400 support
(e.g., remote debugging), and Daniel covers VisualAge for Java details
throughout the examples he presents.

This tight focus of the book lets Daniel concentrate on the details most
useful to the target audience. I think you will appreciate that Daniel didn't
attempt the "galactic Java book" by adding AS/400 and Java tutorials or cov-
ering multiple IDEs. Even with the book's focus, programmers from other platforms, or who use other IDEs, will still find lots of useful information about
AS/400 Java programming. And, the examples and discussions are kept simple
so even "newbie" Java programmers should be able to follow them without
much difficulty.

By not taking up space with material that's well-covered in other books,
Daniel was able to include essential AS/400 topics related to Java, even if they
aren't considered "Java" facilities or tools. He offers great assistance working
with the AS/400's Integrated File System (IFS) and delves into the QShell environment in depth. Knowledge of both AS/400 features is essential to AS/400
Java programming.

The technical content that Daniel has produced is exceptional, but the
book's greatest strength is that Daniel writes from experience. He was an RPG
programmer on the AS/400 who had to learn Java, the VisualAge for Java IDE,
and how to create and deploy *AS/400* Java applications that *really work.* His

writing conveys just what many AS/400 programmers want — a peer who has successfully made it through all this learning process and can explain clearly what those who follow behind should do.

I can't let this opportunity go by without saying what a fine person Daniel is and how enjoyable it has been to get to know and work with him over the past couple of years. I'll treasure both Daniel's writing and his friendship for many years.

Paul Conte
President, Picante Software, Inc.

PREFACE

Exciting changes are happening in the AS/400 world and some of the most exciting involve the Java language. Beginning with OS/400 Version 4, Release 2, the AS/400 has a full-fledged Java Virtual Machine (JVM) built right into it. Even better, IBM has chosen to make the JVM a no-charge feature of the operating system. This fact, coupled with the low cost of development tools, makes the total cost of entry for Java development on the AS/400 minimal.

This is not a book about Java theory or the future of Java, nor is it designed to teach you the Java language. You should spend at least two to six months working with Java before you use this text to tackle Java on the AS/400. That said, I do believe that this book should provide some aid as a secondary reference for those of you just starting out.

As an AS/400 software developer, you can't afford to ignore Java, but you may be wondering just how Java fits in with your legacy applications. Java is a very recent arrival on the AS/400, and it may be unclear to you how the implementation of Java differs from other languages, such as RPG and Cobol. You may also be concerned that everything you know about the AS/400 and programming languages might not transfer to Java. This book answers your questions by putting at your fingertips a practical guide to Java on the AS/400. In this book you work through application examples to learn the techniques and technologies applicable today to AS/400 software development in Java.

Chapter 1

Hello, AS/400 Java World!

In this chapter, you get off to a running start by looking at a start-to-finish example of a Java program created, compiled, and executed on the AS/400. You use nearly all of the AS/400's Java features, although thorough exploration of these features is postponed until later chapters. If the Java language is new to you, or if you have limited practical experience with Java, the Java 101 section of this chapter gives you a quick refresher on the essential concepts.

THE CUSTOMER CLASS

As you begin to explore the AS/400's Java implementation, your traveling companion is the Customer class shown in Figure 1.1.

FIGURE 1.1
Customer Class Source Code

```
/**
 *   The Customer class defines customer contact information and provides
 *   functionality for formatting mailing labels.
 */
public class Customer {

    private int custID = 0; // Customer identifier
    private String custName = null; // Full customer name (e.g. "John Smith")
    private String custStreet = null; // Customer street address
    private String custCityStateZip = null; // Customer city, state and zip

    private static int lastCustID = 10000; // Last customer ID assigned
/*
 * The default constructor is used to create a customer object without
 * specific contact information.
 */
public Customer() {
    this("No Name", "No Street Address", "No City, State, Zip");
}
/*
 * This constructor is used to create a customer object with complete
 * contact information.
 */
public Customer (String name, String street, String cityStateZip) {
    custName = name;
    custStreet = street;
    custCityStateZip = cityStateZip;

    custID = ++lastCustID;
}
```

continued

FIGURE **1.1** *CONTINUED*

```
/*
 * Returns customer contact information in mailing label format.
 */
public String getMailingLabel() {
    return custName + "\n" + custStreet + "\n" + custCityStateZip + "\nID:" +
custID;
}
/*
 * For testing purposes, creates customer objects and prints mailing
 * labels for each.
 */
public static void main(java.lang.String[] args) {

    Customer custArray[] = new Customer[5];

    custArray[0] = new Customer("Dan Darnell",
        "111 Maple Street", "Little Rock, AR 72201");
    custArray[1] = new Customer("John Smith",
        "12 Oak Drive", "Little Rock, AR 72202");
    custArray[2] = new Customer("Bill Jones",
        "115 Willow Way", "Little Rock, AR 72201");
    custArray[3] = new Customer();
    custArray[4] = new Customer("Jane Gibson",
        "1741 Pine Place", "Little Rock, AR 72202");

    for(int i = 0; i < custArray.length; i++)
    {
        System.out.println(custArray[i].getMailingLabel());
        System.out.println();
    }

}
}
```

We build on the Customer class in later chapters, but for now it serves simply as a way to track customer contact information such as any business might keep. Each customer has an identification number, a name, and an address. The Customer class has built-in functionality to perform a small-scale self-test — the class's **main** method creates sample customer objects and prints mailing labels.

For a more detailed explanation of the Customer class and a brief Java fundamentals refresher, see "Java 101" later in this chapter.

NOTE: You can find all the software in this book on the companion CD or on the Web at www.29thStreetPress.com/java400.

Nickel Tour

It takes a few steps to make the Customer class run on the AS/400. First you must enter the Java source code into a source member. This step is probably familiar to you, because it is the starting point for almost all languages on the AS/400. The next step probably isn't as familiar. Before you can compile the Customer class, you have to move it to a directory in the Integrated File System (IFS). This chapter won't delve into the reasons behind this step, but rest assured, you learn all about it in Chapter 3. After moving the source code to the IFS, you can compile it and then run the compiled program. These steps are not difficult, but they do take some practice. Are you ready to begin?

Here is a list of the steps you must perform to create the Customer class:

1. Create a library and a source physical file.
2. Create and edit a source member using Source Entry Utility (SEU).
3. Type the Customer source code and save it.
4. Create a directory in the IFS.
5. Copy the source member to the IFS directory.

Then, to run the Customer class, you must perform these steps:

1. Start the QShell Interpreter.
2. Compile the Customer source code.
3. Execute Customer class.

Finally, as an additional exercise, you can

1. Exit the QShell Interpreter.
2. Create a native, optimized executable for the Customer class.
3. Execute the optimized Customer class.

Create and Compile Customer Source

Let's dive right in by going to an AS/400 command prompt and creating a library.

```
CRTLIB LIB(EXAMPLES)
```

Now create a source physical file inside the library.

```
CRTSRCPF FILE(EXAMPLES/QJVASRC) RCDLEN(112) +
        TEXT('Java source')
```

You're ready to start SEU and type the Customer Java program.

```
STRSEU SRCFILE(EXAMPLES/QJVASRC) SRCMBR(CUSTOMER) TYPE(TXT) +
        TEXT('Customer class Java source')
```

Type the source code for the Customer class as it appears in Figure 1.1 into the source member. Java is a free-format language, so an extra space or blank line here and there normally won't hurt anything. Do make sure that you don't leave out any parentheses or braces; they're important. Also, Java is case sensitive. Unless you strictly follow the changes between upper and lower case in the source code, you will get compile errors. SEU is not Java-aware and is therefore incapable of catching syntax and other errors for you. When you're done typing, save the source member.

NOTE: Advanced readers can copy source code for the Customer class directly to the IFS from the CD-ROM accompanying this book.

Next, you must create a directory in the IFS and copy the source member into it. Back at the AS/400 command line, type the following Make Directory command:

```
MD DIR('/myjava')
```

This command creates a directory called myjava in the root file system of the IFS. Now you can copy the Customer source member to this directory.

```
CPYTOSTMF FROMMBR('/QSYS.LIB/EXAMPLES.LIB/QJVASRC.FILE/CUSTOMER.MBR') +
          TOSTMF('/myjava/Customer.java')                              +
          STMFCODPAG(819)
```

This Copy to Stream File command takes the Customer source member and copies it to a file called Customer.java in the myjava directory. The source member is in EBCDIC, but if you were to look at the Customer.java file with a text editor like Windows Notepad, you would see that the Copy command has translated the file to ASCII format.

NOTE: In V4R2, it is necessary to explicitly specify a code page on the STMFCODPAG parameter of the CPYTOSTMF command for translation to ASCII. Code page 819 is normally used for this purpose.

In V4R3, the *PCASCII special value was added as an option on the STMFCODPAG parameter. In V4R3, you can use a command such as the following to copy a source member to a file and have it translated from EBCDIC to ASCII.

```
CPYTOSTMF FROMMBR('/QSYS.LIB/EXAMPLES.LIB/QJVASRC.FILE/CUSTOMER.MBR') +
          TOSTMF('/myjava/Customer.java') STMFCODPAG(*PCASCII)
```

EXECUTING THE CUSTOMER CLASS

So far you have been using common AS/400 commands — no surprises there. Now you are going to enter a world new to the AS/400, the world of the Unix shell. A shell in Unix provides a protected environment for entering commands and running programs. IBM's implementation of a Unix shell on the AS/400, called Qshell, is closely tied to the AS/400's Java support. For this reason, Chapter 4 looks at QShell in depth.

Your next two tasks, compiling and executing the Customer class, are both accomplished from within QShell. You start QShell with the following simple command.

```
QSH
```

Your display should look like the one shown in Figure 1.2.

FIGURE 1.2

QShell Interpreter Command Entry Screen

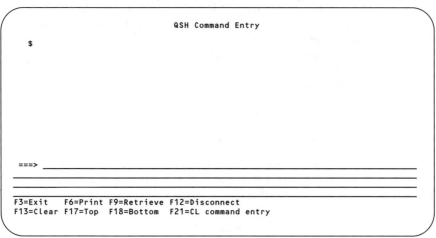

```
                          QSH Command Entry

   $




   ===> _____
        _____
        _____
   F3=Exit    F6=Print F9=Retrieve F12=Disconnect
   F13=Clear F17=Top   F18=Bottom  F21=CL command entry
```

Don't be fooled into thinking that this is a normal AS/400 command line. From
this command prompt, you can use only the commands defined to QShell. Also,
unlike the AS/400 command line, both commands and command parameters
are case-sensitive. The first command that you want to try is one to compile
your Java program.

```
javac /myjava/Customer.java
```

Remember that QShell makes a distinction between the javac and JAVAC
commands. Often, if you receive an error message such as "Error found searching
for command JAVAC," correcting it is simply a matter of going back and
checking carefully the required case of the command and command parameters.

It is somewhat annoying, but you do not get a completion message when
the Customer class compiles successfully. When the display comes back with
no messages except >>>, that is your indication that the command executed
successfully — in this case, the compile command was successful. A normal
compile creates an executable Java bytecode file with the name Customer.class
in the same IFS directory as your Customer.java source code. Bytecodes are the
symbolic instructions created from your source code by a compiler for execution
in a Java Virtual Machine.

If the Customer class does not compile, your display lists the compile errors.
You can page up to see messages if they fill more than one screen. To correct
errors in your Customer class source code, exit QShell and return to a normal
AS/400 command prompt by pressing F3 (Exit). Go back into your source
member with SEU, check your typing, correct any errors, copy the source
member back to the IFS, and then return to QShell to attempt another compile.

> **CAUTION: If you modify the Customer source member to correct compile errors, be sure to specify the file replacement option when you copy it back to the IFS. On the CPYTOSTMF command specify *REPLACE on the STMFOPT parameter. If you fail to specify the file replacement option, a "file exists" message will display and you can try the command again using the appropriate option.**

If the Customer class compiled successfully, you are now ready to execute it. Still in QShell, type the following command to invoke the AS/400's Java Virtual Machine for the Customer class.

```
java -classpath /myjava Customer
```

After the Customer class runs, your display should look like the one in Figure 1.3. You can page up to see the sample customers that scrolled off the display.

FIGURE 1.3
Customer Class After Execution

```
                          QSH Command Entry

    Little Rock, AR 72201
    ID:10003

    No Name
    No Street Address
    No City, State, Zip
    ID:10004

    Jane Gibson
    1741 Pine Place
    Little Rock, AR 72202
    ID:10005

    >>>$

 ===> _____
      _____
      _____

 F3=Exit    F6=Print F9=Retrieve F12=Disconnect
 F13=Clear F17=Top   F18=Bottom   F21=CL command entry
```

If you get an error message, such as "Unable to find class Customer," double-check the command and parameters, paying particular attention to case and spacing. If you are still unable to execute the program, try the following Work with Object Links command to view the files in the IFS directory.

```
WRKLNK OBJ('/myjava/*')
```

You should see the Customer.java and Customer.class files. If not, repeat the steps to copy the source member to the IFS and compile it, making sure that no errors occur along the way.

That's it! You've done the hard part, running your first AS/400 Java program. Next, you are going to optimize your compiled program and then you'll run it again, this time from an AS/400 command line.

Optimize and Run Again

Exit QShell and return to the AS/400 command line by pressing F3 (Exit). Now take your previously compiled Customer class and optimize it with the following Create Java Program command.

```
CRTJVAPGM CLSF('/myjava/Customer.class') OPTIMIZE(40)
```

Unlike other create program commands you might be used to (e.g., Create RPG Program), the Create Java Program command does not operate against source code. This command takes an already compiled Java bytecode file and optimizes it in place. This feature is one of the most remarkable and innovative aspects of the AS/400's Java implementation and you'll learn all about it in subsequent chapters.

To make sure the optimization worked, try the following Display Java Program command.

```
DSPJVAPGM CLSF('/myjava/Customer.class')
```

You should see the display shown in Figure 1.4.

FIGURE 1.4
Display Java Program Screen

```
                    Display Java Program Information
 Class file name . . . . . . . . . . . . . :   /myjava/Customer.class
 Owner  . . . . . . . . . . . . . . . . . :   DAN


 Java program creation information:
   Class file change date/time  . . . . . . . . . :   07/03/99  12:38:16
   Java program creation date/time  . . . . . . . :   07/03/99  12:38:40
   Java program current . . . . . . . . . . . . . :   *YES
   Optimization . . . . . . . . . . . . . . . . . :   40
   Enable performance collection  . . . . . . . . :   *NONE
   Coded character set identifier . . . . . . . . :   65535
 Java program statistics:
   Java program size  . . . . . . . . . . . . . . :   28672
   Java program state . . . . . . . . . . . . . . :   *USER
   Java program domain  . . . . . . . . . . . . . :   *USER
                                                                   Bottom
 Press Enter to continue.

 F3=Exit   F12=Cancel
 (C) COPYRIGHT IBM CORP. 1998, 1998.
```

In addition to change date and time, creation date and time, and program statistics, you can see that the optimization level of the class file is now 40, just like you told it to be on the CRTJVAPGM command.

Only one thing is left to do on this whirlwind tour of AS/400 Java — execute the optimized version of your Customer class. Do so from an AS/400 command line with the following command.

```
JAVA CLASS(Customer) CLASSPATH('/myjava')
```

You should see a decent performance improvement when you run optimized Java code. The downside is that optimized code can't always be debugged. You'll learn the optimization levels and what they mean in Chapter 3.

If the steps required to edit a source member, get it to the IFS, and compile it seem a little cumbersome, don't worry. The next chapter shows you a more practical way to create and work with your Java applications.

JAVA 101

Hundreds of books deal with the Java programming language and many of them do an admirable job of explaining the basics. Because this material is covered so well and so extensively in other texts, we'll just hit the high points of the Customer class's program structure.

Class Definition

Classes are the basic building blocks of Java applications. With the exception of a few primitive data types (like int, the integer data type), everything in Java is defined as a class. Classes can be simple, like the Customer class, or they can be extended and combined using object-oriented design techniques. Once you get the hang of it, programming with an object-oriented language like Java is less error prone than programming in a procedural language like RPG or Cobol.

Unfortunately, many of the skills developed by a procedural programmer don't transfer directly to object-oriented programming. For this reason, if you don't have a solid foundation in object-oriented analysis and design, you should consider spending at least as much time in this area of study as in your study of Java — at least until you get the hang of thinking in terms of objects.

A class definition serves as a template for the creation of objects. The Customer class in Figure 1.1 is a template for the creation of any number of customer objects. Each object created from the class template has its own data in the form of variables. This data is operated on using the methods defined by the class. Methods are similar to functions in C and subprocedures in RPG IV.

The Customer class begins with the following statement:

```
public class Customer {
```

This statement defines the class as publicly accessible and gives it a name. When a class is public, other classes can use it, no matter what package they are in.

Non-public classes can be used only by other classes in the same package. The class definition continues until the final closing brace in the source file.

A package is a collection of classes, normally classes with a related purpose. The Java language and Application Programming Interface (API) are defined in packages such as java.lang, java.io, and java.net. You might choose to use packages to collect related classes of an application. For example, you might place your order-entry and accounts-payable applications in separate packages. Because packages can complicate program compilation, we purposely avoid them in this book's early examples.

Variables

Just after the Customer class's class definition, variables are defined. Technically, variables don't have to be defined at the beginning of a class. Some would even say that object-oriented programming theory demands that variables come at the end. After all, in a good object-oriented design, data is hidden except to the class itself, and the outside world should be looking for your method definitions, not your variables. In the end, personal preference determines where you define the variables or, as is often the case, the development tool you use imposes a specific place for the definition.

```
private int custID = 0;
private String custName = null;

private static int lastCustID = 10000;
```

Two kinds of variables are defined in the Customer class. Both custID and custName are the first kind, instance variables. Every customer object that is instantiated carries its own custID and custName. The second kind of variable, lastCustID, is a class variable, as indicated by the "static" modifier. The variable lastCustID is accessible to all customer objects but it is a part of the class, not of individual object instances.

All the variables defined by the Customer class carry the "private" modifier, which indicates that they cannot be modified directly by anything outside this class. This setup is in keeping with the object-oriented design concept of encapsulation (i.e., self-containment). As soon as you make a variable public, your class is no longer self-contained, encapsulation is broken, and you've obviated one of the primary benefits of object orientation.

For in-between levels of access protection, you can use the "protected" modifier and a default, which carries no modifier. A variable with the protected modifier can be modified by other classes in the same package and by subclasses of the class it is defined in, even if the subclass is in another package. If you leave off the modifier entirely, the default access is implied and the variable is accessible only to other classes in the same package.

It isn't necessarily wrong to declare a variable with protected or default access. At times in an object-oriented design, you need a variable to be accessible to other, closely related classes (e.g., a subclass or another class in the same package). Planned, limited accessibility, determined by a particular design, is very different from public accessibility where your variables can be directly modified by anyone, potentially in a way you don't anticipate.

All variables in Java are defined with a data type. Both custID and lastCustID are defined as the *int* primitive data type, while the custName variable is a *String* class type. The major difference between the primitive data types and a class type is that primitive variables hold actual values (e.g., an integer type can hold values ranging from -2,147,483,648 to 2,147,483,647), while a class type is a reference to an object. In the case of custName, the value of the variable when it is defined is null, indicating that it does not yet refer to a String object. The variables custID and lastCustID cannot be null — they are not object references — so they are set to initial values of 0 and 10000, respectively. Setting lastCustID initialization at a value of 10000 isn't magic; 10000 is just the beginning number arbitrarily chosen for identifiers assigned to customer objects.

Methods

Just as variables define the data of a class, methods define the functionality. Moreover, in a good object-oriented design, method calls are the only way that other classes can manipulate the data in an object of your class type. A method in Java has a signature defining its name, input parameters, and return value. It is possible to have more than one method in Java with the same name as long as the input parameters are different. Different return values are not enough to uniquely identify methods; input parameters are the primary distinguishing feature of like-named methods.

The Customer class in Figure 1.1 has four methods. These are their signatures:

```
public Customer ()
public Customer (String, String, String)
public String getMailingLabel()
public static void main(String[])
```

The first two methods are special types of Java methods called *constructors*. Constructors are executed by the Java runtime when an object is instantiated. The first Customer class constructor accepts no parameters and, consequently, creates a customer object with a customer identifier but no name and address information. The second constructor requires you to provide a customer's information, which then becomes a part of the customer object.

You might find the first constructor's code somewhat confusing:

```
public Customer () {
  this("No Name", "No Street Address",
      "No City, State, Zip");
}
```

Simply stated, this code calls the second constructor and passes it parameter data to initialize the customer object with valid, albeit useless, information.

The code for the second constructor is more meaningful:

```
public Customer (String name, String street,
     String cityStateZip) {
          custName = name;
          custStreet = street;
          custCityStateZip = cityStateZip;

          custID = ++lastCustID;
}
```

This code takes the input parameters to the constructor and retains them as the object's instance variables. The final statement increments the identifier used by the last customer object created and assigns it to the new customer object. The first constructor is included in the Customer class only to serve as a sort of default; it has limited practical value. To create meaningful customer objects, the second constructor is obviously the one you want to use.

The **getMailingLabel** method returns a customer's contact information formatted as a mailing label. This method is an instance method, which means that it is defined to operate on a particular object's instance variables. Contrast this method with the **main** method. The **main** method is defined as static, which makes it a class method. Just like the lastCustID class variable, the **main** method is a part of the class definition, not a part of individual customer objects. A static method can operate only on class variables of its class, not on its instance variables.

The **getMailingLabel** method is one line of executable code.

```
public String getMailingLabel() {
     return custName + "\n" + custStreet + "\n" + custCityStateZip
     + "\nID:" + custID;
}
```

In the return statement, a string is constructed and returned to the method's caller. The string contains the customer contact information and customer identifier with linefeeds ("\n") inserted for formatting purposes.

The **main** method, when coded with the signature used here, has a special purpose. It is the common entry point for all Java classes that execute as applications. The Customer class's **main** method is used just to test the class; it doesn't add functionality to customer objects, nor does it provide real application value.

As you can see in the following code, the code in the **main** method begins by instantiating an array to hold five customer objects. Next, five customer objects are instantiated and stored in the array. Finally, a For loop prints sample mailing labels by executing the **getMailingLabel** method on each of the five customer objects and routing the results to the default output device.

```
     public static void main(java.lang.String[] args) {

          Customer custArray[] = new Customer[5];
```

```
custArray[0] = new Customer("Dan Darnell",
    "111 Maple Street", "Little Rock, AR 72201");
custArray[1] = new Customer("John Smith",
    "12 Oak Drive", "Little Rock, AR 72202");
custArray[2] = new Customer("Bill Jones",
    "115 Willow Way", "Little Rock, AR 72201");
custArray[3] = new Customer();
custArray[4] = new Customer("Jane Gibson",
    "1741 Pine Place", "Little Rock, AR 72202");

for(int i = 0; i < custArray.length; i++)
{
    System.out.println(custArray[i].getMailingLabel());
    System.out.println();
}
}
```

All four of the Customer class's methods use the public modifier in their signatures. This modifier makes these methods visible to other classes that might wish to use the methods. You have several options for method access modifiers, just as you do for variable access modifiers. It is not bad form to make methods public, as long as they are intended for public use. However, any methods of a class that implement internal functionality should probably be coded private.

Comments

You can mark comments in Java in three ways. The first method is commonly used to insert a multiline comment in a class. It begins with /* and continues, over multiple lines if necessary, until you code a */.

The second comment style is much like the first except that is begins with /** and ends with */. This comment can also be continued over multiple lines if necessary. This style of comment is used to create Web browser-based or hardcopy documentation when used with a tool such as javadoc, provided by Sun Microsystems in their Java Development Kit.

A third comment style begins with // and continues to the end of a line. This style of comment is often used on the same line as a variable declaration or some executable code.

Here are examples of the three comment styles as used in the Customer class.

```
/*
 * The default constructor is used to create a
 * customer object without specific contact information.
 */

/**
 *  The Customer class defines customer contact
 *  information and provides functionality for
 *  formatting mailing labels.
 */

private int custID = 0; // Customer identifier
```

Chapter 2

Products and Tools

In Chapter 1 you saw the AS/400's Java support in action. In this chapter, you take a peek at the product behind that support and learn more about its features. You also look at other products and tools that are indispensable to Java development on the AS/400. At the end of this chapter, you revisit the Customer class and, using IBM's VisualAge for Java, put it to work in a real application.

AS/400 DEVELOPER KIT FOR JAVA

Java is made available on the AS/400 through an IBM product called the AS/400 Developer Kit for Java (LPP 5769-JV1), or ADK for short. The ADK is a Licensed Program Product and, starting with V4R2, is available at no charge. At first blush, the ADK might seem like a strange bedfellow for the AS/400 — a box with deep ties to the procedural RPG and Cobol languages. If you have wondered how a modern language like Java fits in with the AS/400's architecture, you aren't the first. Happily, the fit is a good one, due in no small part to the flexibility of the AS/400.

You might know that the AS/400 is designed around a Technology Independent Machine Interface (TIMI). The TIMI protects OS/400 by acting as a layer between it and underlying hardware. With the TIMI, IBM can slide new hardware technology beneath OS/400 without rewriting the operating system.

The TIMI also provides a direct benefit to you: Your applications, like OS/400, ride above the TIMI and are ignorant of hardware implementations. Therefore, you don't have to recompile your programs, even when the hardware changes. If you moved from the AS/400's older CISC hardware technology to the new RISC technology, you saw this benefit in action. Your applications were converted for you internally from CISC to RISC, without recompilation.

If you think about it, there is a striking similarity between the AS/400's TIMI and the concept of a Java Virtual Machine (JVM). A JVM is also designed to provide a layer of abstraction between software and underlying hardware. After you compile a Java program, you can execute the compiled file of byte-codes on any platform with a compatible JVM. No recompilation is necessary. We who use the AS/400 have been running a virtual machine since the beginning, so it is no wonder that IBM has been able to implement Java on the AS/400 in record time. IBM has had a lot of practice in this area; it's what the architecture of the AS/400 is all about!

The rest of this section discusses individual aspects of the ADK and its implementation, including the JVM, Java Database Connectivity (JDBC), and System Debugger.

Java Virtual Machine

An illustration might help you see where the JVM fits into the AS/400 architecture. Figure 2.1 shows the architecture of the AS/400 with a JVM. Notice that the JVM is not above the TIMI with OS/400, ILE programs, and Java programs. The AS/400's JVM is below the TIMI, part of the System Licensed Internal Code (SLIC), talking directly to the hardware.

FIGURE 2.1
AS/400 Architecture with JVM

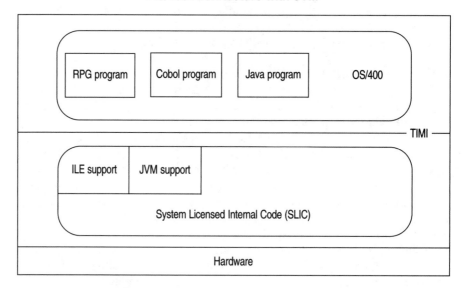

This design has two major implications. First, if the AS/400 changes hardware technology again, like the change from CISC to RISC, the JVM will almost certainly require rewriting. This isn't necessarily bad; it's just a fact. The second implication is undeniably good. By placing the JVM below the TIMI and directly on top of the hardware, IBM has made it possible for Java's performance to be out of this world.

You know that the JVM is responsible for executing Java programs and that Java programs are platform independent. The AS/400 JVM is compatible with Sun Microsystems' JDK 1.1.6. IBM has the mechanism in place to upgrade the JVM between OS/400 releases — the Program Temporary Fix (PTF). This ability is crucial in the world of Java, where language updates come rapidly.

GARBAGE COLLECTOR

One feature of the AS/400's JVM not found on any other platform is a scaleable garbage collector. Every JVM supports garbage collection, which is the process

JDK RELEASE LEVELS

When V4R2 shipped, the JDK release level of the AS/400 JVM was 1.1.4. A PTF is available to bring the JDK in V4R2 up to the JDK 1.1.6 release level. The PTF number is SF49635 for product 5769-JV1 (AS/400 Developer Kit for Java). V4R3 shipped with the JDK at release level 1.1.6. You can search the technical information database on the IBM AS/400 Worldwide Technical Support Web site (http://as400service.rochester.ibm.com) to determine whether a more recent JDK update is available.

of releasing storage back to the operating system when a Java program no longer needs it. For example, an application may create an object and then discard it. In some languages, your applications are responsible for explicitly releasing unused storage back to the operating system. In Java, the JVM detects when objects are no longer referred to by your applications and releases storage automatically.

This process works reasonably well on a small platform like a PC, but IBM found that the standard garbage collection mechanism in Java performed horribly on a larger scale. It is relatively time-consuming for the garbage collector to locate and dispose of unused objects. When the number of objects in a system scales from hundreds to thousands or even millions, garbage collection becomes a serious performance issue. The JVM on the AS/400 addresses performance with pioneering technology in its garbage collection mechanism to scale reliably as the number of objects in a JVM grows exponentially.

THREADS

The AS/400's JVM provides full support for multithreaded Java applications. The advantage of using threads is the low overhead incurred by the operating system when starting and switching between them, as compared to starting and multitasking standalone jobs. The disadvantage of multithreaded programs is that they are often complex and are inherently more difficult to debug. For an explanation of the relationship between threads and jobs, see "Jobs and Threads."

CLASS VERIFIER

Bytecode verification is a way for the JVM to ensure that only "legal" bytecodes are contained in a class file and that the bytecodes manipulate the system in an acceptable manner. The AS/400's JVM performs bytecode verification on every class file it executes — not all JVMs do — which makes for a great security feature. Without verification, rogue programs or viruses could attempt to corrupt memory and generally wreak havoc in the JVM.

JOBS AND THREADS

On the AS/400 we are all familiar with jobs — interactive jobs, batch jobs, system jobs, etc. In some ways, jobs are very simple. A simple Submit Job command starts a job and a simple End Job terminates one. Jobs can also be very complex, involving subsystems, job queues, routing entries, and classes of work. We deal with these issues when we learn to manipulate jobs for the best performance and the most efficient utilization of system resources.

Because threads are a recent addition to the AS/400, you might not know much about them. A thread is a subprocess within the larger process defined as a job. In other words, a thread can't exist on its own; it is always contained within a job. Conversely, every AS/400 job has at least one thread but may have many, many more. Threads share most of the resources allocated to their parent job but carry some attributes of their own, such as a run priority. A thread's run priority is used when the system is doling out processor time.

Threads also retain separate call stacks. This gets to the heart of what threads are all about — executing separate code paths within a single job. To really use the threading support in OS/400, you need a multithreaded language like Java. Every Java application has a main thread, but applications often create additional threads to perform actions of variable duration. When an action completes, its associated thread is destroyed, but the main thread keeps going.

An example of a multithreaded application is a TCP/IP server program that listens on a socket for client connections in its main thread. Each time a client request comes into the server, a new thread is started to handle communications with that client. After the new thread is spawned, the server can go back to waiting in the main thread for more client connection requests. A single server job might have a hundred threads actively talking to clients and still be waiting to take on more. As each client disconnects from the server, the thread handling that client is destroyed.

In many ways, threads came in and quietly took over the way jobs work on the AS/400. It's a testament to the engineers at IBM that most people didn't even notice. One thing is for sure — you can't avoid threads on the AS/400 any longer. Languages such as Java can't live without them, and it won't be long before they make their way into RPG and Cobol.

TRANSFORMER

Another pioneering technology delivered with the ADK is the Java bytecode Transformer. This mechanism takes normal Java bytecodes and translates or transforms them into instructions that can be executed directly by the AS/400's hardware. The transformation can be done on the fly when a Java class executes, or you can transform a class before running it. The Transformer is capable of producing optimized output. In Chapter 1, when you executed the Create Java

Program command on the Customer class, you were using the Transformer to create an optimized executable.

Native JDBC Driver

A standard part of Java is the Java Database Connectivity (JBDC) API, which allows access to database data through a Structured Query Language (SQL) interface. Several types of JDBC drivers are on the market, and each has a different level of database support and integration with Java.

The ADK includes a native JDBC driver for access to DB2/400. The goal of a native JDBC driver is to give applications the fastest possible access to the database. Contrast the native driver with the JDBC-ODBC bridge that comes with Sun Microsystems' JDK. The bridge gives client workstations access to any ODBC-compatible database (including DB2/400). The downside is that all Java calls made to JDBC functions must first be interpreted to ODBC calls and must pass through middleware on the client before reaching the host database. The obvious result is slower performance than that of a native driver.

Native drivers are also better suited to take advantage of database features than are more generic bridge drivers. For example, the JDBC-ODBC bridge uses a lowest common denominator approach to field access. Columns within a JDBC Record Set can be retrieved only once and only in the same order in which they are defined in the database table. The bridge is forced to impose this limitation because it is a defined limitation of ODBC. The native JDBC driver does not impose this limitation because it isn't a requirement for DB2/400.

QShell Environment

As mentioned in Chapter 1, the Unix-like shell on the AS/400, QShell, is closely allied with Java. Two products make up the full QShell environment — the QShell Interpreter and the QShell Utilities. The QShell Interpreter is option 30 of OS/400 (LPP 5769-SS1). The QShell Utilities for AS/400 (5799-XEH) are available as a separate PRPQ.

The QShell Interpreter provides an environment for running multithreaded applications and has a basic set of built-in utilities, including commands to change working directories in the IFS and to compile Java programs. The QShell Utilities are more extensive; they include a full set of commands for working with the IFS. The QShell Utilities are nice but not essential to running Java on your AS/400.

Native Methods

The ADK includes support for invoking C functions contained in service program modules. The Java Native Interface (JNI) defined by Sun Microsystems is the mechanism used on the AS/400 for native method calls.

You might want to use native method calls to take advantage of existing C libraries or to execute C functions, which, in turn, execute system APIs.

Otherwise, there isn't a particularly compelling reason to use JNI on the AS/400. It's a mistake to think that native method calls are a fast way to access AS/400 resources. Because the JVM resides below the TIMI and native methods originate in the layer above, native calls are not speed demons.

Another downside to using JNI on the AS/400 is that C is the only language supported, and C programming skill is rare among AS/400 programmers. RPG and Cobol are not supported for JNI because they are not "thread safe" — programs written in these languages are not capable of protecting their variables and properly avoiding certain types of locks. A Java program that tried to execute an RPG subprocedure directly could trample on data made by other Java calls to the same subprocedure. This conflict is also possible if you execute an RPG or Cobol program out of a C function invoked with JNI.

IBM is working quickly to address the thread safety of RPG and Cobol and will then make these languages work more closely with Java. Even taking into account the performance issues surrounding native method calls, it will be nice to leverage legacy code written in languages other than C.

The alternatives to native method calls are program calls using the AS/400 Toolbox for Java and TCP/IP Sockets communications. Examples of both alternatives are shown in Chapters 5 and 6.

System Debugger

IBM had a head start when they added Java support to the System Debugger — it already supported the C language, and major elements of Java's syntax have analogues in C. Even knowing that IBM had a head start, the Java support in the System Debugger is impressive. True, it is nongraphical and devoid of some slick features found in PC debugger products, but the System Debugger remains a solid workhorse. Provisions for Java in the debugger include thread and object support. For example, you can set breakpoints in specific threads and then, from a breakpoint, evaluate the nature and equality of objects.

As Java and other AS/400 languages start to work together more, the System Debugger provides a single interface for working with them all. Already the debugger can switch between Java programs and programs running in other language environments. If your Java program uses native method calls, you can set breakpoints and perform debug functions in Java and in C in a single debug session.

Remote AWT

In the Java language defined by Sun Microsystems, the Abstract Windowing Toolkit (AWT) provides a core set of graphical components — buttons, text boxes, labels, and so forth. The ADK contains a mechanism called Remote AWT, which allows graphical applications created using AWT components to run on the AS/400.

We should make a distinction here between graphical applications accessing AS/400 resources and graphical applications running on the AS/400. A graphical application can run on a PC or a network computer — any Java-capable workstation — while accessing AS/400 resources. In this case, the functions of the graphical components are handled by a JVM running on the workstation. This type of graphical application performs very well. However, in Remote AWT applications, the AS/400's JVM executes the graphical instructions and then, through Remote Method Invocation (RMI), the graphical functions are farmed out to the workstation. At first blush this approach probably sounds good, but in practice it performs poorly and requires cumbersome workstation configurations.

To IBM's credit, they don't claim that Remote AWT is a feasible way to implement graphical client applications. According to IBM, Remote AWT should be considered only for extremely lightweight client applications such as software installation utilities or configuration displays. The Remote AWT facility is mainly a way for IBM to claim Java compatibility, including graphics support, on the AS/400, a platform without a native graphical interface.

Operations Navigator

Operations Navigator is a feature of AS/400 Client Access for Windows 95/98/NT (LPP 5763-XD1). With the Operations Navigator, you can access AS/400 resources, such as the IFS, through a Windows Explorer-style interface. Operations Navigator also lets you work with and configure AS/400 hardware and software.

Starting with the V3R1M3 release of Client Access, Operations Navigator includes support for creating, deleting, and running Java programs. The Java feature for Operations Navigator is not installed automatically with the product. To install the Java feature, go to the Accessories folder within the Client Access folder and run the Selective Setup program. Using either a Client Access CD-ROM or your managing AS/400 system, Selective Setup will search for additional components. Choose to see the details of the Operations Navigator component. On the subcomponents display, choose to install the IBM Java feature. After a reboot, the Java support is available to you in Operations Navigator.

To try out the Java feature, access your /myjava directory in the IFS through Operations Navigator. Locate the Customer class used in the example in Chapter 1. When you right-click over the Customer class, a pop-up menu appears. The menu has options for creating, deleting, and running Java programs.

The Create and Delete options execute the Create Java Program (CRT-JVAPGM) and Delete Java Program (DLTJVAPGM) commands. You used the CRTJVAPGM command in Chapter 1 to optimize the compiled Customer class. The DLTJVAPGM command gets rid of a previously optimized class (you'll learn all about this in Chapter 3). The Run option executes the Run Java Program (JAVA) command you used in the Chapter 1 example.

If the Java program you execute prints something to the standard output device, the way the Customer class does, it is written as a spooled file when you run it through the Operations Navigator.

Add It Up

What do the features of the ADK add up to? With the ADK, the AS/400 delivers a complete and robust Java platform. It is obvious that IBM took its time and got this implementation right. It is also quite clear that they aren't stopping here. There is every reason to believe that future Java language and technology improvements will find their way quickly to the AS/400.

Today's ADK is nothing to sneeze at. Certainly, you can design and develop server-side functionality with the AS/400 as your target for deployment. The ADK provides a world-class JVM, native JDBC driver, a solid debugger, and all the other features necessary to make it a serious contender for your Java application development projects. Combined with the products and tools outlined in the rest of this chapter, the AS/400 is the best Java platform on the market today.

AS/400 TOOLBOX FOR JAVA

The AS/400 Toolbox for Java (LPP 5763-JC1) is a library of Java classes that provides access to AS/400 resources. The Toolbox can be used in programs written to run on the AS/400, but it is used more commonly to enable client applications. The Toolbox is supported on the AS/400 through OS/400 server jobs that are a part of the base operating system. The Toolbox depends on TCP/IP, because it uses socket connections internally to communicate with the OS/400 server jobs. Because of these roots in TCP/IP, no middleware is required on a client workstation to use the Toolbox.

It is important for you to understand that the Toolbox is not a platform-specific modification to a JVM, nor is it an extension of the Java language. Rather, the Toolbox is a standalone library of AS/400-specific classes. Using the Toolbox does not tie you to a particular vendor for a Java runtime or compiler. It is true that using the Toolbox makes your code less portable to other platforms. However, designing your application so that Toolbox calls are segregated will help make porting to other platforms easier.

The following features are supported by the AS/400 Toolbox for Java V3R2M0 release:

- Program and command execution
- Data queues
- JDBC
- Record-level access
- Integrated File System
- Print resources

The V3R2M1 release adds these features to the Toolbox:

- Message queues
- Active job information retrieval
- User profile information retrieval
- User space access
- Digital certificate management

In addition, the V3R2M1 release adds graphical interface classes for access to AS/400 resources in list views.

Both versions of the Toolbox provide facilities for users signing on to AS/400s and for converting data between AS/400 and Java data types. The latter feature is indispensable. Converting to the AS/400's packed and zoned decimal types can be harrowing without the Toolbox.

The features available in the V3R2M0 Toolbox release are described individually in Chapter 5, which also includes example code for using the features. Chapter 7 provides examples that use the Toolbox in graphical applications.

VISUALAGE FOR JAVA

Sun Microsystems created Java, and Sun continues to create the language specifications that define the "standard" Java platform. With periodic releases of an updated Java Development Kit (JDK), they provide a reference point for companies who make Java development environments and other tools. The JDK, with its command-line compiler and debugger, is not by itself intended to be a serious tool for software development.

Several vendors now provide Integrated Development Environments (IDEs) for Java. An IDE typically consists of a software application with built-in functions for source editing, compilation, execution, and debugging. Most IDEs have a facility for source change management, either built in or through an interface to another product. Often, vendors try to distinguish their IDEs with unique approaches to "visual" programming. Visual designers are real time-savers, because they let programmers put together graphical applications without writing every line of code from scratch.

The examples in this book use IBM's VisualAge for Java (VAJ) as the IDE. As this book is written, Version 2.0 is the current version of the product. VAJ is available in Entry, Professional, and Enterprise editions. The capabilities and features of each are shown in Table 2.1.

The free Entry edition is designed to give you a taste of the product and to get you hooked so that you will license either the Professional or Enterprise edition. Don't expect to run very far with the Entry edition; you will hit the 500-class limitation relatively quickly.

TABLE 2.1

VisualAge for Java Product Features

VAJ Edition	Capabilities/Features
Entry	Limited to 500 classes. Otherwise the same as Professional edition. Free.
Professional	Editor, repository, debugger, class browser, and Visual Composition Editor.
Enterprise	All of Professional edition plus Data Access Builder, RMI Access Builder, OS/390, Enterprise Toolkit/400, Team Support, and other features.

The Professional edition is well suited to small development efforts. You won't find all the AS/400 integration bells and whistles in the Professional edition, but you can still import the Toolbox and write applications of reasonable size and complexity.

For large development projects and those involving more than one or two developers, you need the Enterprise edition. The Enterprise Toolkit/400 provides fully integrated AS/400 support and team development. If you get serious about doing Java on the AS/400, you won't want to live without these features.

Editor and Repository

VAJ takes an approach to hosting software development unlike the approach of any other tool on the market. Instead of editing source files, you import all source code into a central repository and edit it in a closely linked workspace. The workspace and repository are essentially a database of source and object code maintained by VAJ. One advantage of this database is that you can view and work with your Java projects from many different perspectives. Table 2.2 shows the major views available in VAJ.

TABLE 2.2

VisualAge for Java Views

View	Perspective
Workbench	A collection of projects. Open a project, package, or class view.
Project	A collection of packages. Within packages, work with classes and methods.
Package	A collection of classes. Within classes, work with methods.
Class	A collection of methods.
Method	A single method.
Repository	Archived and current versions of projects, packages, classes, and methods.
Debug	A way to work with running Java programs.
Scrapbook	A way to experiment with fragments of Java code without creating or compiling a complete class.

The repository really shines when you begin to take advantage of the built-in version control. As you change and save source code, older versions of the code called *editions* are maintained for you in the repository. You can always revert to an old edition of source code or compare the current code to an old edition.

NOTE: Appendix A describes the steps you need to perform to import the VAJ examples in this book.

Another great feature of VAJ is incremental compile support. Compilation in VAJ is performed at the class definition or the method level. When you change the definition of a class or the code in a method, VAJ performs a compile when you save your change. If your change broke something, even if it is in another place, you see this information right away. For example, if you change the signature of a method, and the old method is referenced by a class in another project and package, you are told of the problem immediately. Because you discover errors caused by your changes right away, you are much more likely to fix your problems as you go.

Debugger

The debug feature includes most features found in other products on the market, including conditional breakpoints. You can even inspect variable values just by placing the mouse pointer over a variable in the debug source view.

The debugger fully participates in VAJ's incremental compile model. With support for incremental compilation, you can debug a Java program and make program changes while the program is running. Your changes take effect immediately, without requiring you to stop and restart the program. The repetitive steps of coding, compiling, running, and debugging are combined into one seamless act.

Visual Composition Editor

As mentioned in the introduction to this section, many Java tool vendors distinguish their products by citing the features of their visual designer. In VAJ, the visual designer is called the Visual Composition Editor (VCE). Like most products on the market today, the VCE is dependent upon the JavaBeans component architecture, in which components have data features called *properties*, code features called *methods*, and action features called *events*.

IBM went quite a bit further than competitors with their visual designer. Designing a graphical application in the VCE is a matter of dropping bean components on a form and establishing connections between the beans. Connections are represented by lines or "wires" between bean components. The VCE generates code to handle connections based on events, like button clicks, but then goes one step further to generate code on property connections and for connections to arbitrary methods you create. The connection types and their VCE color codings are shown in Table 2.3.

TABLE 2.3
Visual Composition Editor Connection Types

Connection	Purpose	Color
Event to method	Based on an event (e.g., a button click), executes a method of a bean.	Green
Property to property	Links the property of one bean to the property of another. Can be based on an event (e.g., focus lost on a text field).	Blue
Event to code	Based on an event, executes an arbitrary method.	Green
Parameter from property	Supplies a method parameter with the value of a property.	Purple

The connection types in VAJ are so varied, and the code generation capabilities so complete, that it is possible to design very sophisticated applications in the VCE with very little hand coding.

Data Access Builder (Enterprise Edition)
The Data Access Builder, commonly called DAX, is a facility for generating database access classes using the JDBC API. Once they are created, you can use these classes as beans in your VCE-designed applications or in the Java code that you write by hand.

The classes created by DAX range from simple beans with read, write, delete, and update capabilities to beans with complex transaction services, such as commit and rollback. You have a great deal of control over DAX-generated classes. For example, you can add your own methods to the generated classes to customize data access or call Stored Procedures.

RMI Access Builder (Enterprise Edition)
Remote Method Invocation (RMI) is a standard feature of the Java language and a big part of Java's future in enterprise application development. With RMI, code running on a client can execute methods in Java objects running on a server. RMI is the mechanism for establishing and maintaining connections between objects and for passing parameters back and forth. VAJ's RMI Generation tool, a part of the RMI Access Builder, creates for you the stubs and proxies that sit on client and server and are an integral part of object-level communications.

Creating even a simple RMI application by hand can be time consuming. VAJ's RMI Access Builder takes away the grunt work involved and makes it much easier to get RMI up and running. Chapter 8 shows you how to use RMI-based applications on your AS/400.

Enterprise Toolkit/400 (Enterprise Edition)

Version 2.0 of VAJ introduced the Enterprise Toolkit/400 (ET/400), adding integrated AS/400 support to the product. Among the notable features of ET/400 are

- The AS/400 Toolbox for Java
- The ability to export Java source and class files to the AS/400
- The ability to compile, run, and debug a Java program residing on the AS/400
- The Toolbox Program Call SmartGuide
- The Convert Display File SmartGuide for converting Display Files to Java GUI applications
- The Create Subfile SmartGuide

NOTE: SmartGuides are step-by-step panels for walking you through a specific task. They are sometimes called wizards in other software packages. In addition to the ET/400 SmartGuides, VAJ has integrated SmartGuides that guide you through many common tasks such as creating projects, packages, classes, methods, and fields (i.e., variables).

Access ET/400 by selecting a project, package, or class in VAJ and right-clicking to display a pop-up menu. From the menu, select Tools, ET/400 to access the SmartGuides and other features of ET/400. To deploy Java code to an AS/400, select the ET/400 Export option. The ET/400 Compile option invokes the Java Transformer on the AS/400 to create native execution objects from class files exported to the IFS. The ET/400 Run option lets you execute a remote AS/400 Java program, with all console input/output routed to the VAJ console.

Perhaps the greatest ET/400 feature is the remote debugger. From your PC, you can debug a Java program running on the AS/400's JVM. The remote debugger is based on the debugger in IBM's CODE/400 product and is separate from VAJ's built-in debugger.

You can reuse existing AS/400 code with ET/400's Convert Display File SmartGuide, which takes an AS/400 display file and generates classes to recreate the user interface. This SmartGuide is a quick way to create a Java application with the same basic look as a nongraphical AS/400 program. The Create Subfile SmartGuide creates a subfile bean using a DB2/400 table that you specify. You select the columns to include in the subfile and you can even have "hidden" fields associated with subfile rows.

IBM's AS/400 Toolbox for Java is a part of ET/400 and is fully integrated into VAJ 2.0. Working from the VCE, all the V3R2M1 Toolbox beans are available on the bean pallet, including the new visual access beans. The Program Call SmartGuide generates the Java code that calls an AS/400 program using the Toolbox. Coding such calls manually is certainly possible, but it is easier with the SmartGuide.

CUSTOMER TRACKING APPLICATION

To give you a chance to fully appreciate the power of VisualAge for Java, let's walk through the construction of an example application. Our application is a simple customer contact list. The finished product is shown running in Figure 2.2. If you import the examples from the CD-ROM into VAJ, you can run this application yourself from a VAJ project or package view. In the Examples project, select the CustomerTracking class in the examples.app package, then right-click the class. From the menu choose Run, Run.

FIGURE 2.2
Customer Tracking Application

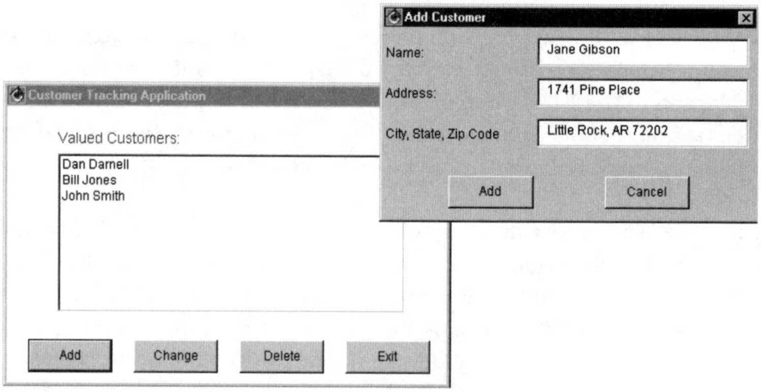

Click Add to enter contact information for a new customer. As you add customers, they appear on the list. To change or delete a customer, select the customer on the list and click Change or Delete. Close the application by clicking Exit or by closing the window.

NOTE: For now, you can ignore the other packages in the CD's Examples project. They will be used in later chapters.

Design Notes

The purpose of the Customer Tracking Application is to keep a list of customers and to allow additions, changes, and deletions to the list. The list shows customer names, but we want to keep track of customer addresses, too. To track addresses, we use the Customer class from Chapter 1 as the basis for the CustomerItem class we create here. With the CustomerItem class, we will create objects to represent customers and keep up with all relevant customer information.

The CustomerItem class includes methods for getting and setting individual properties such as name, address, and the combined city/state/zip. The **getXXXX** methods, called *accessor methods,* and the **setXXXX** methods, called *mutators*, subscribe to the method-naming standards defined by the JavaBeans specification. By following these conventions, our CustomerItem class readily becomes a bean for use in the VCE.

The CustomerItem class adds the methods shown in Table 2.4 to those of the original Customer class.

Table 2.4
Methods of CustomerItem Class

Method	Purpose
getID	Accessor method for custID field
getName	Accessor method for custName field
getStreet	Accessor method for custStreet field
getCityStateZip	Accessor method for custCityStateZip field
setName	Mutator method for custName field
setStreet	Mutator method for custStreet field
setCityStateZip	Mutator method for custCityStateZip field

The list displayed by the application is capable of showing only the customer name, a simple string, so we have to devise another way to store complete CustomerItem objects. The CustomerListKeeper bean keeps a cross-reference between the customer names on the list and corresponding CustomerItem objects. The methods defined by the CustomerListKeeper class are shown in Table 2.5.

Table 2.5
Methods of CustomerListKeeper Class

Method	Purpose
addItem	Adds a new customer object to an internal cross-reference table
removeItem	Removes an existing customer object from an internal cross-reference table
fetchItem	Retrieves for update a customer object from an internal cross-reference table

To implement the cross-reference of customer names to customer objects, we use a hash table. Hash tables are searchable lists of objects supported by the Hash table class defined in the java.util package. Currently, the customer objects kept by the CustomerListKeeper bean are only temporary. Because they are stored in a hash table and are never written to a stream or database file, the customer objects go away forever when you exit the application. Later in this book, you will see this application expanded to make the customer objects permanent by writing their contents to a DB2/400 database file.

If you spend much time with the Customer Tracking Application, you will discover a few limitations. For example, you can't have two customers with the same name. In addition, because the customer name is used to locate a corresponding customer object, the name cannot be modified. At this stage, we've used an intentionally simple application so that you can concentrate on the VCE and not get overwhelmed by an overly complex design pattern. When we revisit the application later in the book, you will see we have addressed these limitations.

Visual Composition

The Customer Tracking Application is built in the VCE part of VAJ. In this section, we dissect the application. The complete VCE design screen, including all of the "wires" or connections, is shown in Figure 2.3.

FIGURE 2.3
VCE Display — All Connections

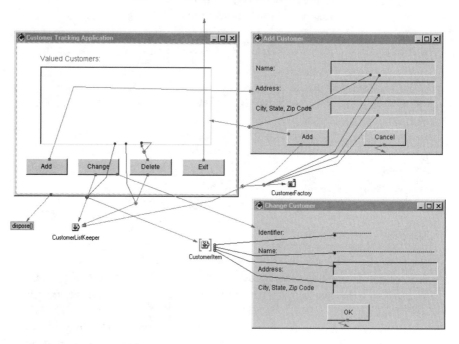

VISUAL BEANS

The Customer Tracking Application begins with a class called, appropriately enough, CustomerTracking. This class inherits its functionality from the AWT's Frame class. Because we extend the Frame class to make the CustomerTracking class, our application is also a Frame. In addition to our frame, we also have two dialog boxes — Add Customer and Change Customer. An assortment of buttons, labels, and text boxes reside in the frame and dialog boxes.

One of the first things you should do with this application is look at the property settings of the various beans. Start with the Add Customer dialog box. To view the properties of this bean, double-click the title bar. You see the window shown in Figure 2.4. Here you can set properties of the dialog box, including the title, colors, and modal state. The modal state is set to True, which disallows input on other panels while the dialog box is displayed. In this application, the Add Customer and Change Customer dialog boxes have their modal state set to True to prevent you from potentially harmful actions, such as deleting a customer item while you have it selected for a change.

FIGURE 2.4
VCE Display — Dialog Box Properties

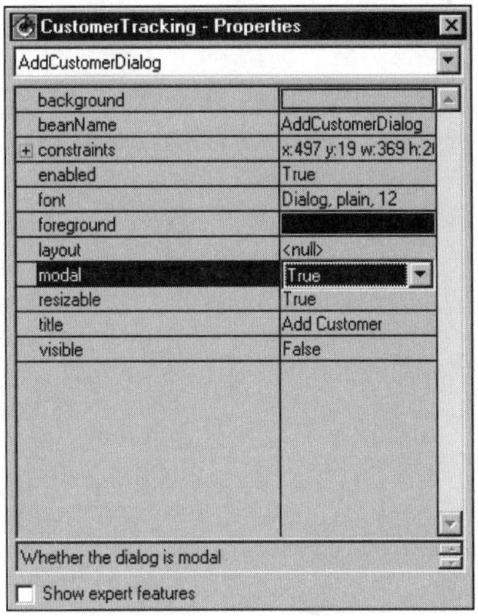

Almost all visual beans and most nonvisual beans have a set of associated properties. You can access them the same way that you accessed the properties of the Add Customer dialog box.

NOTE: You can also select properties for a bean by clicking it and then right-clicking to display a pop-up menu of options. From the pop-up menu, select the Properties option.

NONVISUAL BEANS

In addition to the visual elements of the design, the application includes a few nonvisual elements. Our CustomerListKeeper and CustomerItem classes are represented by nonvisual beans. The CustomerFactory (shown in Figure 2.3) looks like a bean, but it is not. The CustomerFactory is a construct of the VCE that creates objects of a particular type in response to some event. In our case, the factory is used to create a new CustomerItem object when you click the Add button on the Add Customer dialog box. (For a fundamental description of the different varieties of beans used in the VCE, see "Beans, Beans, Beans."

FIRST STEPS WITH THE VCE

A VCE display can become cluttered with connections. The best way to deal with this situation is to hide all the connections except those you are interested in. In Figure 2.5, you see a connection from the Add button of the frame to the Add Customer dialog box. This event-to-method connection causes the dialog box to appear when the button is clicked.

FIGURE 2.5
VCE Display — First Step with Add Button Connection

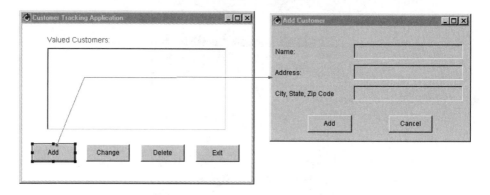

To see just this connection, as in the figure, right-click the VCE design surface and select Browse Connections, Hide All from the pop-up menu. Next, select the Add button and then right-click it. Select Browse Connections, Show To/From, and the VCE display will show you only the connections to and from this bean.

To see what it takes to wire a VCE connection, let's walk through the steps required to connect the Add button to the dialog box. Figure 2.6 shows the pop-up menu displayed when you right-click the frame's Add button. Selecting the actionPerformed event from the Connect menu lets you connect this event, which is a button click, to another component in the VCE.

FIGURE 2.6

VCE Display — Connection Features

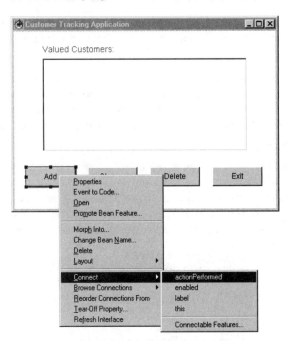

When you select the actionPerformed event, a dashed black line with a spider on the end appears. You use the spider to select a target for the event. Dropping the spider on the Add Customer dialog box makes a pop-up menu appear; from this menu you can select an action to take on the component. To see all the component's features, select Connectable Features from the menu. The "End connection to (AddCustomerDialog)" window appears. From here, you can select any applicable method, property, or event of the target component. For this particular connection, the **setVisible** method is selected.

Now a dashed green line is drawn from the source component, the Add button, to the target component, the Add Customer dialog box. A dashed line indicates an incomplete connection. To complete the connection, you must supply a parameter to the **setVisible** method. Double-click the dashed line to bring up the Event-to-Method Connection Properties window. This window shows the event, **actionPerformed**, and the method to which it is connected, **setVisible**. Click the Set Parameters button to see the Constant Parameter Value Setting window and to specify the Boolean value required by the **setVisible** method. The Boolean parameter needed to show the dialog box is True. Click OK on the Constant Parameter Value Setting window and OK

BEANS, BEANS, BEANS

With all of the discussion about visual beans, nonvisual beans, and bean lookalikes, you may be wondering just where the theoretical lines between these components are drawn.

Visual Beans

Visual beans are the windows, buttons, lists, and other components that comprise a GUI. You can create customized versions of the basic GUI components by extending them through Java's inheritance mechanism or by creating your own from scratch. GUI component libraries are also available for sale and for free download from a variety of companies.

Nonvisual Beans

Nonvisual beans are normally where you implement business logic or some other type of processing. True to their name, nonvisual beans do not display any graphics. In a typical application design, visual beans interact with nonvisual beans — visual beans provide an interface between the user and the business logic contained in the nonvisual beans. On the VCE design display, nonvisual beans are represented by the symbol in Figure 2.A.

FIGURE 2.A
Symbol for Nonvisual Bean

At heart, both visual and nonvisual beans are simply Java classes that conform to Sun's JavaBeans specification. The specification is a guideline for the way classes should define their property, method, and event features so that visual design tools can assist developers in combining them to create applications.

Bean Lookalikes

To accommodate some common programming needs that are not implicitly supported by visual and nonvisual beans, the makers of VAJ decided to create bean lookalikes. You can drop these bean lookalikes on a VCE design display and use them in much the same way that you use nonvisual beans. The two main bean lookalikes supported in the VCE today are the Factory and the Variable.

A Factory is a fundamental design pattern that is usually implemented by writing a class whose purpose is to create object instances of some other class. The VCE takes a slightly different approach, embedding object creation code in its connection logic, but the results are the same. You can use the Factory bean lookalike when you need objects created on the fly as your application runs.

A Variable is a bean lookalike used in the VCE to hold references to objects. As the name "variable" implies, the object this pseudo-bean refers to can change. You might, for example, have a variable linked to a factory that creates a new object. The variable becomes a reference to the object so that other components in the VCE can manipulate it.

again on the Event-to-Method Connection window. The dashed line is now solid and the connection is complete.

When the VCE design is saved, the following code is generated for this connection:

```
getAddCustomerDialog().setVisible(true);
```

Not much code for all of the gyrations with the mouse, is it? Certainly, there are times when hand coding seems faster than using the VCE. VAJ does not prevent you from hand coding and indeed, many applications are a mixture of both "wires" and handwritten code. You'll find, though, that wiring even simple connections has some advantages over writing the equivalent code by hand. For example, in the VCE you can see the design of your application much more readily by wiring connections than if you do a lot of hand coding. In addition, if you're working in a team environment, using the VCE enforces a design and coding standard that is shared by all team members. Obviously, a standard makes it much easier to get into and understand someone else's application.

ADD CUSTOMER

When you type a new customer's information and click the Add button on the Add Customer dialog box, two things happen, as shown by the connections in Figure 2.7.

FIGURE 2.7
VCE Display — Add Customer Connections

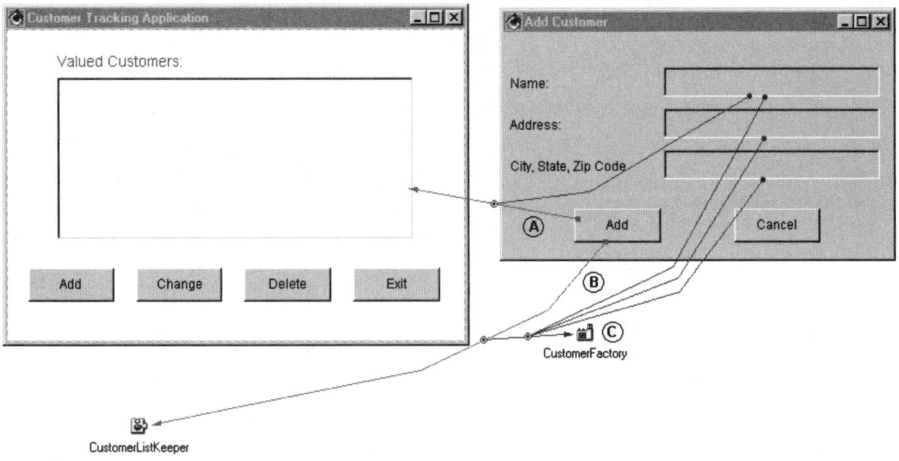

First, at A, the customer is added to the list in the frame. Second, at B, the **addItem** method of the CustomerListKeeper bean is executed. The factory at C supplies a new customer object to **addItem**, taking the text box properties for customer name, address, and city/state/zip and passing them to the CustomerItem class's constructor.

Consider the code generated by the VCE for the second connection:

```
getCustomerListKeeper().addItem(new CustomerItem(getAddName().getText(),
getAddStreet().getText(), getAddCityStateZip().getText()));
```

In contrast to the simple method call generated for the Add button to show a dialog box, this call is substantially more complicated and better illustrates the benefits of working with the VCE.

The Cancel button of the Add Customer dialog box simply causes the dialog box to go away.

CHANGE CUSTOMER

Now consider the connections shown in Figure 2.8.

FIGURE 2.8
VCE Display — Change Customer Connections

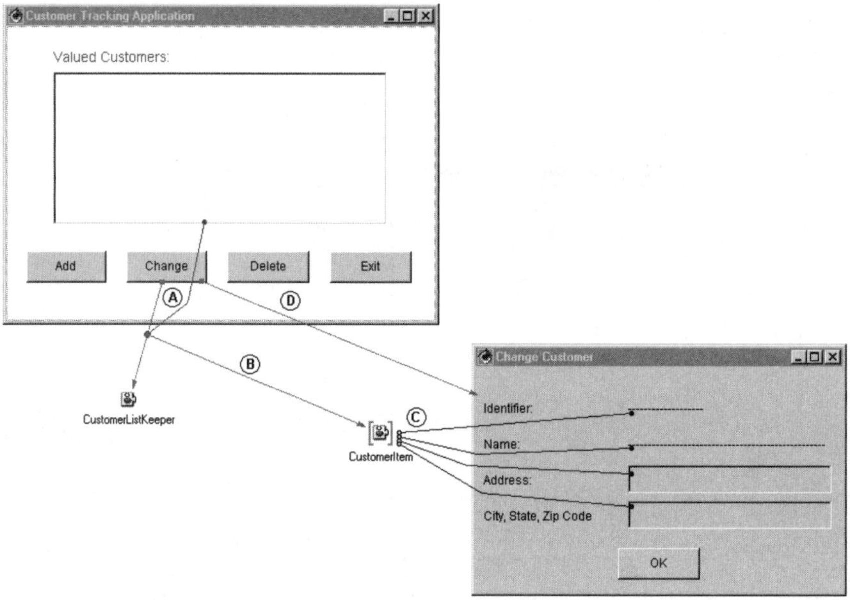

These connections perform the following steps to change a customer object:

1. Retrieve the customer object from CustomerListKeeper using the customer name selected in the list box.

2. Set the CustomerItem bean variable to selected customer object.

3. Set the Customer Change dialog text box and label properties with customer object property values.

The first step is easy enough. When the Change button on the frame is clicked, the **fetchItem** method is called in the CustomerListKeeper bean. This action is represented by the connection at A. Remember that as we added items to the list box, objects were added to an internal hash table of objects in the CustomerListKeeper bean. Now we're asking the CustomerListKeeper bean's **fetchItem** method to return a reference to one of its saved customer objects.

Notice that the CustomerItem bean has brackets around it. The brackets indicate that the CustomerItem bean is a variable — it can be set to any instance of a CustomerItem object. At B, the customer object reference returned by **fetchItem** is used to set the value of the CustomerItem variable.

The data properties of the CustomerItem bean are connected to the text properties of the labels and text boxes on the Change Customer dialog box at C. Selecting a customer from the list and clicking Change sets the CustomerItem variable to the appropriate CustomerItem object and changes the properties of the dialog box components to reflect customer object values. These property-to-property connections are a function of the VCE, and its code generation capabilities save a lot of time. Here is the code generated for the customer identifier in a property-to-property connection:

```
private void connPtoP1SetTarget() {
/* Set the target from the source */
try {
        getChangeID().setText(String.valueOf(getCustomerItem().getID()));
        // user code begin {1}
        // user code end
} catch (java.lang.Throwable ivjExc) {
        // user code begin {3}
        // user code end
        handleException(ivjExc);
}
}
```

Notice that the VCE-generated code converts the customer identifier, an integer, to label text, a string.

The timing of the property change is also a function of the VCE-generated code. In this case, the property connection happens only when the CustomerItem variable bean's reference to a customer object changes. Here is the VCE-generated code, including the property change link, for changing the value of the CustomerItem variable bean.

```
private void setCustomerItem(CustomerItem newValue) {
if (ivjCustomerItem != newValue) {
        try {
                ivjCustomerItem = newValue;
                connPtoP1SetTarget();        ◄── Customer ID property
                connPtoP2SetTarget();
                connPtoP3SetTarget();
```

VCE Naming Conventions and Default Exception Handling

The **connXXtoXX** methods are generated by the VCE. The convention for naming methods reflects the type of connection generated. For example, the first event-to-method connection generates a method named **connEtoM1**. Similarly, the first property-to-property connection generates **connPtoP1**. A method parameter supplied by a property connection generates a connection method called **connPfromP1**. You can change the name of any connection by right-clicking the connection and choosing Change Connection Name from the menu.

VCE-generated code usually attempts to handle exceptions gracefully. The **handle-Exception** method, shown below, is a catch-all for hiccups in the connection code.

```
private void handleException(Throwable exception) {
    /* Uncomment the following lines to print uncaught exceptions to
       stdout */
    // System.out.println("-------- UNCAUGHT EXCEPTION -------");
    // exception.printStackTrace(System.out);
}
```

By default, exceptions are ignored. If you want to handle them yourself, you can. Alternatively, you can uncomment the statements in the **handleException** method so that, at the very least, you know when exceptions occur.

```
                connPtoP4SetTarget();
                // user code begin {1}
                // user code end
        } catch (java.lang.Throwable ivjExc) {
                // user code begin {2}
                // user code end
                handleException(ivjExc);
        }
};
}
```

As the customer address or city/state/zip information is modified on the Change Customer dialog box, the customer object referred to by the CustomerItem variable is kept in sync. The VCE allows unidirectional or bidirectional property connections. At design time, the property-to-property connections between the CustomerItem object and the Change Cutomer dialog box components were established as bidirectional (two-way) connections.

A second connection, at D, exists between the Change button on the frame and the Change Customer dialog box. This simple connection makes the dialog box appear when the Change button is clicked. As you might imagine, when multiple connections are triggered by the same event, the order of the connections can be crucial. In this case, we want the dialog box to appear after the customer object has been retrieved from the CustomerListKeeper bean. You control the execution order of connections by right-clicking the Change button and selecting Reorder Connections From on the pop-up menu.

Figure 2.9 shows the Reorder Connections window for the Change button. This window shows the connections originating with a bean in the VCE and lets you rearrange their order by dragging and dropping listed connections. For the Change button, the connections are already in the order we want.

FIGURE 2.9
VCE Display — Reorder Connections

Source Bean	Source Feature	Target Bean	Target Feature
ChangeCustButton	actionPerformed	CustomerListKeeper	fetchItem(java.lang.String
ChangeCustButton	actionPerformed	ChangeCustomerDialog	setVisible(boolean)

Button(ChangeCustButton) - Reorder connections

Drag connections to reorder

DELETE CUSTOMER

Figure 2.10 shows the connections for deleting a customer entry.

FIGURE 2.10
VCE Display — Delete Customer Connections

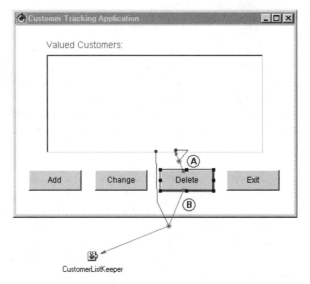

When the Delete button on the frame is clicked, the connection at A takes care of removing the selected customer entry from the list. With the connection at B, the selected customer entry on the list is passed to the **removeItem** method of the CustomerListKeeper bean. The **removeItem** method removes the customer object from the internal hash table of customer objects maintained by the CustomerListKeeper bean.

FINAL CONNECTION DETAILS

Two components that we haven't looked at are the OK button in the Change Customer dialog box and the Exit button on the frame. When it is clicked, the OK button on the dialog box simply hides the Change Customer dialog box. The Exit button executes the **dispose** method of the frame, which causes the application to end.

Back in Figure 2.3, notice the connection in lower left portion of the design area leading from the frame to a small label with the method name **dispose**( ). This connection is an Event-to-Code connection. Such connections are used to execute arbitrary methods of your creation or methods of the application class. This particular connection begins with the "window closing" event and targets the **dispose** method of the application class. The event is triggered when you click the X on the window to close the frame. Recall that our application is inherited from the Frame class, so this connection causes the application to end, just as the Exit button connection to **dispose** does.

HANDWRITTEN CODE

Only one line of Java code in this application was coded by hand. You can find it in the **initConnections** method:

```
setCustomerItem(new CustomerItem());
```

This line sets the CustomerItem bean to a valid object reference so that initial property connections can take place without triggering a null pointer exception. A side effect of creating this object is that the first customer identifier, number 10001, is taken up by a dummy customer object. Real customers added with the application start with identifier 10002. If it were important to start at 10001, we could have set it up that way; it wasn't necessary for our purposes.

NEXT STEPS

In this section you saw how to use the VCE of VAJ to construct a simple application. You saw how to set bean properties, connect events to beans, and supply parameters to methods with bean properties. You also saw an example of manipulating nonvisual beans representing objects and lists of objects. These skills are essential to working in the VCE. In later chapters, the VCE examples get more complicated. If you aren't already skilled with VAJ and the VCE, spend some time on the basics before moving on.

WORKING WITH THE INTEGRATED FILE SYSTEM

In Chapter 1, you saw how to write a Java program on the AS/400 with SEU, and then use the Copy to Stream File command to move it to the IFS for compilation and execution. Now that we've established that VAJ is a better way to edit and compile your Java programs, it's time to discuss better ways to get your programs to the AS/400 for execution.

The first three ways we will look at require that you first copy the code out of VAJ to your local file system by exporting source files, class files, or both. You can export files from the project, package, or class view. To export, just click the projects, packages, or classes and select Export from the File menu. The type of export that you want to do is called a "directory" export.

After your project has been exported to the local file system, you can copy or move it to the IFS in one of these three ways:

- File Transfer Protocol (FTP)
- Client Access
- Network Neighborhood Server

We also look at the ET/400 Export feature.

File Transfer Protocol

File Transfer Protocol (FTP) is a function of TCP/IP that lets you transfer a file from one system to another. If you are using an operating system such as Windows 95/98 or Windows NT, you have a built-in FTP client. Figure 2.11 shows the display you see when transferring a Java class file to the IFS.

FIGURE 2.11
File Transfer with FTP

```
C:\WINDOWS>ftp
ftp> open MYSYSTEM
Connected to MYSYSTEM.
220-QTCP at MYSYSTEM.
220 Connection will close if idle more than 16666 minutes.
User (MYSYSTEM:(none)): dand
331 Enter password.
Password:
230 DAND logged on.
ftp> put d:\book\chapter1\Customer.java /myjava/Customer.java
200 PORT subcommand request successful.
150-NAMEFMT set to 1.
150 Sending file to /myjava/Customer.java
250 File transfer completed successfully.
1927 bytes sent in 0.00 seconds (1927000.00 Kbytes/sec)
ftp> quit
221 QUIT subcommand received.

C:\WINDOWS>
```

After running the FTP command, you use the Open command to establish a connection with your host AS/400.

```
open MYSYSTEM
```

You are then prompted to supply a user ID and password. Once logged on, you use the Put command to copy a file to the IFS.

```
put d:\book\chapter1\Customer.java /myjava/Customer.java
```

In this case, the local file, Customer.java, resides in the directory d:\book\chapter1. The target of the Put command is the /myjava IFS directory. You use the Quit command to exit the FTP utility.

Because the IFS includes more than just the root file system and each file system has its own idiosyncrasies, using FTP can sometimes be tricky. For example, it is easy to confuse FTP into thinking that your target is the library file system (where AS/400 libraries reside). Targeting the right file system is largely a matter of using the right syntax.

The FTP client on the AS/400 is one of the best sources of information for getting the naming convention just right. To access this information, start the FTP client from an AS/400 command line with the FTP command, then type **HELP** to see details about file system naming conventions.

Client Access

IBM's Client Access/400 product includes support for the IFS. With a Windows 95/98 or Windows NT client, you can access the IFS through the Explorer or Network Neighborhood. This method is often a very comfortable way to move Java files to the IFS. IFS directories appear in Explorer just like any other network directories, and the familiar Copy, Cut, Paste, and Delete functions work without surprises. Figure 2.12 shows the IFS as it looks to Explorer.

FIGURE 2.12
Explorer View of AS/400

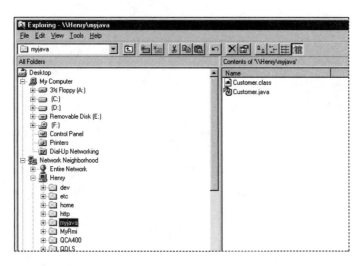

Network Neighborhood Server

Starting with V4R2, a feature of OS/400 makes the IFS available to Windows clients without the need for special software, like Client Access, installed on the client. When the Network Neighborhood Server (NetServer) function is turned on, you can access the IFS through Windows Explorer. For more information about NetServer support, see the IBM publication *Getting Your AS/400 Working for You* (SC41-5161-01).

NOTE: Using either Client Access or NetServer, you can map a drive letter to an IFS directory. Mapping a drive in this way makes it possible to export from VAJ directly to the IFS.

ET/400 Export

Perhaps the easiest way to export Java code to an AS/400 is with the ET/400 Export feature found in VAJ 2.0. Unlike the regular VAJ directory export, the ET/400 Export lets you target the IFS directly, without middleware such as Client Access or NetServer and without mapping a network drive.

For the ET/400 export to work properly, you must first set properties for the tool. Figure 2.13 shows the AS/400 Properties page, which you access by clicking the Project menu and selecting Tools, ET/400, and Properties.

FIGURE 2.13
AS/400 Export Properties

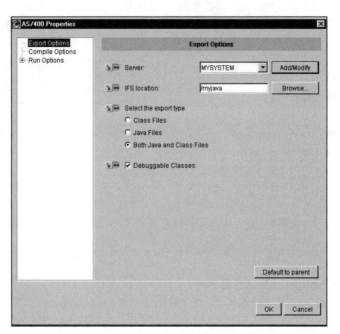

At a minimum, supply an AS/400 system name in the Server field and a valid IFS path in the IFS location field. You can export source files, class files, or both and include debugging information in exported class files.

Chapter 3

Java Environment

When it comes to Java on the AS/400, you've seen the big picture but only a few of the details. In the next three chapters, we look at the AS/400's Java features in depth. This chapter begins with the Integrated File System (IFS). You'll learn what the IFS means to you as a Java programmer and see where the supporting code for the ADK resides. Next, we explore the full spectrum of Java commands on the AS/400. Then we take a walk with the System Debugger and learn its Java features. Finally, we look at the configuration issues that you will encounter in single and multiple AS/400 deployments.

INTEGRATED FILE SYSTEM

The IFS on the AS/400 combines several diverse file systems. Table 3.1 shows the file systems covered by the IFS umbrella. OS/400 brings to the table a way to administer these often dissimilar file systems with a set of universally applicable commands.

TABLE 3.1
IFS File Systems

File System	Characteristics
Root	DOS-like file system. Supports stream files in a hierarchical directory structure. File names are not case sensitive.
QOpenSys	Unix-like file system. Supports stream files in a hierarchical directory structure and supports case-sensitive file names. Posix (open systems standard) compatible.
QSYS.LIB	Supports libraries and objects. DB2/400 database files reside within this file system.
QDLS	Document Library Services file system. Supports folders and documents.
QLANSrv	LAN Server for OS/400 (LPP 5769-XZ1) file system.
QFileSvr.400	Provides access to remote AS/400 file systems.
QNetWare	Novell NetWare file system.
NFS	Network File System. Provides access to data on a remote NFS server.
User-defined	A file system created and managed by the user.

For the purposes of writing and deploying Java programs, the root and QOpenSys file systems are practical choices. These are stream-based file systems

— as opposed to record or database file systems — with hierarchical directory structures. The major difference between the root and QOpenSys file systems is that QOpenSys is case-sensitive when it comes to file names, while the root file system is not.

It's no fluke that the IFS keeps coming up as a topic in this book on AS/400 Java. Java and the IFS are inextricably linked, and the better your understanding of the IFS, the better prepared you are to write and deploy Java applications on an AS/400. Later in this chapter, we complement this IFS section with a discussion of AS/400 configuration.

Naming Conventions

Each file system has its own naming conventions and restrictions. For example, the QDLS file system restricts document names to a maximum of 8 characters with an optional 1- to 3-character extension. A valid name in the QDLS file system, then, is DOCUMENT.DOC. Libraries and objects in the QSYS.LIB file system can have a maximum of 10 characters, with an extension ranging from 1 to 6 characters. Extensions in the QSYS.LIB file system equate to object types (e.g., LIB, FILE, PGM). In the root and QOpenSys file systems, file names can have total of 256 characters in the file name and an optional extension.

Directory structure is another major difference between the file systems. The QSYS.LIB file system has no directories at all, only libraries, and libraries cannot be nested. In the QDLS file system, folders are the equivalent of directories. The QDLS, root, and QOpenSys file systems all support a hierarchical directory structure, which means that you can nest directories within other directories to form a tree, such as the one shown below:

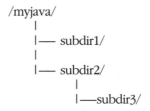

You can manipulate all the file systems with a common set of commands. Targeting a particular file system with a command is largely a matter of getting the naming convention right. The Work with Object Links (WRKLNK) command, for example, shows you the directories and files or their equivalents (for QDLS, folders and documents; for QSYS.LIB, libraries and objects) contained in a file system. To see the directories in the root file system, type

```
WRKLNK OBJ('/*')
```

The slash (/) targets the root file system. Scroll down the list of the root file system directories. You should see the other file systems listed here too. You can create directories and files in the root file system, but the root system also acts as a kind of stepping-off point for access to the other file systems.

To see the contents of the QDLS file system, try this:

```
WRKLNK OBJ('/QDLS/*')
```

You should see all the folders in the Document Library Services file system.

To target your EXAMPLES library in the QSYS.LIB file system, use this command:

```
WRKLNK OBJ('/QSYS.LIB/EXAMPLES.LIB/*')
```

You should see the source file (QJVASRC) that you created for the first Java program example.

You gained access to the EXAMPLES library by going through the QSYS.LIB file system. It doesn't work to use a command like this:

```
WRKLNK OBJ('/EXAMPLES.LIB')
```

You haven't told the WRKLNK command enough information to find the EXAMPLES library — you must specify the file system as a part of the path.

You should take away two main concepts from this discussion. First, each file system has its own naming conventions. Second, the way you specify the path name on a command determines, and is determined by, the file system you are targeting.

Save/Restore

One of the ways that the IFS unites the file systems is by providing a common backup and recovery mechanism. In this section, we look at the Save and Restore commands (SAV and RST) and their essential parameters.

You use the Save and Restore commands from an OS/400 command line to back up and restore IFS information. The target of these operations can be a physical device, such as a tape drive, or a logical device, such as a save file.

SAVE (COMMAND SAV)

The essential parameters of the Save command are the device, the objects, and the directory subtree.

Device (parameter DEV)

This parameter specifies the path to a device or save file. However, you don't simply specify the name of your tape device — say, TAP01. You need to specify the IFS path to your tape device description in a way that conforms to the naming conventions described in the previous section. Therefore, to save IFS data to your TAP01 tape device, you can use the following command:

```
SAV DEV('/QSYS.LIB/TAP01.DEVD')
```

This example points the device parameter to the device description TAP01 contained in the QSYS.LIB file system.

Saving to a save file requires a similar parameter entry, as shown below.

```
SAV DEV('/QSYS.LIB/EXAMPLES.LIB/MYSAVF.FILE')
```

This entry is the device parameter to a save file called MYSAVF in the EXAMPLES library in the QSYS.LIB file system. (This example assumes that you have previously created a save file in the EXAMPLES library using the Create Save File — CRTSAVF — command.)

Objects (parameter OBJ)

This parameter specifies one or more objects to save. It has two parts:

- Name — Specifies the name of an object or a pattern
- Include/Omit — Indicates that the name part should be used to include objects or to exclude objects from a previously specified include statement

An object in this parameter is any component of the IFS. In the QSYS.LIB file system, an object could be a library or an OS/400 object. In the QDLS file system, an object could be a folder or a document. In the root or QOpenSys file systems, an object could be your Java directories or files.

To save the Customer.class file from the root file system to tape, use the Objects parameter in this way:

```
SAV DEV('/QSYS.LIB/TAP01.DEVD')                    +
    OBJ(('/myjava/Customer.class' *INCLUDE))
```

You can also specify a pattern for the object parameter. Using a pattern lets you save more than one object using generic selection criteria. In the example below, the Objects parameter selects all objects in the /myjava directory that begin with Customer.

```
SAV DEV('/QSYS.LIB/TAP01.DEVD')                    +
    OBJ(('/myjava/Customer*' *INCLUDE))
```

The Objects parameter is extremely versatile. It lets you specify multiple criteria to include, and it lets you omit objects matching particular names or patterns. The example below includes all files that begin with Customer but omits files that have .class as the extension.

```
SAV DEV('/QSYS.LIB/examples.lib/mysavf.file')   +
    OBJ(('/myjava/Customer*' *INCLUDE)            +
        ('/myjava/*.class' *OMIT))
```

This example is very simple, but when you consider that you can specify up to 300 separate include/omit criteria, the power of the Objects parameter becomes evident.

Directory Subtree (parameter SUBTREE)

This parameter is especially useful if you specify a directory name on the Objects parameter. You can use the Directory Subtree parameter to provide additional direction to the Save command. If you specify a pattern for the Objects parameter, more than one directory matching the pattern can be saved.

- *ALL (default) — Top-level directories, subdirectories, and objects within the directories are saved.

- *DIR — First-level directories and objects are saved. Subdirectories are saved, too, but not the objects within the subdirectories. Basically, this option saves the entire directory tree structure but saves objects only from the directories at the topmost level.

- *NONE — Only top-level directories and objects are saved.

- *OBJ — Only objects that exactly match the name or pattern specified on the Objects parameter are saved. If the objects are directories, only the directories are saved, not the objects within the directories.

RESTORE (COMMAND RST)

As you might expect, the Restore command lets you get back what you previously saved. Again, the essential parameters of the Restore command are the device, the objects, and the directory subtree.

Device (parameter DEV)

This parameter specifies the IFS path to a device or save file. The same naming considerations apply here as on the Save command.

Objects (parameter OBJ)

Where the Objects parameter on the Save command has two parts (a name and an include/omit indicator), the Objects parameter on the Restore command has three parts:

- Name — Specifies the name of an object or a pattern. The name or pattern must correspond to objects previously saved to a device or save file.

- Include/Omit — Indicates that the name part should be used to include or exclude objects during the restore.

- New object name — Specifies a new name. If you specify a single object in the name part, you can use this entry to rename the object as it is restored. If you specify a pattern in the name part, you can use this entry to restore objects to a different directory than the one containing the objects when they were saved.

To restore one object, use the Objects parameter as shown below.

```
RST DEV('/QSYS.LIB/TAP01.DEVD')                    +
    OBJ(('/myjava/Customer.class' *INCLUDE))
```

To restore more than one object using a pattern, use the following Objects parameter.

```
RST DEV('/QSYS.LIB/TAP01.DEVD')                    +
    OBJ(('/myjava/Customer*' *INCLUDE))
```

This example restores from a tape device all previously saved objects that begin with Customer. You can specify multiple criteria to include or omit objects matching particular names or patterns. For example, to restore all files that begin with Customer but omit files with an extension of .class, use the example below.

```
RST DEV('/QSYS.LIB/examples.lib/mysavf.file')  +
    OBJ(('/myjava/Customer*' *INCLUDE)           +
        ('/myjava/*.class' *OMIT))
```

As with the Save command, you can specify up to 300 separate include/omit criteria on a single Restore command.

Directory Subtree (parameter SUBTREE)

This parameter is especially useful if you specify a directory name on the Objects parameter. You can use this parameter to provide additional direction to the Restore command. If you specify a pattern for the Objects parameter, more than one directory matching the pattern can be restored.

- *ALL (default) — Top-level directories, subdirectories, and objects within the directories are restored.

- *DIR — First-level directories and objects are restored. Subdirectories are restored, too, but not the objects within the subdirectories. This option restores the entire directory tree structure but restores objects only from the directories at the topmost level.

- *NONE — Only top-level directories and objects are restored.

- *OBJ — Only objects that exactly match the name or pattern specified on the Objects parameter are restored. If the objects are directories, only the directories are restored, not the objects within the directories.

Keep in mind that you are not required to mirror the Save operation with the Restore command. For example, if you save with the *ALL value but restore with the *NONE value, only top-level directories and objects are restored — even if the save medium contains subdirectories. Of course, if you saved with the *NONE value, you couldn't restore with the *ALL value and expect to get any subdirectories.

ZIPs AND JARs

You can deploy Java classes in three basic ways:

- Collection of class files in a ZIP archive
- Collection of class files in a Java Archive (JAR)
- Individual class files

Collecting class files in a ZIP archive lets you group related classes in a single file. Then you simply handle one file instead of many individual class files.

A JAR is similar to a ZIP archive containing multiple Java classes. In fact, the JAR format is based on the ZIP format and ZIP utilities can usually read JARs without difficulty. The JAR standard also lets you supply a manifest of a JAR's contents within the JAR itself. The JAR standard is designed to be cross-platform and is supported by most Web browsers. Both ZIP and JAR archives let you include related application resources like sounds and images along with your Java classes.

Unlike archive files that you may be used to, ZIPs and JARs don't require you to unpack your code before running it. JVMs are smart enough to look inside ZIP and JAR archives to execute the classes inside directly.

Using separate class files in one or more directories can clutter up the file system and make administration difficult. When the number of classes in an application climbs over two dozen, deploying classes as individual files begins to get troublesome. In almost all cases, a ZIP archive or JAR is preferable.

System Java Directories

The ADK, described in Chapter 2, stores its Java classes in the IFS just like you do. It's a good idea to get familiar with how IBM set up the directory structure and where it placed the core ADK classes. You never know when you might need to troubleshoot a problem that goes all the way back to the ADK. To simplify matters, IBM uses archives in the ZIP format to store Java code.

JVM

The Java runtime support used by the AS/400's JVM is implemented using the ZIP archives shown in Table 3.2.

TABLE 3.2
JVM Implementation

Path and ZIP File (appended to QIBM/ProdData/Java400)	Purpose
/lib/jdkptf.zip	When it exists, provides PTF-style fixes to Java implementation.
/lib/rawt_classes.zip	Remote AWT classes.

continued

TABLE 3.2 *CONTINUED*

Path and ZIP File (appended to QIBM/ProdData/Java400)	Purpose
/lib/java.zip	Core Java implementation.
/lib/sun.zip	Sun Microsystems' JDK classes.
/com/ibm/db2/jdbc/app/db2_classes.zip	Native DB2/400 JDBC driver classes.

The ZIP archives are listed here in the order that they appear on your classpath (more about this feature in the "Configuration" section). Notice that the jdkptf.zip file appears first on the list (and on the classpath). In this way, IBM can provide PTF-style fixes to the ADK simply by placing updated class files in this ZIP archive. For example, IBM would not need to replace the entire java.zip file if only a few classes in the ZIP archive require a fix.

AS/400 TOOLBOX FOR JAVA

The AS/400 Toolbox for Java resides in the IFS, but in a different location than the core ADK support. It's in /QIBM/ProdData/Http/Public/jt400/lib/jt400.zip.

The Toolbox is most often used in applications running on client workstations. You can either use the AS/400 as a file server to access the jt400.zip file from a client or download the jt400.zip file to each client workstation.

NOTE: The Toolbox is provided in both ZIP and JAR formats. Both files reside in the same directory in the IFS and provide identical functionality.

It is often convenient to access the Toolbox from a client by mapping a drive to the IFS. Mapping a drive requires either Client Access installed on a Windows 95/98/NT PC or NetServer support running on the AS/400. If Client Access and NetServer are not options for you, or if you simply want to gain the best possible performance from your applications, you might install the Toolbox locally on a workstation. The AS400ToolboxInstaller is a part of the Toolbox that automates updates to client-installed Toolbox configurations.

Common IFS Commands

IBM took an interesting approach to the IFS commands. In addition to providing IFS commands that follow OS/400's verb-subject naming standard, IBM provided DOS/Unix-style commands as aliases. Table 3.3 shows the OS/400 commands described in this section and their aliases.

TABLE 3.3

Common IFS Commands Summary

Command (DOS/Unix Aliases)	Description	Comments
CHGCURDIR (CD, CHDIR)	Change current directory	Change the directory established as the current directory
DSPCURDIR	Display current directory	See the name of the directory established as the current directory
CRTDIR (MD, MKDIR)	Make directory	Create an IFS directory
RMVDIR (RD)	Remove directory	Remove (delete) an IFS directory
WRKLNK	Work with object links	Locate and work with IFS files and directories
MOVE (MOV)	Move an object	Move (relocate) IFS files and directories
COPY (CPY)	Copy an object	Copy IFS files
REN (RNM)	Rename an object	Rename an IFS file or directory
RMVLNK (DEL, ERASE)	Delete an object	Remove (delete) IFS files

Although you can use the commands described here with any file system, this discussion is concentrated on the stream file systems (root and QOpenSys). Notice that some commands, like CHGCURDIR, have more than one alias. Where alias commands exist, they function exactly like the OS/400-style commands.

CURRENT AND HOME DIRECTORY

As a Java programmer on the AS/400, you can put your source and class files into any directory in the root or QOpenSys file systems. You create directories in the IFS using the Create Directory (CRTDIR) command or one of its aliases (MD, MKDIR). For example, the following command creates the myapp directory in the QOpenSys file system.

```
CRTDIR DIR('/QOpenSys/myapp')
```

When working with the IFS, you always have a current directory. This directory supplies a default path when used with IFS commands. Setting a current directory lets you type fewer keystrokes. If your current directory is already set to /QOpenSys, you can achieve the same results as in the previous example by typing

```
CRTDIR DIR('myapp')
```

To change your current directory, use the Change Current Directory (CHGCURDIR) command or one of its aliases (CD, CHDIR). For example, the following command changes your current directory to the myapp directory.

```
CHGCURDIR DIR('/QOpenSys/myapp')
```

To determine your current directory, use the Display Current Directory (DSPCURDIR) command. This command displays a screen showing the name of your current directory, not the contents of the current directory.

When you first sign on to the AS/400, your current directory defaults to the home directory specified in your user profile. Home directories are often created in the root file system as subdirectories under the directory /home. For example, the home directories for Tom, Dick, and Harry are

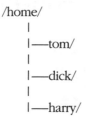

```
/home/
  |
  |—tom/
  |
  |—dick/
  |
  |—harry/
```

When Tom signs on, /home/tom is his home directory and, by extension, his current directory. If a user profile specifies a home directory that does not exist, the root directory (/) becomes the current directory.

As shown in the example below, you can use the Remove Directory (RMVDIR) command to delete an existing directory.

```
RMVDIR DIR('/mydir')
```

The RMVDIR command has one additional parameter, Remove link (RMVLNK). Specify *NO for this parameter (the default) to remove the directory only if it is empty. If you change the parameter to *YES, all objects contained in the directory are deleted along with the directory. The RMVLNK parameter is file-system dependent. Currently, neither the root nor the QOpenSys file systems support deleting a directory while it contains objects.

IFS OBJECT LINKS

At times, the terminology used in IFS command parameters can be confusing. For example, the Remove Link (RMVLNK, DEL, ERASE) command deletes a file in the IFS. Most people don't equate files and links. However, IBM has a good reason for its terminology — the IFS truly does keep track of files via links (i.e., cross-references) in a table.

You'll see an advantage to this internal link mechanism when we discuss symbolic links later in this chapter. For now, links are just an annoying impediment to understanding simple copy, move, rename, and delete commands.

COPY

You can use the Copy Object (COPY, CPY) command to copy a single file or a group of files. The essential parameters of the COPY command are listed below.

- Object (OBJ) — Specify either a single file to copy or a pattern to copy multiple files. If you use a pattern, you must specify the To Directory parameter instead of the To Object parameter.
- To Directory (TODIR) — Specify the target directory for the copy operation. If you specify a pattern for the OBJ parameter, you must also specify this parameter.
- To Object (TOOBJ) — Specify the target directory for the copy operation and a new name for the copied file. This parameter and the TODIR parameter are mutually exclusive; the TOOBJ parameter is valid only if a single file is specified in the OBJ parameter.

The next example copies the Customer.class file by itself to the /myjava-backup directory and gives it the new name Customer.backup.

```
COPY OBJ('/myjava/Customer.class')            +
    TOOBJ('/myjavabackup/Customer.backup')
```

To copy more than one file, use a pattern on the OBJ parameter, as shown below. Notice that the TODIR parameter is required instead of the TOOBJ parameter.

```
COPY OBJ('/myjava/*') TODIR('/myjavabackup')
```

This command copies all files from the /myjava directory to the /myjavabackup directory.

MOVE

The Move Object (MOVE, MOV) command is much like the COPY command except that it relocates files instead of copying them. You can move a single file, with the option of renaming it at the target location, or you can specify a pattern to move more than one file at a time.

To move the Customer.class file by itself to the /myjavabackup directory and give it the new name Customer.backup, the parameters are identical to those used on the COPY command:

```
MOVE OBJ('/myjava/Customer.class')            +
    TOOBJ('/myjavabackup/Customer.backup')
```

The same holds true for moving more than one file using a pattern. Again, the only change is the command name from COPY to MOVE:

```
MOVE OBJ('/myjava/*') TODIR('/myjavabackup')
```

One difference between the MOVE and COPY commands is that the MOVE command lets you move entire directories and their contents, not just files. For example, the following command moves the /myjava directory and makes it a subdirectory of /myjavabackup.

```
MOVE OBJ('/myjava') TODIR('/myjavabackup')
```

After this command is executed, the directory structure appears this way:

/myjavabackup/

|

|—myjava/

Moving the /myjava directory back to the top level is a simple matter:

```
MOVE OBJ('/myjavabackup/myjava') TODIR('/')
```

RENAME

You can use the Rename Object (REN, RNM) command to rename a single file. If you try to rename more than one file by using a pattern on the command, you are shown a list of files and must choose only one to rename.

The REN command has two parameters:

- Object (OBJ) — The name of a file to rename
- New object (NEWOBJ) — A new name for the file

The following example of the REN command renames the Customer.class file in the /myjavabackup directory to Customer.backup.

```
REN OBJ('/myjavabackup/Customer.class')      +
    NEWOBJ('Customer.backup')
```

As with the MOVE command, the REN command lets you manipulate directories as well as files. To rename the /myjava directory, use this command:

```
REN OBJ('/myjava') NEWOBJ('/myrenamedjava')
```

DELETE

The Remove Link (RMVLNK, DEL, ERASE) command deletes files in the IFS. It has only one parameter, Object link (OBJLNK). As with the MOVE and COPY commands, you specify a single file or specify a pattern to delete multiple files at once. For example, the following command removes the Customer.class file from the /myjavabackup directory:

```
RMVLNK OBJLNK('/myjavabackup/Customer.class')
```

All the files beginning with Customer are removed from the /myjavabackup directory with this command:

```
RMVLNK OBJLNK('/myjavabackup/Customer*')
```

WORK WITH OBJECT LINKS

The Work with Object Links (WRKLNK) command lets you access the various file systems contained in the IFS. This command lists the objects in a file system and lets you apply the copy, move, rename, and delete functions to one or more items on the list. For the root and QOpenSys file systems, the

WRKLNK command serves mainly as a directory list utility. Use it to browse a directory and manipulate the files in it.

The parameters provided by the WRKLNK command are listed below.

- Object (OBJ) — Specify either a single directory or file to list or specify a pattern to list multiple directories and files.
- Object Type (OBJTYPE) — Choose to see both directories and files in a list, just directories, or just certain types of objects. Your options for this parameter are

  - *ALL — Includes both directories and files in the list.

  - *ALLDIR — Includes only directories in the list.

  - Object-type — Includes only objects of the type you specify in the list. In file systems such as the QSYS.LIB file system, you can use this option to specify object types such as programs (*PGM) or output queues (*OUTQ). In the root and QOpenSys file systems, your options are limited to objects found in a stream file system such as stream files (*STMF) and symbolic links (*SYMLNK).

- Detail (DETAIL) — Specify the amount of information that you want to see pertaining to each list item. Your options for this parameter are

  - *NAME — Shows only the names of directories and files in the list.

  - *BASIC (default) — Shows type, attribute, and text, along with the name of each directory and file in the list.

  - *EXTENDED — Shows an extended type, plus name, attribute, and text for each directory and file in the list. The extended type shows the relationship between a symbolic link and the file or directory that it is linked to.

  - *PRV — Uses the value specified when the command was last executed.

- Display Option (DSPOPT) — This parameter pertains mainly to PC systems linked through the IFS and is of limited value in the root and QOpenSys file systems. Your options for this parameter are

  - *USER (default) — Does not show the current directory marker (.) and parent directory marker (..) in the list of files and directories unless explicitly selected on the Object parameter.

  - *ALL — Shows the current directory marker (.) and parent directory marker (..) in the list of files whenever a generic pattern (*) is used on the Object parameter.

  - *PRV — Uses the value specified when the command was last executed.

It is always preferable to get the most information possible from the WRKLNK command. Therefore, specifying *ALL for the object type and an *EXTENDED level of detail are your best bets. The following command shows detailed information about the contents of the /myjava directory:

```
WRKLNK OBJ('/myjava/*') OBJTYPE(*ALL) DETAIL(*EXTENDED)
```

STREAM FILES

In Chapter 1 you used the Copy to Stream File (CPYTOSTMF) command to copy a source member to a stream file.

IBM distributes a handy utility, Edit File, for editing stream files in the IFS. This utility, shown in Figure 3.1, looks and acts similar to SEU. Using this utility, you can edit text and Java source files in the IFS directly from a terminal or emulation session. When you need quick access to text or source files residing in the IFS, or when you are away from a client workstation with IFS access, this utility is a real lifesaver.

FIGURE 3.1
Edit File Utility

```
 Edit File: /myjava/Customer.java
 Record . :       1 of      59 by   9            Column:    1 of   77 by  74
 Control  :

CMD  ....+....1....+....2....+....3....+....4....+....5....+....6....+....7....+
     ****************** Beginning of data ********************
     /**
     *  The Customer class defines customer contact information and provides
     *  functionality for formatting mailing labels.
     */
     public class Customer {

       private int custID = 0; // Customer identifier
       private String custName = null;  // Full customer name (e.g. "John Smith")
       private String custStreet = null; // Customer street address
       private String custCityStateZip = null; // Customer city, state and zip co

       private static int lastCustID = 10000;  // Last customer ID assigned


     /*

F2=Save F3=Save/Exit F10/11=Left/Right F12=Cancel F16=Find F17=Chg F15=Copy
```

The Edit File utility is a part of the User Tools shipped with V4R2. Look for instructions to create the tool in the QUSRTOOL library. The source member TGPAESFI in source file QATTINFO provides detailed instructions for creating the EDTF command. You might also find the utility already created in a directory called QGPTOOLS on your system.

NOTE: The Edit File utility is also available as a PTF for V4R2 and V4R3. In V4R2, the PTF number is SF45296 for product 5769-SS1 (OS/400). In V4R3, the PTF number is SF49052, also for product 5769-SS1.

JAVA COMMANDS

Only a handful of AS/400 commands are directly related to Java. They are summarized in Table 3.4. In this section, we examine these commands and their parameters.

TABLE 3.4
Java Commands Summary

Command	Description	Comments
CRTJVAPGM	Create Java program	Transform a class file into a native executable
DLTJVAPGM	Delete Java program	Delete a native executable associated with a class file
DSPJVAPGM	Display Java program	Determine whether a class file has been "transformed" and at what optimization level
RUNJVA (JAVA)	Execute Java program	Run Java programs

Native Compiler

Recall from Chapter 2 that the AS/400 uses a unique technology called a byte-code Transformer to translate Java class files into optimized, directly executable objects. You learned that the Transformer can translate Java class files at run-time or before execution. This section discusses the commands you can use to create and manipulate direct execution objects for your own Java classes.

We first consider the Create Java Program (CRTJVAPGM) command. This command is not a source code compiler for Java. Rather, the CRTJVAPGM command translates already compiled Java class files (bytecodes) into objects containing 64-bit RISC instructions that the AS/400's hardware can execute directly.

These direct execution objects (DE objects) are not exactly like the program objects you create with languages such as RPG or Cobol. For one thing, you can't even see these objects! The AS/400 keeps up with DE objects for you by associating DE objects with the class files used to construct them. When you move a class file in the IFS, the associated DE object moves with it; when you save a class file, the DE object is saved, too.

The primary reason for using the CRTJVAPGM command is to optimize programs. On most platforms, Java is an interpreted language. Some JVMs include just in time (JIT) compilers that create native code from Java class files at runtime. A JIT must compile the classes that make up a Java program every time the program runs. Also, the amount of optimization a JIT can perform is limited by performance constraints. The time it would take for a JIT to do a really thorough job of optimization could negate the resulting runtime performance gains. In contrast, the AS/400's Transformer saves the optimized results of the compile and, because the Transformer compiles class files only once, it can take the time to optimize thoroughly.

CREATE JAVA PROGRAM (COMMAND CRTJVAPGM)

Use this command to create a DE object from a Java class file before the program executes. The parameters of the CRTJVAPGM command are class file, optimization, replace program, enable performance collection, and licensed internal code options.

Class File (parameter CLSF)

You can specify a single class file for this parameter or use a pattern to optimize more than one class file. You can also specify a ZIP or JAR file containing one or more class files.

An example of this parameter for a single class file is shown below.

```
CRTJVAPGM CLSF('/myjava/Customer.class')
```

This command optimizes the class file called Customer.class at the default optimization level of 10. The command below is an example of this parameter using a pattern.

```
CRTJVAPGM CLSF('/myjava/Customer*.class')
```

This command optimizes all class files that begin with Customer at the default optimization level.

Say that we've taken the Customer Tracking Application from Chapter 2 and placed its class files into a JAR file called CustApp.jar for convenience. To optimize the entire JAR file, the CLSF parameter is

```
CRTJVAPGM CLSF('/myjava/CustApp.jar')
```

This command demonstrates another good reason to use ZIP or JAR files to package your applications on the AS/400 — you can optimize entire applications with a single CRTJVAPGM command!

Optimization (parameter OPTIMIZE)

As with ILE language programs, Java programs have more than one optimization level from which to choose. Higher optimization levels make your programs run faster, but they carry with them potentially inconvenient debugging trade-offs. Your options are listed below.

- 10 (default) — A DE object is created. Minimal optimization is performed. Full debugging capabilities are available.

- *INTERPRET — A DE object is created but no optimization is performed. Bytecodes are interpreted at runtime.

- 20 — A DE object is created. Some optimization is performed. Variables in debug can be displayed but not changed.

- 30 — A DE object is created. Even more optimization is performed. Variables in debug can be displayed but not changed; however, displayed variable values may not be current.

- 40 — A DE object is created. Full optimization is performed. Source-level debugging is not possible.

The default optimization level for the CRTJVAPGM command is 10 — a DE object is created but only minimal optimization is performed. At level 10, all debugging functions are allowed. At higher optimization levels, program performance increases but debugging becomes more difficult. For example, at levels 20 and 30, program variables can be displayed but not changed. At level 30, the displayed values of program variables may not even be the current values of the variables! This discrepancy is caused by register-level optimization, in which the memory containing the value of a variable is not necessarily updated every time the value changes. At optimization levels above 20, debugging is impractical.

One often-used technique for optimizing programs is to leave the optimization level at 10 or 20 while programs are in development. When you deploy your software into production, you can optimize the code at a level of 30 or 40 for the best performance.

Replace Program (parameter REPLACE)
This parameter determines whether you want to replace an existing DE object. Your two options are

- *YES (default) — This value forces an existing DE object to be replaced. If a DE object doesn't exist, one is created.

- *NO — The meaning of this value is a bit deeper than you might expect. If the class file associated with a DE object has changed since the DE object was created, the DE object is replaced. If the associated class file has not changed since the DE object was created, the DE object is not replaced. If a pattern was used to select more than one class, and one of those classes didn't change (resulting in a DE object not being replaced), subsequent classes are still considered for DE object replacement. If a DE object doesn't exist when this command is executed, one is always created.

Enable Performance Collection (parameter ENBPFRCOL)
This parameter creates the DE object in a way that allows for collection of program performance data with a product such as IBM's Performance Tools/400

(LPP 5769-PT1). Collecting performance data during program execution is a way for you to locate bottlenecks in your applications.

Your options for this parameter are

- *NONE — No performance data can be collected for this program.
- *ENTRYEXIT — Performance data can be collected before and after internal procedure calls.
- *FULL — Performance data can be collected before and after internal and external procedure calls.

Be forewarned that collecting performance data during program execution can decrease the program's performance. This effect is caused by the amount of time it takes for a performance tool to log the data it is collecting. However, because performance monitors tend to slow a program predictably and uniformly, the statistics they generate are still valid.

Licensed Internal Code Options (parameter LICOPT)

Used properly, this parameter lets you fine-tune a DE object's performance. This parameter affects the internal representation of the DE object and should be used only by advanced programmers with an understanding of the internal workings of the AS/400's Java runtime environment.

This parameter does not exist in V4R2; it is introduced in V4R3. Your option for this parameter is

- *OPTIMIZE (default) — Perform optimization based on the Optimization (OPTIMIZE) parameter alone.

You can also specify one or more Licensed Internal Code optimization strings to use when creating the DE object. At the time of this writing, the optimization strings allowed and their effect on the DE object were not fully defined by IBM.

DISPLAY JAVA PROGRAM (COMMAND DSPJVAPGM)

Use this command to check for the existence of a DE object associated with a class file and to determine the attributes of the DE object. If you use this command on a class file before it has been optimized, you receive the escape message "No Java program associated with the class file."

The parameters of the DSPJVAPGM command are listed below.

- Class file (parameter CLSF) — Specifies a class file to display. You can specify only a single class file for this parameter; patterns are not allowed. You can also specify a single ZIP or JAR file.
- Output (parameter OUT) — A target for output from the command. You can either specify the local display or direct the output to be printed.

DELETE JAVA PROGRAM (COMMAND DLTJVAPGM)

Use this command to delete an existing DE object from the system. The class file used to create the DE object is not deleted.

The only parameter of the DLTJVAPGM command is the class file.

Class File (parameter CLSF)

This parameter lets you specify one or more class files. You can specify a single class file for this parameter or use a pattern to select more than one class file. You can also specify a ZIP or JAR file containing one or more class files.

OPTIMIZATION "GOTCHA"

You might encounter an annoying "gotcha" when creating and deleting DE objects. Here is the scenario:

- Using the CRTJVAPGM command, you compile a Java class and optimize it to level 40.
- You delete the DE object.
- You run the Java class with the Run Java (RUNJVA) command specifying to optimize at level 10.

What do you expect to happen? If you expect to end up with a DE object optimized at level 10, you're sadly mistaken. Even though you deleted the level 40 optimized object and you said to optimize at level 10 on the RUNJVA command, the Transformer optimizes at the previous optimization level. This is also the case in the reverse scenario described below.

- Using the CRTJVAPGM command, you compile a Java class and optimize it to level 10.
- You delete the DE object.
- You run the Java class with the RUNJVA command specifying to optimize at level 40.

The result is a DE object optimized at level 10. The thinking is that the last explicit optimization of a Java class is where all subsequent optimizations should revert. The best way of dealing with this is to avoid the OPTIMIZE parameter of the RUNJVA command entirely and always control optimization with the CRTJVAPGM command.

ANOTHER LOOK AT SAVE/RESTORE

The IFS section of this chapter described the Save and Restore commands and how to use them with your Java projects. In light of the new information about hidden DE objects that go along with optimized Java classes and JAR files, we need to revisit the Backup and Restore discussion.

What happens to the optimized DE object when a Java class (or JAR) is saved from the IFS? Good news! The optimized object goes along for the ride. You can easily confirm this fact by performing the following steps:

1. Create a Java class without optimization.
2. Save the class to a save file.
3. Display the contents of the save file and check the file size.
4. Optimize the Java class.
5. Save the class to a save file.
6. Compare the size of the save file contents to the earlier save.

Try it. First, compile the Customer class from Chapter 1. If it's already compiled, delete any optimization with the DLTJVAPGM command.

Now, create a save file:

```
CRTSAVF FILE(EXAMPLES/MYSAVF)
```

Save the Customer.class file to it:

```
SAV DEV('/QSYS.LIB/EXAMPLES.LIB/MYSAVF.LIB')    +
    OBJ(('/myjava/Customer.class' *INCLUDE))
```

Display the contents of the save file:

```
DSPSAVF FILE(EXAMPLES/MYSAVF)
```

Note the size of the Customer.class file.

Figure 3.2 shows the DSPSAVF command results for the non-optimized Customer.class file.

FIGURE 3.2
Display Save File Results Before Optimization

```
                    Display Saved Objects - Save File

Display level . . . . . :   1
Directory . . . . . . . :     /myjava


Type options, press Enter.
  5=Display objects in subdirectory   8=Display object specific information

Opt  Object             Type        Owner         Size  Data
  _    Customer.class    *STMF       DAND          4096  Yes




                                                                  Bottom
 F3=Exit    F11=Display names only   F12=Cancel   F16=Display header
 F22=Display entire field
 1 objects saved on media file.
```

Now, optimize the Customer class, clear the save file, and repeat the save.

```
CRTJVAPGM CLSF('/myjava/Customer.class') OPTIMIZE(40)

CLRSAVF FILE(EXAMPLES/MYSAVF)

SAV DEV('/QSYS.LIB/EXAMPLES.LIB/MYSAVF.LIB')    +
    OBJ(('/myjava/Customer.class' *INCLUDE))

DSPSAVF FILE(EXAMPLES/MYSAVF)
```

Figure 3.3 shows the Display Save File command results for the optimized Customer.class file.

FIGURE 3.3
Display Save File Results After Optimization

```
                      Display Saved Objects - Save File
Display level . . . . . :   1
Directory . . . . . . . :    /myjava


Type options, press Enter.
  5=Display objects in subdirectory   8=Display object specific information

Opt   Object              Type        Owner          Size  Data
  _   Customer.class      *STMF       DAND           32768  Yes



                                                            Bottom
F3=Exit    F11=Display names only   F12=Cancel   F16=Display header
F22=Display entire field
1 objects saved on media file.
```

The difference in the size of the Customer.class file is the DE object saved as a part of the class file. You can rest assured that although you can't see the optimized DE object listed as a separately saved object, it is there.

Java Program Execution

Your interface to the AS/400's JVM is the Run Java (RUNJVA, JAVA) command. This command is the equivalent of the "java" command that you might have used with Sun Microsystems' JDK. The parameters are many, so let's get right to them.

Class (parameter CLASS)

With this parameter, you specify the name of a class to run. If the class is part of a package, you must qualify the class name with the package name. An example of this parameter with an unqualified class name is

```
RUNJVA CLASS('Customer')
```

This command executes the Customer class from the example in Chapter 1. To specify a package-qualified class name, separate each element of the package name with periods, as in this example

```
RUNJVA CLASS('package.anotherpackage.MyClass')
```

Instead of a class name, you can specify the special value *VERSION for this parameter. This value causes the command to return information about the current version of the JVM and JDK compatibility, such as, "Version JVM V4R3M0 JDK 1.1.6."

PARAMETERS (PARAMETER PARM)

Using this parameter, you can specify up to 200 parameters that you want passed to the Java program. These parameters can be accessed by the Java program as an array of Strings passed as an argument to the **main** method.

CLASSPATH (PARAMETER CLASSPATH)

This parameter specifies the classpath, consisting of IFS path names, used to locate Java classes at runtime. The classpath may also contain the path to one or more ZIP or JAR archive files.

A special value for this parameter is *ENVVAR. This value, the default for the parameter, indicates that the environment variable CLASSPATH is used to determine the classpath. We discuss how to use this environment variable in "Configuration," later in this chapter.

You can specify one or more IFS path names to construct a classpath. If you specify more than one path, use colons (:) to separate the path names. The JVM looks for classes in the classpath by searching directories and archive files in the order specified.

Examples of the CLASSPATH parameter using one and more than one path name are listed below.

```
RUNJVA CLASS('Customer') CLASSPATH('/myjava')

RUNJVA CLASS('Customer')                                       +
       CLASSPATH('/myjava:/myDir2/subDir2a/subDir2b')

RUNJVA CLASS('Customer')                                       +
       CLASSPATH('/myDir2/subDir2a/subDir2b:                   +
                  /myDir3/myJar.jar:/myjava')
```

CLASSPATH SECURITY LEVEL CHECK (PARAMETER CHKPATH)

This parameter specifies the level of protection you desire when the classpath contains directories with public write authority. Directories in the classpath with public write authority represent a significant security risk.

Consider a scenario in which your classpath is established with the following directories:

```
/pubjava/:/myjava
```

Assume that the directory /pubjava has been granted public write authority and that the two directories contain a class called Customer.class. At runtime, the class is loaded from the first directory found to contain the class, in this case /pubjava. With public write authority, classes in /pubjava could be replaced by someone with malicious intentions. The AS/400's JVM is happy to help you minimize this security risk.

Your options for this parameter are

- *WARN (default) — A warning message is issued for every directory in the classpath found to have public write authority; however, the Java program is not prevented from running.

- *SECURE — A warning message is issued for every directory in the classpath found to have public write authority. If any directory in the classpath has public write authority, an escape message is issued after the warning messages and the Java program is not allowed to execute.

- *IGNORE — No warning or escape messages are issued for directories in the classpath with public write authority. The Java program is allowed to run.

OPTIMIZATION (PARAMETER OPTIMIZE)

In this parameter, you specify the optimization level to use when creating a DE object. Recall that the AS/400's JVM creates a DE object at runtime if one was not created ahead of time using the CRTJVAPGM command. The DE object created at runtime for a single class is retained by the system after the command is run. Any DE objects created at runtime for classes inside ZIP or JAR files are discarded by the system after the command is run.

Because it is costly in terms of performance for the system to create DE objects at runtime, it is a good idea to always create them ahead of time with the CRTJVAPGM command, especially if your classes are packaged in ZIP or JAR files.

If a DE object already exists when the RUNJVA command is run, this parameter is ignored. Optimization levels allowed on this parameter are the same as those allowed on the like-named parameter of the CRTJVAPGM command.

INTERPRET (PARAMETER INTERPRET)

This parameter provides a finer degree of control over when Java classes are executed in an interpreted fashion. When a Java class is interpreted, the bytecodes making up the class are read and executed without any optimization taking place. This parameter does not exist in V4R2; it is introduced in V4R3. The options for this parameter follow.

- *OPTIMIZE (default) — The OPTIMIZE parameter is used to determine whether Java classes are executed in an interpreted fashion.

- *YES — All Java classes are executed in an interpreted fashion, regardless of the optimization level on associated DE objects.

- *NO — Java classes are not interpreted unless they have associated DE objects and the DE objects were created with an *INTERPRET optimization level.

No matter which parameter value is specified, if a class does not have an associated DE object, an object is created and the OPTIMIZE parameter determines its level of optimization.

PROPERTIES (PARAMETER PROP)

This parameter specifies runtime property values and consists of two parts:

- Property name — The name of a runtime property
- Property value — A value assigned to the runtime property

The JVM maintains a list of runtime properties, some of which you can set. To see all the default runtime properties, execute this short Java program.

```
class ShowMeProperties {
public static void main(String[] args)
    {
        java.util.Properties p = System.getProperties();
        p.list(System.out);
    }
}
```

For the purposes of illustration, set the JVM's user.dir property to the /myjava directory and then display the results with the ShowMeProperties program:

```
RUNJVA CLASS(ShowMeProperties) CLASSPATH('/myjava')    +
    PROP((user.dir '/myjava'))
```

You can also establish your own properties and then interrogate them in applications, just as you might do with system properties. The following command creates a property called someproperty and establishes a value for it of somevalue. This new property appears in the property list along with the default system properties.

```
RUNJVA CLASS(ShowMeProperties) CLASSPATH('/myjava')    +
    PROP((someproperty 'somevalue'))
```

GARBAGE COLLECT INITIAL SIZE (PARAMETER GCHINL)

Understanding the garbage collection control parameters is not critical for running most Java programs, but you'll want to become familiar with their purpose anyway. Balancing the garbage collection mechanism is a black art and you'll find that, in practice, successfully setting it depends on your system hardware (processor speed and number of processors) and system resources (memory).

Garbage collection works by looking for objects with no references in other objects and then reclaiming the storage allocated to the non-referenced objects.

On the AS/400, garbage collection is an asynchronous process; it runs in separate threads and can therefore work continuously as a Java program runs.

This parameter specifies the initial amount of storage, expressed in kilobytes, assigned for garbage collection. Essentially, garbage collection does not take place at all until at least this much storage is allocated by a Java program.

The default value for this parameter is 2048, IBM's minimum recommended setting. The larger the number specified for this parameter, the longer it is before garbage collection takes place in a given Java program. Specifying a larger number in this parameter can improve application performance.

GARBAGE COLLECT MAXIMUM SIZE (PARAMETER GCHMAX)

This parameter specifies the maximum amount of storage, expressed in kilobytes, which can be accumulated for garbage collection. If this maximum is reached, the JVM takes it as an indication that a runaway program is sucking up all available storage and takes action rather aggressively — the JVM stops all active program threads while garbage collection takes place. To avoid such a performance crunch, this parameter and the Garbage Collection Priority parameter should be carefully managed to avoid reaching the maximum.

The default settings for this parameter are

- 32768 (V4R2 default) — IBM's minimum recommended setting for this parameter. It should always be set large enough to avoid reaching the maximum.

- *NOMAX (V4R3 default) — Added in V4R3, this setting indicates that the system will determine an appropriate amount of storage to use for garbage collection.

GARBAGE COLLECTION FREQUENCY (PARAMETER GCFRQ)

This parameter was introduced in V4R2 but was advertised as an "unimplemented feature." In other words, it didn't do anything. It was expected that this feature would be implemented in V4R3 but instead, IBM decided that this feature would never be necessary. The parameter exists today only to ensure that the RUNJVA command parameters remain compatible in all releases.

In V4R2 and V4R3, this parameter is ignored by the JVM.

GARBAGE COLLECTION PRIORITY (PARAMETER GCPTY)

Garbage collection threads have run priorities just like threads in any other AS/400 job. This parameter determines the run priority assigned to garbage collection threads. However, the values specified for this parameter do not directly equate to AS/400 run priorities. In fact, they might seem backwards to you. On an AS/400 job, a job with a run priority of 10 is a "high priority" job, compared to a "low priority" job with a run priority of 99. A high priority for garbage collection is 30 and a low priority is 10.

The AS/400 interprets this parameter into a real run priority for the garbage collection threads relative to the run priority of the job in which the JVM is running. As a job priority is changed, the threads within the job, including the garbage collection threads, are adjusted relative to the job priority.

This parameter is supported in V4R2 but ignored in V4R3. The options are listed below.

- 20 (default) — Considered normal garbage collection priority. At this setting, garbage collection threads are set to the same run priority as application threads.

- 10 — The lowest priority for garbage collection. At this setting, garbage collection threads are typically set to a lower run priority than application threads. Garbage collection may not run as frequently as it would at a priority of 20 or 30. Take care to ensure that garbage collection is happening frequently enough to avoid reaching the maximum storage size specified on the GCHMAX parameter.

- 30 — The highest priority for garbage collection. At this setting, garbage collection threads are typically set to a higher run priority than application threads.

Option (parameter OPTION)

With this parameter, you specify the options to be exercised when executing the class that is specified. You can specify multiple values for this parameter. Your options are listed below.

- *NONE (default) — No special options are exercised.

- *VERBOSE — A message is sent to the display each time a class is loaded by the JVM. This value is extremely useful for tracking down errors occurring as a result of an erroneous classpath. Figure 3.4 shows just a few of the messages issued when the Customer Java program is executed.

- *DEBUG — This option starts the source-level debugger for the class specified. Debugging is covered in the next section.

- *VERBOSEGC — With this option, a message is sent to the display each time garbage collection takes place. Use this option to determine the frequency and extent of garbage collection while fine-tuning performance. This option does not exist in V4R2; it is introduced in V4R3.

- *NOCLASSGC — This option turns off garbage collection for unused classes. Using this option can improve performance in situations where classes are garbage collected and then used again, obviating the need to garbage collect them in the first place. This option does not exist in V4R2; it is introduced in V4R3.

FIGURE 3.4
Verbose Java Program Execution

```
                    Java Shell Command Entry
    Loading class: java/util/Hashtable.clas
    Loading class: java/util/Dictionary.class
    Loading class: java/lang/CloneNotSupportedException.class
    Loading class: java/util/Enumeration.class
    Loading class: java/util/HashtableEnumerator.class
    Loading class: java/lang/InternalError.class
    Loading class: java/util/Date.class
    Loading class: java/util/HashtableEntry.class
    Loading class: sun/io/ConversionBufferFullException.class
    Loading class: sun/io/CharToByteConverter.class
    Loading class: java/io/UnsupportedEncodingException.class
    Loading class: java/lang/ClassNotFoundException.class
    Loading class: java/lang/IllegalAccessException.class
    Loading class: java/lang/InstantiationException.class

    ===>



    F3=Exit    F6=Print F9=Retrieve F12=Disconnect
    F13=Clear F17=Top   F18=Bottom  F21=CL command entry
```

Debugging Java Programs

Historically, the System Debugger has been used for debugging Old Program
Model (OPM) and Integrated Languages Environment (ILE) programs. Now
the System Debugger is fully capable of debugging Java programs too. This
section walks you through the basic features of the System Debugger as they
apply to Java.

STARTING DEBUG

Before you try to debug a Java program, make sure that it was compiled with
the debug option. (When you export class files from VisualAge for Java, select
the "Include debug attributes in class files" option on the "Export to directory"
SmartGuide.) If you're using the ADK compiler, use the -g option to compile
with debug information.

Going back to the example from Chapter 1, compile the Customer class in
the /myjava directory using the modified compile command below, which
includes the debug option:

```
javac -g /myjava/Customer.java
```

Remember, to compile Java programs on the AS/400, you must be in the
QShell interpreter. The -g option includes special debugging tables in the compiled class file. This process is roughly akin to compiling an ILE program with
the *SOURCE debugging view option. For the System Debugger to provide a

THREAD PRIORITIES

Each thread running in the JVM is assigned a run priority by the AS/400. In OS/400 V4R2, the formula used by the AS/400 to calculate a thread's run priority is

ThreadRunPriority = JobPriority + (11 − JVMThreadPriority).

Job Priority is the run priority of the AS/400 job running the JVM. Values can range from 1 to 99, with 1 being a high priority and 99 being a low priority. A normal interactive job priority is 20. A normal batch job priority is 50.

JVMThreadPriority is the internal thread priority kept for each thread by the JVM. Values can range from 1 to 10, with 1 being a low priority and 10 being a high priority. A normal priority for a thread in the JVM is 5.

For a normal thread running in the JVM interactively, the AS/400 run priority assigned to the thread is 26. You can adjust the priority of the AS/400 job running the JVM to increase or decrease thread priorities.

The thread priority for garbage collection is determined by the Garbage collection priority (GCPTY) parameter of the RUNJVA command. For the purposes of calculating run priorities for garbage collection threads, a garbage collection priority of 10 (low priority) equates to a JVMThreadPriority of 10. A garbage collection priority of 20 (normal) is a JVMThreadPriority of 5, and a garbage collection priority of 30 (high priority) is the equivalent of a JVMThreadPriority of 0.

source view for your Java program, the source code must be in the same IFS directory as your class file.

Starting debug on a Java program is as simple as specifying *DEBUG for the Option parameter of the RUNJVA command.

```
RUNJVA CLASS(Customer) CLASSPATH('/myjava') OPTION(*DEBUG)
```

You should see the Display Module Source screen, as shown in Figure 3.5.

The source code in the debugger has line numbers that you will use to perform debug operations. As we work through the Customer program, we refer to these line numbers, so if you modified the Customer program source code or formatted the source code with more or fewer blank lines, you need to adjust accordingly.

SETTING AND CLEARING BREAKPOINTS

An appropriate place to begin debugging the Customer class is in the **main** method. To set a breakpoint, position the cursor on a line where you want to break and press the F6 key. During program execution, the breakpoint is triggered before the code in the breakpoint line is executed. Instead of using the F6 key, you can set a breakpoint from the debug command line by typing **BREAK X,** where *X* is the statement number on which you want the breakpoint.

Set a breakpoint at line 54 (either with F6 or using the BREAK command).

FIGURE 3.5
Display Module Source Screen

```
                        Display Module Source
Class file name:    Customer
   1  /**
   2   *  The Customer class defines customer contact information and provid
   3   *  functionality for formatting mailing labels.
   4   */
   5  public class Customer {
   6
   7    private int custID = 0; // Customer identifier
   8    private String custName = null;  // Full customer name (e.g. "John Sm
   9    private String custStreet = null; // Customer street address
  10    private String custCityStateZip = null; // Customer city, state and z
  11
  12    private static int lastCustID = 10000;  // Last customer ID assigned
  13  /*
  14   * The default constructor is used to create a customer object without
  15   * specific contact information.

Debug . . .

F3=End program    F6=Add/Clear breakpoint    F10=Step    F11=Display variable
F12=Resume        F17=Watch variable    F18=Work with watch    F24=More keys
```

```
54  custArray[4] = new Customer("Jane Gibson",
```

You remove a breakpoint by repeating the same procedure used to add it; either press F6 on a line where a breakpoint has been set or type **BREAK X** on the command line. For now, leave the breakpoint at line 54 in place.

Set a second breakpoint at line number 59.

```
59  System.out.println(custArray[i].getMailingLabel());
```

This time, make it a conditional breakpoint by specifying an expression after the BREAK command.

```
BREAK 59 WHEN i == 3
```

This command tells the debugger to halt on line 59 when the local variable "i" is equal to 3. Notice that you use a Java-style comparison operator for equality (==) on the breakpoint command and not just an equal sign (=).

Set the program in motion by pressing the F12 (Resume) key. When the first breakpoint at line 54 is reached, you can begin working with variables.

DISPLAYING AND CHANGING VARIABLES

To display variables, place the cursor on a variable and press the F11 key. Try this at the current breakpoint with the custArray variable. You can also display the value of a variable with the EVAL command:

```
EVAL custArray
```

The message line of the debug display shows the results of the evaluation. Note that because the custArray variable is an array, the address of the variable in memory is shown rather than the contents of the array. It should appear something like this (although the exact address of the array will differ from one program execution to the next):

```
custArray = ARR:E3C22F165215C680
```

To see the contents of the array, evaluate each array element. For example, to see the first element of the array (array indexes are zero-based), use this debug command:

```
EVAL custArray[0]
```

The debug display should switch to the Evaluate Expression page to show the multiline evaluation of the array element, like this:

```
custArray[0] = Customer:E3C22F165215C700
custArray[0].custName = Dan Darnell
custArray[0].custStreet = 111 Maple Street
custArray[0].custCityStateZip = Little Rock, AR 72201
custArray[0].custID = 10001
custArray[0].lastCustID = 10005
```

The address of the customer object is displayed, along with the variables defined by the object.

Set the program in motion again by pressing the F12 key. It should stop again when it reaches the conditional breakpoint at line 59. Examine the local variable "i" to make sure the conditional breakpoint worked properly.

```
EVAL i
```

The message line should read i = 3.

Changing the value of a variable such as "i" is a simple matter. Use the arithmetic equality operator (=) with the evaluate command to assign a new value to a variable.

```
EVAL i = 4
```

The message line should read "i = 4 = 4". If you check it again, the value of "i" should now be 4.

OBJECT RULES

Simple local variables, such as the integer "i" in the previous example, are easy enough to deal with, but what about the data that you define as instance variables inside your objects? There is good news and potentially bad news on this front. The good news is that you can display and change object data very easily. The potentially bad news is that the System Debugger does not observe any of the protection rules of Java — even an object's private instance variables can be changed inside the debugger.

Try the following debugger command to display the customer ID variable that's inside the customer object held at custArray element number one.

```
EVAL custArray[1].custID
```

The message line should read "custArray[1].custID = 10002". Now change this private instance variable and then redisplay it.

```
EVAL custArray[1].custID = 12345
```

```
EVAL custArray[1].custID
```

You should see "custArray[1].custID = 12345" on the message line, an indication that the System Debugger has happily allowed this object's private instance variable to be changed.

Now that our experimentation with the Customer class is over, press F12 to allow the Java program to finish running.

NOTE: To prevent users from using the debugger to compromise the integrity of your objects, consider recompiling Java programs without using the debug (-g) option before deploying them in a production environment.

SPECIAL FEATURES

One nice feature of the System Debugger is the ability to compare two object references to see whether they refer to the same object. Let's debug a Java program that includes the following code.

```
String objRef1 = "This is a string";
String objRef2 = objRef1;
String objRef3 = "This is another string";
```

Type the following debug command:

```
EVAL objRef1 == objRef2
```

Notice that you use a Java-style comparison operator for equality (==) and not just an equal sign (=). This evaluation yields "objRef1 == objRef2 = TRUE," indicating that the two object references do indeed refer to the same object.

As you might expect, the debug command

```
EVAL objRef1 == objRef3
```

returns "objRef1 == objRef3 = FALSE," indicating that the two object references refer to different objects.

Another special feature of the System Debugger is its ability to see whether an object is an instance of a particular class. While debugging a Java program that includes the following code (where MyClass is a Java class of your own creation)

```
MyClass objRef1 = new MyClass();
```

try this debug command:

```
EVAL objRef1 instanceof MyClass
```

The result of the evaluation is "objRef1 instanceof MyClass = TRUE."

Use the instanceof function to discover whether an object is of a specific class type or a subclass of another type. Consider an example in which the class MyClass2 inherits from MyClass. With an object created using the following code

```
MyClass2 objRef1 = new MyClass2();
```

the following instanceof evaluations are both true:

```
EVAL objRef1 instanceof MyClass2
EVAL objRef1 instanceof MyClass
```

The real power of the instanceof operator is that it works in a polymorphic fashion. In sophisticated object-oriented designs, it is often crucial while debugging to discover the precise nature of a method parameter that is received as a generic object. Consider a method defined with this signature:

```
public void myMethod(Object objParm)
```

At runtime, polymorphism lets you pass this method a Java object of any type (all Java objects are subclasses of Object). In this example, **myMethod** is executed twice, first with an instance of MyClass and then again with an instance of MyClass2.

```
MyClass objRef1 = new MyClass();
MyClass2 objRef2 = new MyClass2();

myMethod(objRef1);
myMethod(objRef2);
```

Using the System Debugger, you can interrogate the object parameter (objParm) inside **myMethod** to discover its type. Consider the following evaluations:

```
EVAL objParm instanceof MyClass2
EVAL objParm instanceof MyClass
```

When objRef1 is passed to **myMethod**, the first evaluation is false and the second evaluation is true. When objRef2 is passed, both evaluations are true. This is polymorphism at work in the System Debugger!

The last special feature available to Java programs in the System Debugger is a %LOCALVARS function:

```
EVAL %LOCALVARS
```

Use this function to see a display listing all the local variables in a method. In the case of object references and arrays, you see the address of the object or array. If a variable is not initialized when you use this function, the contents of the variable are unpredictable — you see the uninitialized contents of the memory allocated for the variable.

Any time you display local variables, either with the %LOCALVARS function or singly, keep in mind that local variables are subject to scope rules. If a variable value doesn't show up when you are expecting it to, check the Java code to see whether the variable is in scope at the breakpoint where you are trying to display it.

CONFIGURATION

This section focuses on the system and job configuration settings that are necessary for using Java effectively on the AS/400. Table 3.5 shows the configuration commands described in this section.

TABLE 3.5
Configuration Commands Summary

Command	Description	Comments
WRKENVVAR	Work with environment variables	Establish CLASSPATH and other variables
ADDENVVAR	Add environment variable	Create a new environment variable
CHGENVVAR	Change environment variable	Change the value assigned to an environment variable
WRKLNK	Work with object links	Establish symbolic IFS links
ADDLNK	Add link	Create an IFS link
RMVLNK	Remove link	Remove an IFS link
WRKRDBDIRE	Work with relational database directory entries	Configure local and remote databases

Classpath Environment Variable

The classpath is an environment variable Java uses to locate classes at compile time and at runtime. It provides the compiler and JVM with a path to classes in the IFS. The classpath consists of IFS path names and may also contain the path to one or more ZIP or JAR archive files.

Environment variables are a relatively new feature in OS/400, created in large part to support Java. Environment variables on the AS/400 have an analog in the PC and Unix worlds. On those systems, and on the AS/400, environment variables can be established in a job and then queried later by system products such as the JVM.

OS/400 provides commands to add, change, and work with environment variables. Noticeably lacking is a remove command. The only way to get rid of a previously added environment variable completely is to end the job (sign off the interactive job or end the batch job).

A classpath environment variable on the AS/400 is established with this command:

```
ADDENVVAR ENVVAR(CLASSPATH) VALUE('/myjava')
```

Any subsequent uses of the RUNJVA command or a Java compile in QShell uses this pre-established classpath to locate classes. Environment variable names are case sensitive; the classpath environment variable is CLASSPATH with uppercase letters.

You can specify one or more IFS path names to construct a classpath; if you specify more than one path, separate the path names with a colon (:). The JVM looks for classes in the classpath by the searching directories and archive files in the order specified. Here are examples for establishing the classpath environment variable with more than one path name:

```
ADDENVVAR ENVVAR(CLASSPATH)                          +
          VALUE('/myjava:/myDir2/subDir2a/subDir2b')

ADDENVVAR ENVVAR(CLASSPATH)                          +
          VALUE('/myDir2/subDir2a/subDir2b:          +
          /myDir3/myJar.jar:/myjava')
```

With the simple Java program shown below, you can discover what the classpath looks like in your job on the AS/400.

```
class ShowMeClasspath {
   public static void main(String[] args)
   {
           System.out.println("CLASSPATH=" +
               System.getProperty("java.class.path"));
   }
}
```

Here is the output from this program on a typical AS/400 after the /myjava directory has been added to the classpath:

```
CLASSPATH=/QIBM/ProdData/Java400/lib/jdkptf.zip:
/QIBM/ProdData/Java400/lib/rawt_classes.zip:
/QIBM/ProdData/Java400/lib/java.zip:
/QIBM/ProdData/Java400/lib/sun.zip:
/QIBM/ProdData/Java400/com/ibm/db2/jdbc/app/db2_classes.zip:
/QIBM/ProdData/Java400/:/myjava
```

Do you recall the "System Java Files" section earlier in this chapter? The AS/400's important Java runtime archive files are included at the beginning of the classpath automatically. This way, the JVM ensures that system classes can be found no matter what you establish for a personal classpath.

You can use the Work with Environment Variables (WRKENVVAR) command to see the environment variables set for your job. From this display, you can also add or change an environment variable.

When you submit Java programs to run in batch using the Submit Job (SBMJOB) command, you might expect the environment variables from your interactive job to carry over to the batch job. However, default behavior of SBMJOB is not to carry over the environment variables from the interactive job. You can override this setting on the SBMJOB command by using the "Copy environment variables" parameter. Simply change the default value of *NO to *YES, and your interactive job's environment variables are copied to the newly created batch job.

CREATING SYMBOLIC IFS LINKS

Managing the classpath can be a tricky process. For one thing, as your projects and accumulated applications grow in number, the number of path names on a classpath can be substantial. What do you do when your own classpath gets to be unmanageable? If your directories are nested deeply (e.g., /dir1/subdir1a/subdir1b/subdir1c) you can create a symbolic link with the Add Link (ADDLNK) command, which lets you refer to the nested structure with an alias.

```
ADDLNK OBJ('/dir1/subdir1a/subdir1b/subdir1c')    +
    NEWLNK(myshortpath) LNKTYPE(*SYMBOLIC)
```

Now, instead of typing **dir1/subdir1a/**... for a path name on the classpath, you can just type the alias **myshortpath** with the same results.

```
ADDENVVAR ENVVAR(CLASSPATH) VALUE('myshortpath')
```

You can also create aliases for files. For example, use the following command to create a link to the Customer.class file:

```
ADDLNK OBJ('/myjava/Customer.class')              +
    NEWLNK(myclass.class) LNKTYPE(*SYMBOLIC)
```

It is now possible to use the alias myclass.class anywhere that you would have used the qualified /myjava/Customer.class. For example, on the DSPJVAPGM command you could say

```
DSPJVAPGM CLSF(myclass.class)
```

You remove symbolic links with the Remove Link (RMVLNK) command, as shown below.

```
RMVLNK OBJLNK('myshortpath')
```

This command removes only the symbolic link; the directories or files named in the link remain intact.

Database Setup

To access a DB2/400 database with Java, you must first give it a name. To name it, you add an entry to your AS/400's table of databases, called a relational database directory. The Work with Relational Database Directory Entries command (WRKRDBDIRE) is your gateway to the database table. In addition to naming the local database, you use the directory to name and locate remote databases on other systems.

This feature is incredibly powerful when used in conjunction with Java programs running on your AS/400. You can access any compatible database on a system that communicates with your AS/400 by adding a simple entry to this table.

Figure 3.6 shows the directory entries for an AS/400 with a local database and one remote database. The local database, as you can see, is called LILROCK and the remote database is CHICAGO. Let's look at what it took to create the local database entry first.

FIGURE 3.6
Work with Relational Database Directory Entries Display

```
                Work with Relational Database Directory Entries

  Position to  . . . . . .

  Type options, press Enter.
    1=Add    2=Change    4=Remove    5=Display details    6=Print details

            Relational          Remote
  Option    Database            Location                  Text

       _    LILROCK             *LOCAL
       _    CHICAGO             198.1.0.100




                                                                  Bottom
  F3=Exit    F5=Refresh    F6=Print list    F12=Cancel
```

Figure 3.7 shows the prompted Add RDB Directory Entry (ADDRDBDIRE) command. In the Relational database parameter, you type a name for the database. This name must be unique on this system and among the systems that you intend to network. For the Remote location parameter, the local database uses the special value *LOCAL. When you press Enter, the entry is added to the table (you can configure only one local database on a system).

FIGURE 3.7
Local Database Setup

```
                  Add RDB Directory Entry (ADDRDBDIRE)

Type choices, press Enter.

Relational database  . . . . . . > LILROCK
Remote location:
  Name or address  . . . . . . . > *LOCAL



  Type . . . . . . . . . . . . .                    *SNA, *IP
Text . . . . . . . . . . . . . .      *BLANK




                                                             Bottom
F3=Exit    F4=Prompt    F5=Refresh    F12=Cancel    F13=How to use this display
F24=More keys
```

A remote database isn't much harder to establish. Figure 3.8 shows the prompted ADDRDBDIRE command for the CHICAGO system.

FIGURE 3.8
Remote Database Setup

```
                  Add RDB Directory Entry (ADDRDBDIRE)

Type choices, press Enter.

Relational database  . . . . . . > CHICAGO
Remote location:
  Name or address  . . . . . . . > '198.1.0.100'



  Type . . . . . . . . . . . . . > *IP            *SNA, *IP
Text . . . . . . . . . . . . . .      *BLANK

Port number or service program       *DRDA




                                                             Bottom
F3=Exit    F4=Prompt    F5=Refresh    F12=Cancel    F13=How to use this display
F24=More keys
```

In addition to the database name, a TCP/IP address is specified and the type parameter reflects the protocol to be used (*IP). Pressing Enter adds this entry to the table.

NOTE: Instead of using TCP/IP, you can use SNA to connect to a remote database. On systems with OS/400 release levels earlier than V4R2, the SNA protocol is your only option for remote database connectivity.

With a properly configured relational database table, you can access a local or remote database by name in your Java programs. The mechanism behind this database support is called the Distributed Relational Database Architecture (DRDA). It's one thing to enable AS/400-to-AS/400 database connectivity. The beauty of DRDA is that you can also connect seamlessly to relational databases on other platforms.

DRDA supports the following database systems on the AS/400:

- DB2/400
- DB2 Connect
- DB2 Universal Database
- DB2/390
- DB2 for VSE and VM

This degree of connectivity has overwhelming potential. With DRDA, your AS/400-based Java applications can directly access data residing on other AS/400s, PC and Unix servers, and even mainframes.

Chapter 4

QShell Interpreter

The QShell Interpreter is one of the most important recent additions to OS/400. It is new enough that if you are an RPG or Cobol programmer, you might not know it exists. You may be blown away by QShell and the way it acts as a system-within-a-system in relation to OS/400.

Shell environments come from the Unix world, which makes using and configuring them nonintuitive to most AS/400 diehards. In this chapter, you will learn to perform essential tasks in QShell, including compiling and executing Java programs. Once familiar with life in the shell, you'll be able to work easily with Java code and have a better understanding of the execution environment that forms the basis of the AS/400's Java runtime support.

QSHELL REVEALED

To start QShell, type the Start QShell (STRQSH) command from an OS/400 command line. An alias command, QSH, also starts the shell. The STRQSH command accepts only one parameter, a command to execute. Leave this parameter at the default value (*NONE) to enter the shell's command entry screen, shown in Figure 4.1.

FIGURE 4.1
QShell Interpreter

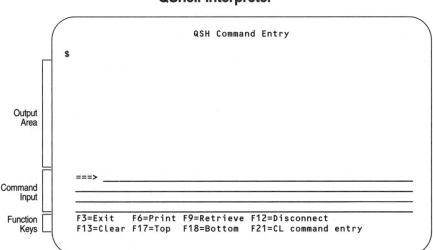

A command prompt and function keys appear in the lower half of the screen. Above the prompt is an output area where commands are logged and program output is displayed.

Commands in the shell environment are divided into two categories: built-in utilities and regular utilities. A built-in utility is one of 30 or so commands that let you accomplish the basic tasks required to navigate in the shell and run scripts, which are executable files containing shell commands. When used in a script, shell commands make up a type of programming language.

Regular utilities augment the built-in utilities, providing more advanced functionality and more links to the AS/400 platform. For example, one regular utility is the find command, which lets you search for a file by name anywhere in the IFS. The regular utilities are available as the QShell Utilities for AS/400, a PRPQ from IBM (5799-XEH). If you find that you need additional reference material on Unix shells, look for information about the Bourne and Korn shells, the two principal shell environments found in Unix systems. The QShell Interpreter is upwardly compatible with the Bourne shell and supports some features of the Korn shell.

If you are familiar with Unix shell commands, you might be interested to know that only the most primitive commands such as cd and pwd made it into QShell's built-in utilities. Such features as the global pattern search utility (grep) and the stream editor (sed) are a part of the regular utilities. Happily, IBM chose to include all the Java-related commands as built-in utilities. Every AS/400 installation of QShell includes the Java tools at no additional charge. This is very significant because nearly all of the JDK's Java tools are represented, including a source code compiler!

Whether you run a Java program from inside the shell or use the Run Java (RUNJVA) command from an OS/400 command line, a multithreaded execution environment is at the foundation of the AS/400's Java support. Java requires a multithreaded environment and the AS/400 uses a unique approach to support threads. For more information about the AS/400's Java execution environment and how it works inside and outside the shell, see "Multithreaded Java."

First Steps

You caught just a glimpse of the QShell Interpreter in Chapter 1. Let's take the time now to look at the function keys available inside QShell and then try a few simple shell commands.

Unlike most AS/400 software, the QShell Interpreter doesn't provide context-sensitive help. Moreover, not all the function keys that you can use in the shell are listed on the QShell command entry screen. The only way to figure out on your own how to use the shell, or what the function keys do, is to look at the help provided for the Start QShell (STRQSH) command.

MULTITHREADED JAVA

The AS/400's support for threads was discussed briefly in Chapter 2. We described how one AS/400 job can have multiple threads and how each thread has its own call stack. Although it isn't immediately apparent, interactive jobs on the AS/400 are not allowed to participate in multithreading — every interactive job on the AS/400 is limited to a single thread. However, it is also true that you can run multithreaded Java applications interactively on the AS/400.

This contradiction is explained by an interesting technique that the operating system uses to make interactive jobs *appear* to be multithreaded when a Java program is running.

Start with the understanding that although interactive jobs are limited to single threads, batch jobs are not. Add to this knowledge a new type of batch job called a *batch immediate job*, or BCI job. BCI jobs are not typical AS/400 jobs; for example, they don't route through a job queue. Instead, BCI jobs are spawned by parent jobs and inherit features, such as the subsystem they run in, from their parent. Like other batch jobs, BCI jobs have a multithreading capability.

When you execute a Java program on the AS/400, a BCI job is spawned to run the JVM in a multithread-capable process. Exactly how this process occurs depends on whether you run Java from a command line or from the QShell Interpeter.

Command Line Java

You use the Run Java (RUNJVA) command to execute a Java program from an OS/400 command line in an interactive job. Doing so sets in motion a three-step process. First, a BCI job named QJVACMDSRV is spawned to run the JVM. Next, a data queue named QP0ZTRML is created in library QTEMP. This data queue is created as a mechanism for the BCI job and the interactive job to exchange information. In the third step, a Dynamic Screen Manager (DSM) session is created in the interactive job. Through the DSM session, Java sends output to the display.

Although your Java program appears to run in the interactive job where you initiated the RUNJVA command, the program actually runs in the secondary BCI job. As your Java program runs, the interactive job keeps up with it via event information passed through the data queue by the BCI job. When your Java program runs to completion, the BCI job ends and the data queue is deleted from QTEMP automatically.

The BCI job creation takes place behind the scenes. If you look at the active jobs on your AS/400 while a Java program is running, you will see the BCI job spawned to run the JVM. Dig a little deeper and look at the threads running in the BCI job by using the "Work with threads" option of the Work with Job display. You will see the JVM threads and any additional threads spawned by your Java program.

continued

MULTITHREADED JAVA, *continued*

If you aren't acquainted with DSM, you should know that it was originally created to support languages such as C on the AS/400. Languages like C, and now Java, come from a world in which displayed output usually takes the form of stream data, often encoded in ASCII. You don't have to learn the inner workings of DSM to use Java. Just know that when you run a Java program interactively, it is capable of sending text, even ASCII text, to your AS/400 display.

If you submit a RUNJVA command to run as a batch job, a data queue is not created and a DSM session is not started. These steps solely support Java running interactively. Note, however, that even when a Java program runs in a batch job, an additional BCI job is still spawned to run the JVM. Just as with interactive Java, the BCI job is the one really running your Java program.

QShell Java

When you run Java from a command line, a new BCI job is spawned every time you execute the RUNJVA command. If you are running a series of Java programs, the process of spawning a BCI job, creating a data queue, and starting a DSM session for each one can be a drain on performance. The environment of the QShell Interpreter is built to support multithreaded languages like Java and to do so in an optimal fashion.

When you enter the shell using the Start QShell (STRQSH) command, a BCI job named QZSHSH is spawned immediately. As with the RUNJVA command, a data queue named QP0ZTRML is created in library QTEMP to communicate between the BCI job and the interactive job. The shell environment is implemented as a DSM session, eliminating the creation of a DSM session as a separate step when you run a Java program. When you execute a Java program in the shell, it is ready to run right away, no more BCI jobs are spawned, no data queues created, and no DSM sessions started — they're already in place!

Command Line or QShell?

IBM has done an excellent job of hiding the technical hoops that the operating system must jump through to run Java. In everyday practice, you won't have to think much about the BCI jobs, data queues, and DSM sessions required to make Java work. What you should think about is where you will run your Java programs — from the command line or from QShell. Because the shell environment eliminates the overhead required to run a program, it is normally the best choice you can make.

Inside the shell environment, the following function keys are available. Function keys labeled as unadvertised are not shown on the command entry screen although they are also available.

- F3=Exit — Exits the command entry display. The shell environment is not preserved (contrast this key with the F12=Disconnect key).

- F5=Refresh (unadvertised) — Refreshes the display by clearing anything entered at the command prompt. The output area of the display is not affected by this key.

- F6=Print — Prints (to a spooled file) the entire contents of the output area of the display. The output area is a scrollable message area where shell commands are logged and program output is displayed.

- F7=Page Up/F8=Page Down (unadvertised) — Pages up or down through the output area of the display. The functional equivalent of the Page Up or Page Down key on a standard keyboard.

- F9=Retrieve — Retrieves the last shell command entered at the command prompt. Pressing the key repeatedly brings up previously entered commands. You can also position the cursor on any command in the output area of the display and press this key to bring the command back to the command prompt.

- F11=Line Wrap Toggle (unadvertised) — In the output area of the display, any command (or program output) that extends beyond the screen display is automatically wrapped to display on subsequent lines. This key lets you toggle between this wrap mode and a mode in which long commands and program output are truncated at the end of a line. Refer to the F19/F20 (Page Left/Page Right) keys for a way to work with output in the truncate mode.

- F12=Disconnect — Closes the command entry display and returns you to where you were when you started QShell. The shell environment is preserved; you can return to the shell and pick up where you left off by re-entering the STRQSH command.

- F13=Clear — Clears the entire output area.

- F17=Top — Immediately moves to the top of the output area.

- F18=Bottom — Immediately moves to the bottom of the output area.

- F19=Page Left/F20=Page Right (unadvertised) — When working with the output area in the truncate mode (see F11=Line Wrap Toggle for output area mode switching), these keys move you left and right in the output area. Press F20=Page Right to see more of a command or output truncated at the display's edge.

- F21=Command entry — Displays an OS/400 command entry window where you can run any OS/400 command.

When a dollar sign ($) appears in the output area, the shell is ready to accept your commands. When a command runs to completion, three greater-than signs (>>>) appear in the output area. For example, if you start the shell and enter the command to compile a Java source file, the output area looks like this after the compile runs to completion.

```
$
javac /myjava/MyClass1.java
>>>$
```

When you enter a command, the session does not stay inhibited even though your command is still running. For example, when you type the javac command to compile a Java source file, you can type another shell command before the compile finishes. The reason is that the shell environment runs as two processes. One process is the interactive shell display — the user interface with the command prompt. The second process is a batch immediate (BCI) job where your requests actually execute.

When you enter commands in the shell environment, they are queued to run in the batch process. After each command is entered, the shell display is immediately available to accept another command. Commands queued to execute in the batch process are executed in a first-in, first-out manner. As a command runs to completion, a completion notification (>>>) is sent to the output area on the shell display.

If you enter three Java compile commands one after another, you should see an output like this:

```
$
javac /myjava/MyClass1.java
javac /myjava/MyClass2.java
javac /myjava/MyClass3.java
>>>$>>>$>>>$
```

The shell environment is tightly linked with the Integrated File System (IFS). The types of operations that you normally perform in the shell are primarily those of the stream file systems — either root or QOpenSys. For this reason, OS/400 libraries and concepts such as the library list have little or no bearing on your activities in the shell. Instead, you need to get used to working with Unix-like concepts of paths, current directories, and home directories.

You saw in Chapter 3 how to establish a home directory and also how to use OS/400 commands to set a current directory. The same concepts apply here, and the commands are similar. Here is the shell command for setting your current directory to the /myjava directory:

```
cd /myjava
```

To change back to the previous setting, you use the Current Directory command this way:

```
cd -
```

The Present Working Directory command displays the name of the directory set as the current directory. Use this command any time you are unsure of the current directory setting:

```
pwd
```

A variety of names are given to constructs in the shell environment, a carry-over from the Unix world. For example, you might find the current directory called just that, or it may be the "current working directory," the "working directory," or, in honor of the pwd command, the "present working directory."

A full description of the shell's many regular utilities (the additional commands available as a PRPQ) is beyond the scope of this chapter. Using the regular utilities, you will find that it is seldom necessary to leave the shell or access an OS/400 command line while you are working with Java. Commands exist to create and delete directories; move, copy, and delete stream files; and even compile C language programs. Essentially, every secondary activity that you might need to perform in the context of developing Java applications is covered by the regular utilities.

A few of the more commonly used regular utilities are shown in Table 4.1. The OS/400 equivalent, where it exists, is listed along with the shell utility. Complete descriptions for most of the OS/400 command equivalents are given in Chapter 3. These descriptions should help you determine the applications for a given shell command.

TABLE 4.1
Useful Regular Utilities

Utility	OS/400 Equivalent(s)	Purpose
mv	MOVE (MOV)	Move a file in the IFS.
cp	COPY (CPY)	Copy a file in the IFS.
ls	WRKLNK	List the contents of an IFS directory.
mkdir	CRTDIR (MKDIR, MD)	Create one or more IFS directories.
rm	RMVLNK (DEL, ERASE)	Remove (delete) one or more IFS files.
rmdir	RMVDIR (RD)	Remove (delete) one or more IFS directories.
chmod	CHGAUT	Change IFS file authorities.
ln	ADDLNK	Create a new link to an existing IFS file or directory.
find	N/A	Locate files by name in the IFS and optionally execute commands against the files.
cc	CRTCMOD/CRTPGM	Compile a C language program.
system	N/A	Execute an OS/400 command.
cat	N/A	Read and print an IFS file to the standard output device.
grep	N/A	Search contents of IFS files.

JAVA UTILITIES

Bundled with the built-in utilities are the tools that you need to work effectively with Java in the shell environment. The syntax and usage of these commands is essentially the same as for the JDK tools provided by Sun Microsystems. Table 4.2 shows the Java utilities supported by QShell.

TABLE 4.2
Java Utilities

Utility	Purpose
javac	Creates a class file made up of executable bytecodes by compiling Java source code.
java	Executes a Java program by invoking the JVM.
appletviewer	Executes a Java program written as an applet. Typically, applets are used as embedded content in Web pages. (This tool works only with Remote AWT support.)
rmic	Creates and compiles stub and skeleton class files to assist with Remote Method Invocation.
rmiregistry	Tracks remote objects and allows clients to locate them (a server-side component of Remote Method Invocation)
jar	Creates an archive of one or more class files and associated resources such as image, audio, or data files.
javakey	Generates digital signatures for JAR files and manages a database of public and private keys and certificates (a security tool).
serialver	Calculates a serial number based on the internal representation of a class file. Used as a type of level-checking when serializing and deserializing objects. (This tool works only with Remote AWT support.)
javah	Creates a C language header file to enable JNI-style native method calls.
javap	Disassembles a class file. May be used to output the bytecode representation of a class file and to discover a class file's variables and method signatures.
javadoc	Parses comments embedded in Java source files to create HTML-based program documentation.
native2ascii	Converts files encoded in other formats to a Unicode encoding.

Two of these Java tools, appletviewer and serialver, require a graphical user interface. For this reason, they can be used only with the ADK's Remote AWT. Remote AWT is a way to run a Java program on the AS/400 and have the graphical user interface presented on an intelligent workstation such as a PC. Remote AWT support is an immature technology on the AS/400 and is not covered in this book; consequently, the appletviewer and servialver utilities are not covered here either. If you are developing applets (Web browser-based Java programs) or you need to identify class files with serial numbers, you might want to look into Remote AWT support elsewhere or use the tools in the Sun Microsystems JDK on another platform.

The rest of the Java utilities can be executed directly from the shell environment with no additional support or configuration. The Java commands used most often in QShell are java and javac; the java command invokes the JVM on a class file, while the javac command is a Java source code compiler. Because of the importance of these two commands, their parameters are covered here in complete detail. The rest of the commands are described here to a lesser degree.

Only one utility commonly distributed by Sun Microsystems isn't supported by IBM in the QShell Interpreter. The jdb utility is a command-line debugger. The AS/400's source code debugger, the System Debugger, more than makes up for the lack of the primitive jdb tool.

Compiling Java Programs

One of the AS/400's best-kept secrets is its Java source code compiler. Because it is embedded in the shell environment, it's not something you're likely to stumble upon accidentally.

The parameters of the javac compile command are essentially those of the like-named tool in Sun Microsystems' JDK. We describe the parameters, pointing out AS/400 specifics, and then give several examples for using the command.

The syntax of the javac command is

```
javac options sourcefile.java
```

The first parameter to the javac command is a set of options, which are described below. The second parameter to the command is the name of a file containing Java source code. The file name should have the extension .java to identify it as Java source. For the compiler to locate a source file, you must either qualify the file name with the directory name or change your current directory to the source directory before invoking the compile command.

The options available for the javac command are:

- -classpath *path_name* — Specifies one or more IFS path names or archive files for the compiler to use while resolving references from the compiled class to other classes. If you specify more than one path, separate the path names with a colon (:). The compiler resolves references to classes by searching the classpath directories and archive files in the order specified.

  If you don't give this option, the OS/400 environment variable CLASSPATH is used by default to locate classes in the IFS. You can override the CLASSPATH variable inside the shell environment. This technique is discussed in "Alias and Export," later in this chapter.

- -deprecation — Directs the compiler to issue a warning message any time a deprecated method is used. Methods are deprecated (made obsolete) by Sun Microsystems as it refines the Java APIs. Because Sun may remove deprecated methods from the API, it is a good idea to identify and clean up these method calls in your code. For almost all deprecated methods, Sun's documentation recommends an alternative method to call or an alternative technical solution.

- -d *output_directory* — Specifies the directory where compiled class files are placed. If this option is not given, the compiled class files are placed in the directory containing the Java source code.

- -depend — Recompiles depended-on classes if they are out-of-date or do not exist. This activity is a sideline for the compiler. As the compiler resolves references to other class files from the class it's compiling, it looks for source code accompanying those other class files. If the date and time stamps on the source files don't match the class files, or if the class files don't exist, the source code is recompiled and the class files are re-created.

  With the -depend option, recompiling out-of-date (or nonexistent) depended-on classes works recursively. In other words, the resolution and recompilation of depended-on classes extends to the dependents of the class specified for compilation, and their dependents. Out-of-date class files referenced inside class files that are current (i.e., the source date matches the class date) are not considered for recompilation.

- -encoding *encoding_scheme* — Specifies the encoding scheme used in the Java source file. As long as the source file is encoded using Latin-1 ASCII or Unicode, this option is not necessary. Use it as a shortcut to converting a source file from one encoding scheme to another using the native2ascii utility.

- -g — Includes debugging tables in the compiled class. This option is required on any classes that you wish to debug using the AS/400's System Debugger. Note: This option is mutually exclusive with the optimization option (-O).

- -nowarn — Turns off warning messages issued by the compiler.

- -verbose — In the output area, displays all the classes loaded to accomplish the compile and the amount of time required to load each class. Also indicates which class files are being compiled and the total amount of time required for the compile.

- -O — Optimizes a class during compilation by making static, final, and private methods inline methods. Instead of creating a call from one method to another, in some instances the code from a called method will be embedded in the calling method. This process normally improves performance but makes debugging more difficult. In fact, compiling with this option automatically disables the debug option (-g). Contrast this type of optimization with the native instruction optimization that the Create Java Program (CRTJVAPGM) performs (see Chapter 3).

If you are used to the commands of OS/400, you might have trouble getting used to the peculiar syntax required for shell options. In particular, it is often difficult to tell when an option specifies a value, like the classpath option, and when the option stands alone, like the verbose messages option. With time and practice, you learn to parse the command-line options mentally. To help you along, here are several examples of the javac command with various options.

The following example simply specifies the directory-qualified Customer.java file for compilation.

```
javac /myjava/Customer.java
```

Here is the same command with options for verbose messages and the debug (-g) option added.

```
javac -verbose -g /myjava/Customer.java
```

Again, the command below compiles the Customer.java source file, this time with the class output redirection (-d) option, the deprecation warning option, and the verbose messages option.

```
javac -d /dand -deprecation -verbose /myjava/Customer.java
```

Running Java Programs

On the flip side of the compiler coin is the shell command to run a Java program. This command, java, is essentially the same as the RUNJVA command in OS/400. Many java command options have analogs in the parameters of the RUNJVA command. Where the options are the same, the RUNJVA command parameter is noted and an abbreviated description is repeated from the parameter descriptions given in Chapter 3.

The syntax of the java command is as follows:

```
java options classfile pgmParm1 pgmParm2 etc.
```

The first parameter to the java command is a set of options. The second parameter is the name of a class file containing Java bytecodes. Do not include the .class extension on the class file name. After the class file, you can include one or more parameters to pass into the Java program as an array argument to the program's **main** method.

The options available for the java command are listed below.

- -chkpath*protection_level* — Serves a purpose similar to that of the Classpath security level check (CHKPATH) parameter of the RUNJVA command. This parameter specifies the level of protection you desire when the classpath contains directories with public write authority. The protection levels are defined below. If this option is not specified, the command defaults to a classpath protection level of 20.

  ○ 10 (ignore) — No warning or escape messages are issued for directories in the classpath with public write authority. The Java program is allowed to run.

  ○ 20 (warning) — A warning message is issued for every directory in the classpath found to have public write authority; however, the Java program is not prevented from running.

- 30 (secure) — A warning message is issued for every directory in the classpath found to have public write authority. If any directory in the classpath has public write authority, an escape message is issued after the warning messages and the Java program is not allowed to execute.

- -classpath *path_name* — Serves the same purpose as the Classpath (CLASSPATH) parameter of the RUNJVA command. The classpath consists of IFS path names and is used to locate Java classes at runtime. The classpath may also contain the path to one or more ZIP or JAR archive files.

  You can specify one or more IFS path names to construct a classpath. If you specify more than one path, separate the path names with colons (:). The JVM looks for classes in the classpath by searching the directories and archive files in the order specified. If you don't specify this option, the OS/400 environment variable CLASSPATH is used by default to locate classes in the IFS. You can override the OS/400 CLASSPATH variable inside the shell environment; this technique is discussed in "Alias and Export," later in this chapter.

- -gcfrq*frequency* — In V4R2 and V4R3, this parameter is ignored by the JVM.

- -gcpty*priority* — Serves the same purpose as the Garbage collection priority (GCPTY) parameter of the RUNJVA command. Specifies the priority desired for garbage collection. If this option is not specified, the command defaults to a garbage collection priority of 20. This parameter is supported in V4R2 but ignored in V4R3.

  - 10 — The lowest priority for garbage collection. At this setting, garbage collection threads are typically set to a lower run priority than application threads.

  - 20 — The normal priority for normal garbage collection. At this setting, garbage collection threads are set to the same run priority as application threads.

  - 30 — The highest priority for garbage collection. At this setting, garbage collection threads are typically set to a higher run priority than application threads.

- -noclassgc — This option turns off garbage collection for unused classes. Using this option can improve performance in situations where classes are garbage-collected and then used again, which obviates the need to garbage collect them in the first place. This parameter does not exist in V4R2; it is introduced in V4R3.

- -verbosegc — With this option, a message is sent to the display each time garbage collection takes place. Use this option to determine the frequency and extent of garbage collection while fine-tuning performance. This parameter does not exist in V4R2; it is introduced in V4R3.

- -help — Displays the command syntax and a list of supported options.

- -ms*size* — Serves the same purpose as the Garbage collect initial size (GCHINL) parameter of the RUNJVA command. This parameter specifies the initial amount of storage, expressed in bytes, kilobytes (k), or megabytes (m), that is assigned for garbage collection. Essentially, garbage collection does not take place at all until at least this much storage is allocated by a Java program.

- -mx*size* — Serves the same purpose as the Garbage collect maximum size (GCHMAX) parameter of the RUNJVA command. Specifies the maximum amount of storage, expressed in bytes, kilobytes (k), or megabytes (m), that can be accumulated for garbage collection.

- -opt*optimization_level* — Serves the same purpose as the Optimization (OPTIMIZE) parameter of the RUNJVA command. This option sets the optimization level to use when creating a direct execution object (DE object). Higher optimization levels make your programs run faster, but they carry with them potentially inconvenient debugging tradeoffs. If this option is not specified, the command defaults to an optimization level of 10.

  - 0 (interpret) — A DE object is created but no optimization is performed. Bytecodes are interpreted at runtime.

  - 10 — A DE object is created. Minimal optimization is performed. Full debugging capabilities are available.

  - 20 — A DE object is created. Some optimization is performed. Variables in debug can be displayed but not changed.

  - 30 — A DE object is created. Even more optimization is performed. Variables in debug can be displayed but not changed; however, displayed variable values may not be current.

  - 40 — A DE object is created. Full optimization is performed. Source level debugging is not possible.

- -v, -verbose — Displays in the output area all the classes loaded as a Java program executes.

- -version — Displays information about the current version of the JVM and JDK compatibility, such as "java version 1.1.6."

- -D*property_name=property_value* — Serves the same purpose as the Properties (PROP) parameter of the RUNJVA command. Specifies runtime property values. This parameter consists of two parts:

  - Property name. The name of a runtime property.

  - Property value. A value assigned to the runtime property.

When you compare the java utility in the shell environment to the utility provided by Sun Microsystems with the JDK, you find a few parameters that are not supported on the AS/400. In most cases, the lack of support is caused by architectural differences between AS/400's JVM and the runtime environment on other platforms. Here is a quick rundown of the unsupported options:

- -cs, -checksource (recompile updated source automatically)
- -debug (start debug support)
- -noasyncgc (turn off asynchronous garbage collection)
- -noverify (do not verify the integrity of classes)
- -oss (set Java stack size)
- -prof (start performance profiling)
- -ss (set native stack size)
- -t (trace executed instructions)
- -verify (verify the integrity of class specified for execution)
- -verifyremote (verify the integrity of all classes used)

The only surprise on this list is the debug option (-debug). To debug a Java program on the AS/400, you invoke the source-level System Debugger by specifying the *DEBUG option on the RUNJVA command.

As for the other options, performance profiling and runtime traces can be obtained with existing AS/400 tools; class verification options do not apply on the AS/400 — classes are always verified at runtime; and stack sizes are irrelevant in OS/400.

Here are several examples of the java command to show you how some of the supported options are used.

The following example executes the Customer class after setting the classpath. Verbose class-loading messages are displayed and the class is executed in an interpreted fashion (i.e., with no optimization).

```
java -classpath /myjava -verbose -opt0 Customer
```

The next example executes the Customer class with the added safety of a secure classpath protection level.

```
java -classpath /myjava -chkpath30 Customer
```

Finally, this example simply returns version information about the JVM and JDK.

```
java -version
```

Remote Method Invocation Tools

Remote Method Invocation (RMI) is a technology for creating and using distributed Java objects. With current technology, creating and using distributed Java objects usually amounts to client Java programs accessing server Java objects to take advantage of server-specific functionality, such as a native JDBC driver.

Two tools are available in the shell environment to enable your work with RMI. The RMI compiler, supported by the rmic command, takes a properly coded Java class file and creates for you the stub and skeleton classes that make the class capable of acting as a remote object. (Stubs and skeletons are explained in Chapter 8.)

The second tool is the RMI registry, supported by the rmiregistry command. The RMI registry is a server function, typically a background process that runs continually, though you must start it running. Through the registry, server objects register themselves so that client applications can locate them and invoke their methods. Application development using RMI is the topic of Chapter 8.

Java Archives

An extremely convenient way to organize your Java applications is to package them into Java Archive (JAR) files. As described in Chapter 3, a JAR file is a collection of classes in a ZIP format. You can package resources such as images or audio files in a JAR along with your class files. The shell environment lets you create your own JAR files on the AS/400 with the jar utility. Again, the parameters of the jar command are those of the like-named tool in Sun Microsystems' JDK, with the one minor exception noted below.

In most cases, JAR files contain a manifest of their contents. You can let the jar command generate a manifest file and place it in the JAR file for you or you can specify a manifest file that you have created yourself. Under normal conditions, it is preferable to have the jar command create the manifest file for you; we follow this practice in the examples presented here.

The syntax of the jar command is shown below.

```
jar options output_file manifest_file input_files
```

The first parameter to the jar command is a set of options. The second parameter is the name and location of the JAR file to be created. The third parameter is the optional name of a file containing a manifest of the JAR file's contents. The fourth parameter specifies the files that are placed in the archive.

If you use the jar command on other platforms, be careful; the output file and manifest file are in reverse order from Sun Microsystems' JDK command.

The options available for the jar command are divided into two parts. You can think of them as action options and modifier options. The action options are:

- c — Creates a JAR file.
- t — Lists the table of contents in an existing JAR file.
- x *filename* — If a file name is given, extracts only that file from an existing JAR file. If a file name is omitted, extracts all files from an existing JAR file.

The modifier options for the jar command are:

- f — Indicates that the second parameter is a JAR file name (rather than a manifest file name).
- v — Displays verbose messages as the JAR file is created.

- m — Indicates that you are supplying a manifest file as the second parameter (rather than a JAR file name). In this case, the JAR file name is specified as the third parameter.
- 0 — Do not compress the JAR file. It is recommended that you always specify this option for JAR files that you intend to use on the AS/400. Compressed JAR files can negatively affect performance because of the amount of runtime decompression that they require.
- M — Indicates that no manifest file is to be created for the JAR file.

For example, the following command creates a JAR file called myjar.jar. The "c" action option indicates that a JAR file is to be created, and the "f" modifier option indicates that the second parameter is the path-qualified JAR file name. The third parameter specifies the files to place inside the JAR file — in this case, all the files in the /myjava directory with a .class extension.

```
jar cf /myjava/myjar.jar /myjava/*.class
```

Here is the same command with verbose messages (the "v" modifier option). For each file placed in the archive, a line is displayed in the shell's output area with the name of the file and the degree of compression achieved.

```
jar cfv /myjava/myjar.jar /myjava/*.class
```

Here is the command again, this time without compression (the "0" modifier option). Each file added to the archive is displayed to the output area with 0 percent compression indicated.

```
jar cfv0 /myjava/myjar.jar /myjava/*.class
```

The next example lists the table of contents for the newly created myjar.jar file by using the "t" action option.

```
jar tf /myjava/myjar.jar
```

In this last example, the table of contents for the myjar.jar file is again listed. The verbose modifier option "v" causes more information about the contents to be displayed.

```
jar tvf /myjava/myjar.jar
```

Other Java Tools

The remaining Java tools supported in the QShell environment are specialized and, depending upon your circumstances, you may never need them. The minimal descriptions of these tools given here should at least tell you whether they apply to your situation.

Java utilities can process only stream files encoded with Unicode or Latin-1 ASCII characters. The native2ascii tool converts files encoded in other formats to a Unicode encoding.

The javadoc tool creates documentation in the form of HTML pages from special comments embedded in your Java source files.

With the javakey tool, you can create and manage the resources that are used for Java program authentication. Use this tool to create public key/private key pairs and certificates, and to manage a database of trusted and untrusted signers. You can also use this tool to create signed JAR files.

The javah tool creates a C language header file to help enable the execution of your Java methods from within a C program. Note that on the AS/400, only Java Native Interface (JNI) header files can be created. Early stub file creation is not a supported option.

The javap tool is a disassembler for class files. The tool accepts a class file as an input parameter and puts out a list of the symbolic bytecodes that comprise the class file. The tool includes options that list the variables and signatures of methods defined to the class. You can use this tool to examine a class that is undocumented and for which you do not have source code. Note that this tool is not a decompiler — you cannot use this tool to regenerate Java source code from a class file.

ALIAS AND EXPORT

Combine a handful of commands (such as cd and pwd) with the Java utilities, and you can be a reasonably productive programmer in the shell environment. Moving to the next level, where the shell actually simplifies your life, requires that you pick up some new concepts and techniques. To start on this course, let's look at creating aliases and then see how to set the shell's environment variables.

Aliases

If you find yourself regularly typing a long shell command with obscure parameters, you can make your job easier by assigning an alias to the construct. The best way to picture this feature is with an example — how about the funky options that go along with Java program execution using the java command? Perhaps you routinely set a classpath and override the defaults for path security and garbage collection minimum storage, like this:

```
java -classpath /myjava -chkpath30 -ms10M classfile
```

To simplify the command, create an alias for the java command that includes your standard options.

```
alias j='java -classpath /myjava -chkpath30 -ms10M'
```

Now you can significantly cut down on the amount of typing you have to do by using the alias "j" instead of the java command. The shell environment expands the alias to execute the java command with your custom parameters. For example, the following command

```
j Customer
```

executes in exactly the same manner as the long-hand version shown below.

```
java -classpath /myjava -chkpath30 -ms10M Customer
```

To see a list of the aliases you have established, use the alias command without specifying any parameters. To remove an alias that you have established, use the unalias command. For example, to remove the j alias, use the command below.

```
unalias j
```

To remove all aliases established in the shell, use the unalias command with the -a option.

```
unalias -a
```

Exports

You can set the classpath used by the shell environment's Java utilities in three ways. You've already seen one of them, the -classpath option of the java and javac tools. This method requires typing the classpath as a part of every Java command or creating command aliases that include the classpath option.

A second way to set the classpath is to create an OS/400 environment variable using the Add Environment Variable (ADDENVVAR) command before you start the shell. When the shell is started, it automatically creates internal variables for every OS/400 environment variable. If you intend to stay in the shell for an extended period of time, this approach is impractical. What if you need to change the classpath setting? You have to exit the shell, change the environment variable and then restart the shell. It doesn't work to change OS/400 environment variables from a disconnected shell or from the shell's CL command entry prompt.

The ideal solution lies in the shell's export command, which lets you update environment variables kept by the shell itself. Set the classpath variable inside the shell using the export command like this:

```
export -s CLASSPATH=/myjava
```

The -s option indicates that the variable is set both for the current shell and for any subprocesses that it spawns. As with any other time that you set the classpath, to include more than one path name, separate the names with colons (:). Also, environment variable names are case sensitive — be sure to use all capital letters when specifying the classpath variable. To see the current setting of the CLASSPATH variable, execute the export command without specifying any parameters.

SCRIPTS

Fundamentally, a script is just a file containing shell commands. Scripts allow some basic control and looping constructs, making them similar to interpreted

CL programs. This section gives you the essential information you need to begin creating scripts of your own.

Creating and Executing Scripts

Scripts are interpreted, not compiled, and there is no fixed syntax for a script the way there is for many programming languages. You can create scripts using the Edit File user tool described in Chapter 3 or any PC-based text editor. For example, the Notepad program bundled with Windows works well as a script editor.

The ideal location for your scripts is in the root file system of the IFS. Personal scripts are often kept in home directories, while scripts that you want to share with others are better placed in a common directory such as /etc.

Execute a script from within the shell by using the dot (.) command. Leave a space between the dot and the name of the script that you wish to execute. For example, to execute the myscript script, use the dot command this way:

```
. myscript
```

You can also execute a script by specifying the dot command and script name on the command (CMD) parameter of the Start QShell (STRQSH) OS/400 command. To execute myscript when you start the shell, using the following STRQSH command:

```
STRQSH CMD('. myscript')
```

The shell environment locates scripts by looking first in the current directory and then in the directories specified on the PATH environment variable. By default, the value of the PATH variable is set to /usr/bin. This variable works in the same way that the PATH variable works in DOS or the CLASSPATH environment variable works in Java. If you specify more than one path name on the PATH variable, the shell looks in each directory in turn until it finds your script.

Here is an example showing you how to set your own PATH variable with two directory names.

```
PATH=/myjava:/home/dand
```

One extremely common command used in a script is the echo command. This command simply displays text in the output area. You might use echo to output a status message as a script executes or to prompt a user for input. Here is a simple echo command.

```
echo "What is your name?"
```

Alternatives to echo are the print and printf commands. The print command is very similar to echo but allows for some basic text formattting. The printf command provides for full text formatting, including formatted numbers.

You can receive input from a user by using the read command in your script. Here is the format for the read command:

```
read variable
```

Combine the echo and read commands to achieve full interactivity. Here is the code for a script that asks for your name and then repeats it back to you.

```
echo "What is your name?"
read name
echo "Hi $name. I'm pleased to meet you."
```

When this script is executed, the results are as follows:

```
. myscript
What is your name?
Dan
Hi Dan. I'm pleased to meet you.
```

In the script, the read command creates a variable called name to contain your input. When it is used on the echo command, the variable name is prefaced with a dollar sign ($). Use the dollar sign syntax with variable names in circumstances where there is a need to distinguish them from constants.

COMMENTS

What would a programming language be without comments? The hash sign (#) is used to indicate a script comment. A simple comment in the scripting language looks like this:

```
# The purpose of this script is to test a loop
```

You can also place comments on the same line as a command.

```
echo "Hi there!"                # display greeting
```

CONDITIONAL STATEMENTS

The primary conditional construct in the shell is the "if" statement. Every "if" statement is followed by a "then" statement and a command. You can nest "if" statements by using the elif (else if) statement or code for an "else" condition. For every "if" you must have an ending "fi" (that's "if" spelled backwards). Here is the complete structure for an if-else-if-else-fi grouping.

```
if condition                    # test for first condition
    then command
elif condition                  # test for second condition
    then command
else
    command                     # default
fi                              # end if
```

The condition evaluated by an "if" statement is the result of the execution of a shell command. Even simple comparisons of string values on an "if" must be evaluated using a shell command called test. Here is the structure illustrated above, this time with actual conditional tests and command responses.

```
echo "What is your name?"
read name
if test "$name" = "Jill"
    then echo "I've always liked the name Jill."
elif test "$name" = "Jack"
    then echo "I once knew a guy named Jack."
else
    echo "Hi $name. I'm pleased to meet you."
fi
```

You can see that the test command evaluates the comparison between the name that you type in and two constants. This code gives special responses to the names "Jill" and "Jack" and a generic response to any other name.

LOOPS

Another often-used construct in a programming language is the loop. In the scripting language, a loop that produces this output

```
. testloop
counter value=0
counter value=1
counter value=2
counter value=3
counter value=4
```

looks like this:

```
i=0                          # initialize counter
while test "$i" -lt "5"      # test for counter < 5
do                           # start body of loop
    echo "counter value=$i"  # display counter
    i=$(($i + 1))            # increment counter
done                         # end body of loop
```

First, a numeric variable "i" is established and initialized to zero. On the "while" statement, the test command evaluates a condition — in this case, the loop is performed as long as the variable "i" is less than the number five. Notice the strange less-than operator (-lt) used on the test command. When dealing with numeric variables on "if" and "while" statements, you use -lt, -gt, -le, -ge, -eq, and -ne as Boolean operators.

The body of the loop is enclosed in "do" and "done" statements. Within the body of this loop, the value of the counter is displayed and then incremented by one. The strange syntax used to increment the counter is necessary because of the way the scripting language parses expressions.

If you think that the syntax of the scripting language seems less than obvious, you are not alone. It can take some time to become comfortable with the idiosyncratic way in which shell commands and control structures are implemented. You can rest assured that you have seen the worst of it. With just a little practice you can be scripting along with the best of the Unix dweebs.

APPLICABILITY TO JAVA

You might be wondering where scripts fit into the Java picture. With a script, you can configure your shell environment before executing a Java program. You might also use a script to execute several Java programs in sequence. Scripts can pass prompted user input to Java programs or use conditional and looping structures to influence when and how a Java program is executed.

For example, consider a script that presents a simple menu and allows you to select a Java program to execute.

```
Menu of Java Programs
1. Display classpath
2. Display properties
Q. Quit
Enter an option (1-2, Q)
```

The Java programs used in this example are two programs shown in Chapter 3; one displays the classpath and the other displays runtime properties.

The script to display and process this menu, called menuscript, illustrates everything you have learned in this chapter.

```
export -s CLASSPATH=/myjava
option=" "
while test "$option" != "Q"
do
    echo " "
    echo "Menu of Java Programs"
    echo "1. Display classpath"
    echo "2. Display properties"
    echo "Q. Quit"
    echo "Enter an option (1-2, Q)"

    read option                          # get user response

    if test "$option" = "1"
        then java ShowMeClasspath
    elif test "$option" = "2"
        then java ShowMeProperties
    elif test "$option" = "Q"
        then :
    else
        echo "Option $option is invalid."
    fi
done
```

To start, the CLASSPATH environment variable is set to the /myjava directory, where the Java programs in this example are assumed to reside. Next, the option variable is established and initialized to blanks. Then a "while" loop, whose condition is that the option variable is not equal to a Q (i.e., the Quit option), is established. Within the body of the loop, the menu is displayed and the menu choice is read as the option variable. An "if" grouping processes the menu choice and executes Java programs for options 1 and 2. The response to the Q option is simply a colon (:), a "do nothing" command ignored by the script interpreter. Using the colon as a response to the Q option allows the conditional test on the "while" statement to end the loop at the appropriate time.

When a Java program ends, it can return a completion status to the program that started it by calling the **exit** method of the System class. For example, here is a Java program that prints a message, then exits with a normal completion status of 0.

```
class NormalExit
{
public static void main(String[] args)
{
    System.out.println("This program always ends normally.");
    System.exit(0);
}
}
```

Here is another Java program that prints a message and exits, this time with an abnormal completion status of 1.

```
class AbnormalExit
{
public static void main(String[] args)
{
    System.out.println("This program always ends abnormally.");
    System.exit(1);
}
}
```

NOTE: Technically, a call to the System.exit method shuts down not just the program but also the current invocation of the JVM. It might not be an appropriate method call in situations where more than one Java program can be active in the JVM.

You can write scripts that react to the normal or abnormal completion status of a Java program. Consider this script, called exitstatus:

```
if java $1
then
    echo "Good news! The Java program exited normally."
else
    echo "Bad news! The Java program exited abnormally."
fi
```

Run this script using the dot command and supply it with the name of a Java program to execute. For the purposes of this illustration, use the NormalExit and AbnormalExit programs.

```
. exitstatus NormalExit
This program always ends normally.
   >>>Good news! The Java program exited normally.

. exitstatus AbormalExit
This program always ends abnormally.
   >>>Bad news! The Java program exited abnormally.
```

In the body of the script, the java command has a strange looking argument of $1. This is a placeholder representing the first parameter to the exitstatus script supplied by you on the command line (e.g., "NormalExit" or "AbnormalExit"). When the java command is parsed for execution, the command line parameter is substituted for the placeholder. The "if" statement interprets the completion status of the program executed by the java command and displays an appropriate message. If you are executing several Java programs in one script, this technique is a way to trap errors and short-circuit the script if one of the programs fails.

You can use scripts in many other ways in conjunction with your Java efforts. Using some of the regular utilities, you might want to create directories or copy files before a Java program's execution. Or you can script cleanup steps that must be performed after a Java program runs to completion.

STARTUP CONFIGURATION

When you start the shell, you may find that you always execute the same commands to establish a customized environment. For example, you probably have a favorite set of aliases to decrease the amount of typing while performing repetitive tasks. Or, working with Java, you probably export the CLASSPATH environment variable as a matter of routine. You might also be in the habit of setting a new default PATH environment variable so that the shell can easily locate your custom scripts.

Consider automating processes such as these by using one of the startup scripts — scripts that are automatically executed when you start the QShell Interpreter. Startup scripts come in three types:

- User profile script
- Environment script
- System profile script

This section examines each startup script type, giving you some hints for using each of them.

User Profile Script

Each person on your system can have his or her own user profile script. User profile scripts let users individualize their shell environments. These scripts reside in the home directory of each user (e.g., home/dand) and .profile is always the script name. The leading period has nothing to do with the dot command that you saw earlier; it's just a part of the file name.

One neat thing you can do in a startup script is change the dollar sign prompt ($) to something a little more meaningful. Because your work with Java requires so much interaction with stream file systems, how about changing the dollar sign prompt to show the current directory name? Place the following statement in your personal .profile script to make this happen.

```
PS1="[$(pwd)]"
```

The variable PS1 is a special variable defined by the shell environment to represent the command prompt. The present working directory (pwd) command is executed and its output is assigned to the PS1 variable. The brackets just spiff up the prompt a little bit.

Now when you enter the shell you should see your current directory in brackets instead of that meaningless dollar sign. It looks like this:

```
[/home/dand]
```

With the prompt change in place, try changing the current directory using the cd command.

```
cd /myjava
[/home/dand]
```

Whoa! The current directory was changed (check it with pwd) but the prompt remains the same (i.e., [home/dand]). The prompt is set in the startup script but the change directory command doesn't know that it is supposed to change the prompt as you go.

The solution is to get a bit more sophisticated with your startup script. The shell lets you create functions that you can use just like built-in utilities. To overcome the cd command problem, create a function, chgdir, that changes both the directory and the prompt.

```
chgdir()
{
cd $1
PS1="[$(pwd)]"
}
```

All you need to do is add the preceding lines to your .profile script. The code is quite simple. All the statements that describe the function are enclosed in a set of braces (just like a method in Java!). Within the braces, the first statement changes the directory using the first positional parameter ($1) passed to the function. The second statement inside the braces changes the prompt variable to the directory name. With this function defined in your startup script, using the chgdir command instead of cd to change the current directory causes the prompt to change as the current directory changes.

```
chgdir /myjava
[/myjava]
```

Functions are a slick and useful feature of the shell environment, but do you really want to remember to type chgdir when you've already become accustomed to the built-in cd command? Of course not, and you've already learned the solution to this problem. Just set up an alias, cd, that overrides the built-in change directory command. Add this statement to your startup script to make it happen.

```
alias cd=chgdir
```

Now when you are working in the shell, you can use either chgdir or cd to execute your new function. By the way, it won't work simply to define your function with the name cd. The shell environment gives precedence to built-in commands over functions with the same name. Aliases, however, take precedence over built-in commands. Therefore, you can define an alias with the name of a built-in command and assign it to a function of your own creation.

Environment Script

The environment script is executed when you start the shell but the name of this script is not predetermined like the name of the user profile script. You provide the name of the environment script by setting the ENV environment variable. Often, you set this variable in OS/400 before issuing the STRQSH command. For example, here is the OS/400 command to establish the ENV environment variable and point it to a script in the /myjava directory.

```
ADDENVVAR ENVVAR(ENV) VALUE('/myjava/myscript')
```

When you start the shell, the myscript script is executed. You can also set the ENV environment variable inside your .profile user profile script, like this:

```
ENV=/myjava/myscript
```

Look at the environment script as an effective way to overcome the limitation of placing user startup scripts in home directories. By using the ENV environment variable to name the environment script, you can execute any script, in any location, when you start the QShell Interpreter.

System Profile Script

Everyone on the system shares the system profile script. Use this script to set options that apply across the board. For example, you might have a standard set of aliases that you want to be available to everyone. You create the system profile script by placing a script named "profile" (no leading period) in the /etc directory.

Chapter 5

AS/400 Toolbox for Java

In this chapter you'll get a guided tour of the AS/400 Toolbox for Java, IBM's library of AS/400 features. Each of the V3R2 product features is explained in sufficient detail for you to get a good handle on the focus and scope of the product as a whole. Example code is presented for you to see how to use portions of each Toolbox feature. In Chapter 7, Toolbox features described here are demonstrated in applications created using VisualAge for Java.

The Toolbox works through TCP/IP sockets connections from a client workstation to a server AS/400. Server jobs listen for communications of a particular type and then service requests on behalf of the client. For example, one type of server job does nothing but execute command and program requests. The AS/400 manages these server jobs for you, typically by starting a new server job for each client and type of service requested. Table 5.1 shows the host server job names and the types of services the jobs provide.

TABLE 5.1
Host Server Jobs

Server Job Name	Subsystem	Service Provided
QPWFSERVSO	QSERVER	Integrated File System (IFS)
QZDASOINIT	QSERVER	Database access (JDBC)
QRWTSRVR	QSYSWRK	Database access (record-level)
QZRCSRVS	QSYSWRK	Command and program calls
QZHQSSRV	QSYSWRK	Data queues
QNPSERVS	QSYSWRK	Network print

NOTE: In addition to using the Toolbox with client-based applications, you can use the Toolbox in Java programs that run entirely on your AS/400 server. Although this chapter is written with client-based programs in mind, the coding techniques described here apply either way.

To enable the server jobs, use the Start Host Server (STRHOSTSVR) command. This command starts several "traffic cop" jobs, which in turn start the server jobs as clients connect to the AS/400.

```
STRHOSTSVR SERVER(*ALL)
```

To enable record-level access, you must also start the TCP/IP server for Distributed Data Management (DDM) using this command:

```
STRTCPSVR SERVER(*DDM)
```

Depending upon the release level of your AS/400, you may need some PTFs to enable certain Toolbox functions. In general, it is a good idea to apply the latest cumulative PTF package for your release before attempting to use the Toolbox. For a list of the specific PTFs required by the Toolbox, see Appendix B.

GETTING CONNECTED

All the Toolbox functions except JDBC require that you construct an object of the AS400 class. Through this object, Toolbox functions communicate with the server jobs on the AS/400. An AS400 object can be created in different ways. A system name, user ID, and password can be supplied by a Java program, or you can arrange for these values to be supplied at runtime. Here is an example of an AS400 object constructed with a program-supplied system name, user ID, and password:

```
AS400 as400 = new AS400("MYSYSTEM", "DAND", "MYPASSWORD");
```

Nothing difficult about that. To have the Toolbox prompt for a system name, user ID, and password, construct an AS400 communications object in your program without supplying any parameters.

```
AS400 as400 = new AS400();
```

When this statement executes, you are not prompted immediately to sign on. The prompt appears only when the Java program first attempts to use a Toolbox service. You can force the AS/400 sign-on by explicitly connecting to a Toolbox service.

```
as400.connectService(AS400.DATAQUEUE);
```

This command forces a connection to the data queue service and causes the sign-on prompt shown in Figure 5.1 to appear immediately.

Once an AS400 communication object is created and you sign on to the AS/400, the same AS400 object can be shared by multiple services. In other words, you create only one AS400 object and sign on only one time for a program to use all the services provided by the Toolbox.

INTEGRATED FILE SYSTEM (IFS) FEATURE

The first Toolbox service we look at is the Integrated File System (IFS) feature. Using this feature, your Java programs can access directories and files in the IFS. You may be wondering why you need this feature if Java already gives you support for stream file systems. The IFS feature of the Toolbox offers a way to access the AS/400's IFS without Client Access or NetServer. You don't get this support in Java's standard stream file access classes.

FIGURE 5.1
Toolbox Sign-On Prompt

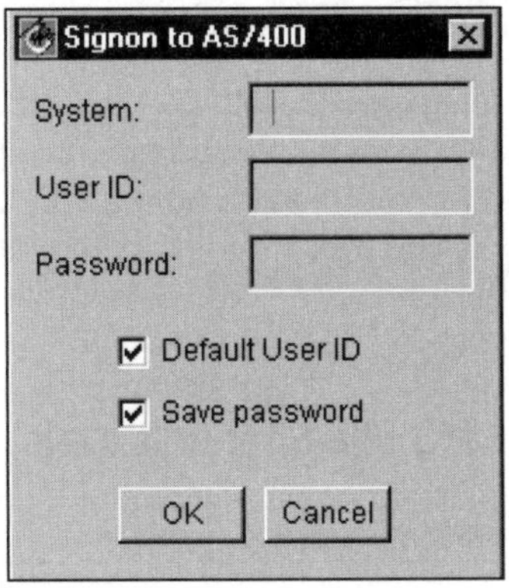

The IFS feature provides a wide range of functionality to your Java programs. The specific functions that we look at in this section are

- Reading and writing stream files
- Manipulating directories and files

Reading Files

Let's start by looking at the Java code required to read a stream file in the IFS. IFS classes in the Toolbox require you to create an AS400 communications object for communicating with your host AS/400.

```
AS400 as400 = new AS400();
```

With an AS400 object constructed, you can get a reference to an IFS file by creating an instance of the IFSFile class.

```
IFSFile myFile = new IFSFile(as400,
    "/myjava/Customer.java");
```

In this example, you are referencing the file containing the source code for the Customer class. With the IFS file object called myFile, you can interrogate the file to discover its properties, such as read and write authorities, length (in bytes), and the date it was last changed.

```
System.out.println("Read capable (true/false) : " +
    myFile.canRead());
System.out.println("Write capable (true/false): " +
    myFile.canWrite());
System.out.println("Length (bytes)             : " +
    myFile.length());
System.out.println("Change date                : " +
    new java.util.Date(myFile.lastModified()));
```

You can access the contents of the file by creating an instance of the IFSTextFileInputStream class.

```
IFSTextFileInputStream st = new IFSTextFileInputStream(as400,
    myFile, IFSTextFileInputStream.SHARE_ALL);
```

The IFS file object myFile is passed to the constructor as a pointer to the file you want to read. The other parameters accepted by the constructor are the AS400 communication object and a constant value indicating the access sharing level to be enforced for the file. Here, access to the file is shared with all other programs. The file-sharing options are shown in Table 5.2.

TABLE 5.2
IFS File-Sharing Levels

Sharing Level	Description
SHARE_ALL	The file is shared with all other programs.
SHARE_NONE	No other programs can access the file.
SHARE_READERS	Other programs can read the file but cannot write to it.
SHARE_WRITERS	Other programs can write to file but cannot read it.

NOTE: File-sharing levels are a part of OS/400, not Java, so when a Java program specifies a restricted sharing level (e.g., SHARE_NONE), more than just other Java programs are restricted. If, for example, you try to edit Customer.java with Windows Notepad (through Client Access) while a Java program has it locked, you receive a message to the effect that the file cannot be opened.

You can print the entire contents of a file with a single compound Java statement. The following tidy bit of Java code says to read and print all available bytes from the input stream:

```
System.out.print(st.read(st.available()));
```

It is interesting to note that the IFSTextFileInputStream class inherits from Java's core InputStream class. Because of this, you can wrap a text input stream object with a buffered input stream for better performance, just as you might with any Java stream.

Objects of the IFSFile class can also be used to interrogate the contents of directories. To determine whether an IFS file object is a directory, use the **isDirectory** method.

```
if(myFile.isDirectory())
{
    // . . . treat as directory
}
```

You may retrieve the contents of a directory as an array of string objects by using the **list** method. It is a simple matter to loop through this array to print the directory contents.

```
String[] dirContents = myFile.list();

for(int i = 0; i < dirContents.length; i++)
    System.out.println("     /" + dirContents[i]);
```

The Java class SimpleIFSExample shown in Figure 5.2 is a complete example for accessing IFS files and directories.

FIGURE 5.2
Simple IFS Example Program

```
import com.ibm.as400.access.*;
import java.io.*;

class SimpleIFSExample {

/*
 * Pass an IFS file or directory name as a command line parameter.
 *
 * Examples:  java SimpleIFSExample /myjava/Customer.java
 *            java SimpleIFSExample /myjava
 */
public static void main(String[] args)
{
    // Create an AS400 connection object
    AS400 as400 = new AS400();

    // Create an IFS object reference
    IFSFile myFile = new IFSFile(as400, args[0]);

    // List IFS object attributes
    System.out.println("Attributes                : " + myFile.getName());

    try
    {
        System.out.println("Path                         : " + myFile.getPath());
        System.out.println("Directory (true/false)    : " + myFile.isDirectory());
        System.out.println("File (true/false)         : " + myFile.isFile());
        System.out.println("Read capable (true/false) : " + myFile.canRead());
        System.out.println("Write capable (true/false): " + myFile.canWrite());
        System.out.println("Length (bytes)            : " + myFile.length());
        System.out.println("Change date               : " +
            new java.util.Date(myFile.lastModified()));
        System.out.println("-------------------------------------------------------------------");

        // If object is a directory, list directory contents
        if(myFile.isDirectory())
        {
            System.out.println("Directory contents      :");

            String[] dirContents = myFile.list();
            for(int i = 0; i < dirContents.length; i++)
                System.out.println("     /" + dirContents[i]);
        }

        // If object is a file, read and print file contents
        if(myFile.isFile())
        {
            try
```

continued

FIGURE 5.2 *CONTINUED*

```
{
    IFSTextFileInputStream st = new IFSTextFileInputStream(as400,
        myFile, IFSTextFileInputStream.SHARE_ALL);
    System.out.print(st.read(st.available()));
}
catch(AS400SecurityException ase)
{
    System.out.println("Not authorized to read file");
}
}

}
catch(java.io.IOException ioe)
{
    System.out.println("Error occurred processing file or directory.");
    ioe.printStackTrace();
}

// Exit gracefully
System.exit(0);
}
}
```

The **main** method of the class accepts an IFS file or directory name as a command-line parameter. If a file name is passed to the program, the contents of the file are listed. If a directory name is passed to the program, the files within the directory are listed.

Unless otherwise noted, the Toolbox classes described in this chapter are all contained in the com.ibm.as400.access package. When you use the Toolbox in your own code, be sure to import this package so that the Toolbox classes are available to you. Recall from Chapter 3 that the Toolbox classes are collected in archive files (both ZIP and JAR) and that you should include one of these archives on your classpath when you run applications that use the Toolbox.

Writing Files

The steps required to write an IFS stream file are nearly the same as the steps to read one, except that the IFSTextFileOutputStream class is used to create an output stream object. Just as with the text input stream, an AS400 communications object, IFS file object, and sharing-level constant are passed to the constructor. A fourth parameter is a Boolean value indicating whether to append data to the file or replace data in the file — "true" appends data, and "false" replaces data.

```
AS400 as400 = new AS400();

IFSFile myFile = new IFSFile(as400, "/myjava/SimpleClass.java");

IFSTextFileOutputStream st = new IFSTextFileOutputStream(as400,
    myFile, IFSTextFileInputStream.SHARE_ALL, true);
```

The next bit of example code uses the text output stream object to write a few lines of Java source code to a stream file in the root file system. For the lines of source code to be readable, they must be converted to ASCII. A text output stream object can translate character sets as bytes are written to the stream. The **setCCSID** method lets you set the target character set before doing any output. The character set 819 used in this example is an ASCII character set. After setting the Coded Character Set Identifier (CCSID), sending data to the output stream is a matter of executing **write** methods.

```
st.setCCSID(819);

st.write("public class SimpleClass {");
st.write("public static void main(String[] args) {");
st.write("System.out.println(\"Made it this far.\");");
st.write("}}");
```

Closing the text output stream writes any buffered data to the file and releases any file-sharing restrictions in place on the file.

```
st.close();
```

Directories and Files

You've seen how IFS file objects let you read and write stream files and list the contents of a directory. You can also use IFS file objects to

- Create directories
- Delete directories
- Rename directories
- Delete files
- Rename files

To create a directory, you first create an IFS file object and then execute the object's **mkdir** (make directory) method.

```
IFSFile myDir = new IFSFile(as400, "/mydir");

myDir.mkdir();
```

You use the **mkdir** method to create a single directory. The **mkdirs** method creates all the directories and subdirectories named in an IFS file object.

```
IFSFile myDir = new IFSFile(as400,
    "/mydir/subdir1/subdir2/subdir3");

myDir.mkdirs();
```

Renaming a directory requires two IFS file objects, one for the old directory name and one for the renamed directory. Execute the **renameTo** method on the IFS file object for the old directory name, passing it the IFS file object for the renamed directory.

```
IFSFile myDir = new IFSFile(as400, "/mydir");
IFSFile myDir2 = new IFSFile(as400, "/mydir_renamed");

myDir.renameTo(myDir2);
```

To delete a directory, you create an IFS file object and then execute the object's **delete** method.

```
IFSFile myDir = new IFSFile(as400, "/mydir");

myDir.delete();
```

The **delete** method removes only a single directory. Unfortunately, there is no analog to **mkdirs** — no method for deleting more than one directory. If you want to delete the entire /mydir/subdir1/subdir2... directory structure, you have to do it one directory at a time.

Files are created automatically when you create and write to output streams. You can use IFS file objects to delete or rename files in a manner similar to directories.

```
IFSFile myFile = new IFSFile(as400, "/mydir/myfile.txt");
IFSFile myFile2 = new IFSFile(as400, "/mydir/myfilerenamed.txt");

myFile.renameTo(myFile2);

myFile2.delete();
```

Use the **renameTo** method, passing it an IFS file object, to rename a file; use the **delete** method to delete a file.

For Further Study

In addition to what you've seen here, the IFS feature of the Toolbox includes classes for reading and writing stream files without character set conversion. These are the IFSInputStream and IFSOutputStream classes. The Toolbox also provides an IFSRandomAccessFile class for you to access stream file data randomly using byte offsets.

Also beyond the scope of this section is a discussion of byte-level locks that you can obtain on the data within stream files. The Toolbox uses the IFSKey class to represent a data lock.

DATABASE ACCESS

A powerful feature of the AS/400 is its integrated database, DB2/400. The Toolbox gives your Java programs two ways to access DB2/400 data:

- JDBC driver
- Record-level access

This section shows you how to code database access using each of these facilities.

JDBC Driver

Java Database Connectivity (JDBC) is a standard defined by Sun Microsystems that determines how Java programs access database management systems. The

JDBC standard lets you use Structured Query Language (SQL) statements to define, manage, and access databases in a cross-platform manner. Both JDBC and SQL are huge topics and are covered in depth in many currently available Java language books.

Instead of attempting comprehensive coverage of JDBC and SQL, this chapter shows you how to perform basic JDBC/SQL functions using the Toolbox driver. After learning how to register the driver and connect to a DB2/400 database, you'll see how to insert a record into a database table and then read the record back as a result set.

REGISTERING THE DRIVER

Before you can start accessing a database with JDBC, you have to register your driver with the JVM. There are different schools of thought on the best way to do this. One common approach is simply to instantiate a JDBC driver object and pass it to the DriverManager class's **registerDriver** method in an application's initialization routine, as shown below.

```
DriverManager.registerDriver(
    new com.ibm.as400.access.AS400JDBCDriver());
```

Another approach to registering a JDBC driver is to set a system property at runtime. Using the Sun Microsystems JDK, you can set properties with the -D option on the java command, as in this example:

```
java -Djdbc.drivers=com.ibm.as400.access.AS400JDBCDriver/myjava/SomeApp
```

Using the AS/400's native JVM, the Run Java (RUNJVA) command lets you do the same thing with the Properties (PROP) parameter.

```
RUNJVA CLASS(SomeApp) CLASSPATH('/myjava')              +
    PROP((jdbc.drivers com.ibm.as400.access.AS400JDBCDriver))
```

Registering the driver in the source code locks an application into using one specific driver. Setting the driver using a system property is generally preferred because this technique lets you substitute one JDBC driver for another at runtime.

WHEN TO USE THE TOOLBOX DRIVER

IBM provides two JDBC drivers for Java access to DB2/400. The subject of this chapter, the Toolbox driver, is one; the other is a native driver shipped as a part of the ADK. How do you decide when to use the Toolbox driver and when to use the native driver?

The Toolbox JDBC driver is a great choice for applications and applets running on client workstations. The alternative on a client workstation is to use the JDBC-ODBC bridge provided by Sun Microsystems. This bridge passes JDBC calls through an ODBC connection to the target database. The added configuration and the overhead of translating JDBC calls to ODBC calls make the Toolbox driver attractive indeed.

When you write applications that run in the AS/400's JVM, you should choose the JDBC driver shipped with the ADK. You certainly can use the Toolbox driver even for host-based Java applications, but you'll find the native JDBC driver to be a better performer.

Because you never really know where your Java application might run — on a client workstation, an AS/400, or an unforeseen future Java platform — the best practice is to soft-code the JDBC driver your application uses. You have several options for soft-coding the driver. For example, you can use the "jdbc.drivers" system property and register your driver at runtime. Or you might query a properties file of your own creation to determine the runtime driver.

JDBC CONNECTION

Before we can go much further with database access, we need to create a table on the AS/400. Use the Data Description Specifications (DDS) shown in Figure 5.3 to create the table CUSTMAST in the EXAMPLES library. "Creating the Customer Table" offers detailed instructions for creating the DDS and compiling it to create the table.

FIGURE 5.3
Customer Master Table DDS

```
*...1....+....2....+....3....+....4....+....5....+....6....+....7....+....8
A                                        UNIQUE
A          R CUSTREC
A            CUSTID        5  0
A            CUSTNAME      40
A            CUSTSTREET    40
A            CUSTCITY      40
A          K CUSTID
```

NOTE: In this book, we use the database terms *table* and *file* to refer to AS/400 physical file objects. Table is commonly used in discussions of SQL-related subjects, such as JDBC, and file is used normally in discussions of record-level access. In addition, when discussing SQL, we use *row* and *column*; in record-level access, the terms are *record* and *field*.

After registering the JDBC driver, you must establish a connection with your AS/400 before you can make database-level JDBC calls. The **getConnection** method of the DriverManager class returns an instance of the Connection class. (Replace *system* with the name of your AS/400 system.)

```
Connection conn =
    DriverManager.getConnection("jdbc:as400://system");
```

CREATING THE CUSTOMER TABLE

To create the table CUSTMAST used by the examples in this book, follow these steps:

1. Create a source physical file in the EXAMPLES library.

   ```
   CRTSRCPF FILE(EXAMPLES/QDDSSRC)
   ```

2. Start the Source Entry Utility (SEU) to create a source member.

   ```
   STRSEU SRCFILE(EXAMPLES/QDDSSRC) SRCMBR(CUSTMAST)        +
          TYPE(PF) TEXT('Customer master table source')
   ```

3. Type the physical file source shown in Figure 5.3.

4. Compile the source to create a physical file object.

   ```
   CRTPF FILE(EXAMPLES/CUSTMAST) SRCFILE(EXAMPLES/QDDSSRC)
   ```

Instructions for restoring the complete EXAMPLES library from the CD-ROM accompanying this book are included in Appendix A.

JDBC is the only component of the Toolbox that does not explicitly require you to create an AS400 object as a way to communicate with the AS/400. When you execute the **getConnection** method, you are prompted to supply a user ID and password. You could also supply the user ID and password on the method call.

```
Connection conn =
    DriverManager.getConnection("jdbc:as400://system",
    "DAND", "MYPASSWORD");
```

JDBC INSERT

With a connection object, you can begin executing SQL statements that operate on the database. The following Java code creates a JDBC statement object and then uses this object to insert a row into the CUSTMAST database table.

```
Statement stmt = conn.createStatement();
stmt.executeUpdate("insert into examples.custmast " +
    "values(12345, 'Dan Darnell', '111 Maple Street', " +
    "'Little Rock, AR 72211')");
```

As you can see, the connection object is used to create an instance of the Statement class. This statement object is then used to execute an SQL insert on the table CUSTMAST.

JDBC SELECT

You can query a database to obtain a collection of rows based on selection criteria. This collection of database rows is made available to your Java program as an instance of the ResultSet class.

```
Statement stmt = conn.createStatement();
ResultSet rs = stmt.executeQuery("select * from " +
    "examples.custmast");
```

Here, a connection object is used to create a statement object, which in turn is used to execute a query. The result set object returned by the **executeQuery** method contains the rows and columns selected by the SQL Select statement. In this instance, all rows and all columns are selected from the CUSTMAST table.

You can access data in the result set object one row at a time using a loop such as this one:

```
while(rs.next())
{
    java.math.BigDecimal custID = rs.getBigDecimal("CUSTID", 0);
    String custName = rs.getString("CUSTNAME");
    String custStreet = rs.getString("CUSTSTREET");
    String custCity = rs.getString("CUSTCITY");

    System.out.println("Customer ID     : " + custID);
    System.out.println("Customer Name   : " + custName);
    System.out.println("Customer Street: " + custStreet);
    System.out.println("Customer City   : " + custCity);
}
```

The **next** method of the result set advances an internal current row pointer from one row to the next. While a row is current, you can parse individual columns from the row.

Depending upon the data type of a column in the underlying database table, you use a different result set method to obtain the data. The loop above uses the **getBigDecimal** method to retrieve packed decimal data from the CUSTID column and **getString** to retrieve character data from the remaining columns. Table 5.3 shows the most commonly used DB2/400 data types, the result set methods used to retrieve these data types, and the resulting Java object types.

TABLE 5.3

Data Types, Result Set Methods, and Object Types

DB2/400 Data Type	Result Set Method	Java Object Type
Binary (2-byte)	getShort	Short
Binary (4-byte)	getInt	Integer
Character	getString	String

continued

TABLE 5.3 *CONTINUED*

DB2/400 Data Type	Result Set Method	Java Object Type
Floating point (4-byte)	getFloat	Float
Floating point (8-byte)	getDouble	Double
Packed decimal	getBigDecimal	BigDecimal
Zoned decimal	getBigDecimal	BigDecimal

In most cases, JDBC can convert from one data type to another as it retrieves information for you from a result set. As a rule, don't try to retrieve a numeric value from a larger data type into a smaller data type (e.g., an integer into a short or a double into a float). Another tip to remember is that all data types can be retrieved as string values with a **getString** method call.

JDBC CLEANUP
You always want to close result set, statement, and connection objects when you are through with them. Closing them releases any holdover table, row, or column locks and frees other resources taken by the objects.

```
rs.close();
stmt.close();
conn.close();
```

FOR FURTHER STUDY
We've covered only a tiny fraction of JDBC's extensive capabilities. Other very useful features of JDBC that you might want to study are

- Stored procedures — Host programs attached to the database, called stored procedures, are supported by JDBC through the CallableStatement class. Using stored procedures is a way for your Java programs to call AS/400 programs written in RPG or Cobol. Another way to call AS/400 programs is with the Program Call feature of the Toolbox discussed later in this chapter.

- Meta data retrieval — You can discover runtime information about the structure of the database as a whole; this information is called meta data. JDBC provides the DatabaseMetaData class for this purpose. One use for this capability is to discover what tables exist in a database. A similar capability exists at the result set level. Use the ResultSetMetaData class to obtain information about the rows and columns contained in a result set.

Record-Level Access
The Toolbox includes classes for accessing DB2/400 just as you do in an RPG or Cobol program. These record-level access classes make it possible to read and write database records using a sequential access method — by relative

record number or with key values. In this chapter, you see an example of record-level access using the keyed access method. This example uses the same CUSTMAST file that you created for the JDBC example.

WRITING RECORDS

Several classes work together to provide record-level access and it takes several steps to get the job done. The basic steps required to write a record to a file are listed below.

1. Create an AS400 communications object.
2. Create a file object.
3. Create a file record description object.
4. Retrieve a record format object using the record description.
5. Associate the record format with the file object.
6. Open the file.
7. Create an empty record.
8. Set field values within the record.
9. Write the record.
10. Close the file.

Before you can write a record to a file, you must first determine which record format to use and associate that record format with a file object. Given this, you might say that the first five steps are preparation for the last five, in which the file is actually opened and a record written.

Let's look at the code required to complete each step. First, you create an AS400 communications object. As described before, this object is used for communications with host server jobs.

```
AS400 as400 = new AS400();
```

Using the AS400 object you then create a keyed file object as a way to access a database file. The constructor of the KeyedFile class includes the IFS-style path to the file (here the CUSTMAST file in the EXAMPLES library).

```
KeyedFile myFile = new KeyedFile(as400,
    "/qsys.lib/examples.lib/custmast.file");
```

Next, create a file record description object using the AS400FileRecord-Description class. Again, the IFS-style path to the CUSTMAST database file is passed to the constructor. The purpose of this object is to link your Java program to the record formats of a particular database file.

```
AS400FileRecordDescription myFileDesc =
    new AS400FileRecordDescription(as400,
    "/qsys.lib/examples.lib/custmast.file");
```

After creating a file record description object, you use it to retrieve the record formats of the database file. Because a database file can have more than one record format (in the case of a multiformat logical file), the **retrieveRecord-Format** method returns an array of record formats. For physical files, the array always contains a single record format in array element zero.

```
RecordFormat recFormats[] = myFileDesc.retrieveRecordFormat();
```

Before you can take the step of opening the file, you must associate a record format from the array with the keyed file object. You perform this step with the **setRecordFormat** method of the keyed file object.

```
myFile.setRecordFormat(recFormats[0]);
```

The preparation steps are over and now you can use the fully described keyed file. The first step toward using the file is opening it.

```
myFile.open(AS400File.WRITE_ONLY, 0,
    AS400File.COMMIT_LOCK_LEVEL_NONE);
```

The parameters accepted by the **open** method of the keyed file object are

- Open type — Valid values for this parameter are READ_ONLY, WRITE_ONLY, and READ_WRITE. Files opened as READ_ONLY do not allow write operations. Files opened as WRITE_ONLY do not allow read operations.

- Blocking factor — With this parameter, you can specify how many records the system should buffer during each read operation or how many records the system should write during a write operation. The Open type parameter influences this parameter. Valid Blocking factors and their relationships to Open types are described in Table 5.4. If the system is required to calculate a blocking factor, it does so using the formula

$$blocking\_factor = (2048 / record\_length) + 16$$

TABLE 5.4
Block Factors by Open Type

Blocking Factor	READ_ONLY	WRITE_ONLY	READ_WRITE
0	A blocking factor is calculated by the system.	A blocking factor is calculated by the system.	Automatically overridden to 1.
1	No blocking occurs.	No blocking occurs.	No blocking occurs.
integer value	The number of records to block during a read.	The number of records to block while writing an array of records.	Automatically overridden to 1.

- Commitment control level — This parameter specifies when an update, delete, or write operation on a record is committed. Valid values for this parameter are described in Table 5.5.

TABLE 5.5
Commitment Control Levels

Level	Description
COMMIT_LOCK_LEVEL_ALL	All records read are locked until a transaction is committed or rolled back.
COMMIT_LOCK_LEVEL_CURSOR_STABILITY	A record read and updated or deleted is locked until a transaction is committed or rolled back. A record read and not changed is unlocked when another record is read.
COMMIT_LOCK_LEVEL_NONE	No commitment control is used.
COMMIT_LOCK_LEVEL_CHANGE	A record read and updated or deleted is locked until a transaction is committed or rolled back. A record read and then released is unlocked.
COMMIT_LOCK_LEVEL_DEFAULT	The level of commitment control specified on the startCommitmentControl method is used.

Before writing data to the open file, you must create a record object and apply values to the fields within the record. To obtain an instance of the Record class, execute the **getNewRecord** method on the record format object that describes the database file.

```
Record addRec = recFormats[0].getNewRecord();
```

This record object contains field descriptions based on the record format used to create it. Values for all the fields in the record are set to default values, either by data type (e.g., zeros for numeric field, blanks for character fields) or using the default value specified for the field when the file was created. You can override these default values using the **setField** method on the record object.

In this example, the field values are set to the identifying information for a new customer.

```
addRec.setField("CUSTID", new java.math.BigDecimal(12345));
addRec.setField("CUSTNAME", "Dan Darnell");
addRec.setField("CUSTSTREET", "135 Any Street");
addRec.setField("CUSTCITY", "Little Rock, AR 72211");
```

The **setField** method accepts a field name and a value with which to set the field. The Toolbox takes care of converting Java data types to DB2/400 data types, but it is your responsibility to pass the correct Java data type to the

setField method. If you fail to do so, a ClassCastException exception is thrown at run time.

The DB2/400 data types and compatible Java data types are shown in Table 5.6.

TABLE 5.6

Data Type Conversions

DB2/400 Data Type	Java Data Type
Binary (2-byte)	Short
Binary (4-byte)	Integer
Character	String
Date	String
Floating point (4-byte)	Float
Floating point (8-byte)	Double
Hexadecimal	byte[]
Packed decimal	BigDecimal
Time	String
Timestamp	String
Zoned decimal	BigDecimal

With values set into the fields, writing the record is a matter of passing the record object to the **write** method of the keyed file object.

```
myFile.write(addRec);
```

By way of cleanup, make sure that you close a file when you are finished with it.

```
myFile.close();
```

NOTE: In addition to writing records to a file one at a time, you can also accumulate an array of records and then write the entire array to a file by using the *write* method with the following signature:

```
write(Record[] records)
```

READ AND UPDATE

Many of the steps you just went through to write records to a keyed file are also required to read and update records. Again, several classes work together. Here are the steps required for reading and updating records in a keyed file.

1. Create an AS400 communications object.
2. Create a file object.

3. Create a file record description object.

4. Retrieve a record format object using the record description.

5. Associate the record format with the file object.

6. Open the file.

7. Create a key array.

8. Read a record using the key array.

9. Retrieve field values from the record.

10. Set new field values in the record.

11. Update the file.

12. Close the file.

The first five steps are the same as for writing records to a keyed file. Here again is the code required:

```
// Construct an AS400 communications object
AS400 as400 = new AS400();

// Create a keyed file object
KeyedFile myFile = new KeyedFile(as400,
    "/qsys.lib/examples.lib/custmast.file");

// Create a file record description object
AS400FileRecordDescription myFileDesc =
    new AS400FileRecordDescription(as400,
    "/qsys.lib/examples.lib/custmast.file");

// Get the record format(s) from the record description object
RecordFormat recFormats[] = myFileDesc.retrieveRecordFormat();

// Associate the record format with the file
myFile.setRecordFormat(recFormats[0]);
```

To open a file for read and update, specify the READ_WRITE open type on the call to the **open** method.

```
myFile.open(AS400File.READ_WRITE, 0,
    AS400File.COMMIT_LOCK_LEVEL_NONE);
```

The Toolbox lets you use full or partial keys to access records. For example, if a DB2/400 file has a key consisting of fields A, B, and C, the file can be read using a key for field A, a key for fields A and B, or a key for fields A, B, and C.

Using Java fields as key data to locate DB2/400 records isn't always a graceful maneuver. If your file key contains character fields, you must pad the Java strings used in the key with blanks to the length of the character field.

In the example below, we construct a key that retrieves the record written in the earlier example. Keys are always defined as an array of objects, even if the DB2/400 file has only one key field. Because the CUSTMAST file has a numeric key, no padding is required.

```
Object[] key = new Object[] {new java.math.BigDecimal(12345)};
```

With a properly constructed key object array, you can begin reading records using the **read** method of the keyed file object. With each read, an instance of the Record class is returned containing the record data. If a record matching the key value that you specified is not found, the **read** method returns null.

```
Record record = myFile.read(key);
```

In addition to the **read** method, the KeyedFile class provides several other methods, summarized in Table 5.7, for working with keyed data.

TABLE 5.7
Additional Keyed File Methods

Method	Purpose
positionCursor(Object[] key)	Position the file pointer to the first record with a key matching the key parameter.
positionCursorBefore(Object[] key)	Position the file pointer to the record just before the record with a key matching the key parameter.
positionCursorAfter(Object[] key)	Position the file pointer to the record just after the record with a key matching the key parameter.
read(Object[] key)	Read the first record with a key matching the key parameter. If the file contains more than one record with the same key, the first record with a matching key is always returned.
readBefore(Object[] key)	Read the record just before the record with a key matching the key parameter.
readAfter(Object[] key)	Read the record just after the record with a key matching the key parameter.
readNextEqual()	Read the next record with a key matching the current record.
readNextEqual(Object[] key)	Read the next record with a key matching the key parameter.
readPreviousEqual()	Read the previous record with a key matching the current record.
readPreviousEqual(Object[] key)	Read the previous record with a key matching the key parameter.
update(Object[] key, Record record)	Update the record with a key matching the key parameter. The record values used to update the record are given as the second parameter.
deleteRecord(Object[] key)	Delete the record with a key matching the key parameter.

A few additional methods are made available by the KeyedFile class's base class, AS400File. These methods are summarized in Table 5.8.

TABLE 5.8
Additional File Methods

Method	Purpose
update(Record record)	Update the record at the current file pointer position. The record values used to update the record are given as the only parameter. Before performing this type of update, you must first position the file pointer to a valid record.
deleteCurrentRecord()	Delete the record at the current file pointer position.
write(Record record)	Write a record to the file.
write(Record[]records)	Write an array of records to the file.

Back to the example. After attempting to read a record by key, check for a null value. If a record was read, you can start retrieving individual field values from the record object. Our example prints each field in a record from the CUSTMAST file to the standard output device.

```
if (record != null)
{
   System.out.println("Customer ID: " +
       record.getField("CUSTID"));
   System.out.println("Name      : " +
       record.getField("CUSTNAME"));
   System.out.println("Address   : " +
       record.getField("CUSTSTREET"));
   System.out.println("City      : " +
       record.getField("CUSTCITY"));
}
```

The **getField** method accepts a field name as a parameter and returns a Java object. The object's data type is determined by the data type of the field in the DB2/400 file. The data type conversion performed by the Toolbox is the opposite of that performed for the **setField** method. Again, see Table 5.6 for a list of compatible DB2/400 and Java data types. Notice in the example that although the customer ID field CUSTID is packed decimal data, it is used as though it were a string.

```
System.out.println("Customer ID: " + record.getField("CUSTID"));
```

This code takes advantage of Java's inherent ability to turn an object of any type into a string. To access the Customer ID field's packed decimal data as its true data type (BigDecimal), cast the result of the **getField** method call like this:

```
java.math.BigDecimal custID =
    (java.math.BigDecimal)record.getField("CUSTID")
```

To update the field values in the current record, use the **setField** method on the record object. The following example modifies the values of the customer name and street address fields.

```
record.setField("CUSTNAME", "Daniel Darnell");
record.setField("CUSTSTREET", "222 Oak Lane");
```

Make the field changes permanent by executing the **update** method on the keyed file object and passing it the record object with the changed field values.

```
myFile.update(record);
```

By way of cleanup, close the keyed file when you are through with it.

```
myFile.close();
```

FOR FURTHER STUDY
As with JDBC, the record-level access features of the Toolbox are extensive. You can create and delete files and members, and commitment control is fully supported.

Working with sequential files is very similar to working with keyed files. The primary difference between the two is that the **read** methods for sequential access are fewer and far simpler than the keyed access methods.

Consider creating classes of your own, one per physical file, that combine the steps for creating file and record formats with the file open. By doing so, you reduce the amount of coding that is required to access a file.

COMMANDS AND PROGRAMS
Two more indispensable features of the Toolbox allow your Java programs to run commands and programs residing on the AS/400. Using the command call feature, you can easily perform operations on the AS/400 such as creating a library or copying a database file. With the program call feature, you can leverage existing Original Program Model (OPM) and Integrated Language Environment (ILE) programs.

Command Call
The command call feature is the easiest of the Toolbox features to use. Executing an AS/400 command is as simple as creating an AS400 communications object, creating a command call object, and executing the command object's **run** method. The only restriction is that you cannot execute commands that send output to a display, for obvious reasons — there is no place for displayed output from a command to display in Java.

Getting right to an example, let's first create an AS400 communications object. This step should be familiar to you by now.

```
AS400 as400 = new AS400();
```

Second, create an instance of the CommandCall class, passing the AS400 communications object to the constructor.

```
CommandCall command = new CommandCall(as400);
```

Now execute the **run** method on the command object. The **run** method accepts as a parameter a string containing the command to execute. The **run** method returns a Boolean value — "true" if the command executed normally and "false" if it did not.

```
if(command.run("DSPLIB LIB(EXAMPLES) OUTPUT(*PRINT)"))
    System.out.println("Command completed normally.");
else
    System.out.println("Command did not complete normally.");
```

If the command fails for some reason, you can retrieve a list of the messages generated by the failed command. The Toolbox includes the AS400-Message class, which acts as a wrapper for AS/400 system messages. Execute the **getMessageList** method on the command object to obtain an array of all the AS/400 messages generated by the command.

```
AS400Message[] messages = command.getMessageList();
```

Using the methods of the AS400Message class, you can print message details, as shown below.

```
if(messages != null)
{
    for(int i = 0; i < messages.length; i++)
    {
     System.out.println(messages[i].getID() + "   " +
        messages[i].getText());
    }
}
```

Program Call

In contrast to making command calls, making program calls is a complicated and cumbersome proposition. The complications arise because you are responsible for converting parameters to and from AS/400 data types. The mechanism for doing so is error prone — it is very easy to mistype a parameter.

Figure 5.4 shows the source code for an RPG IV program. The program doesn't do much; it just receives data in parameters of various data types and passes other data back in these same parameters. We use this program to show you how to call an AS/400 program and make the proper conversions.

FIGURE 5.4
RPG IV Program TESTPGM

```
*...1....+....2....+....3....+....4....+....5....+....6....+....7....+....8
D character       S             10
D packed          S              7P 2
D zoned           S              8S 4
D float           S              4F
D double          S              8F
D short           S              5I 0
D integer         S             10I 0
```

continued

FIGURE 5.4 *CONTINUED*

```
*...1....+....2....+....3....+....4....+....5....+....6....+....7....+....8
C     *entry      plist
C                 parm                      character
C                 parm                      packed
C                 parm                      zoned
C                 parm                      float
C                 parm                      double
C                 parm                      short
C                 parm                      integer

C     character   dsply
C     packed      dsply
C     zoned       dsply
C     float       dsply
C     double      dsply
C     short       dsply
C     integer     dsply

C                 eval      character = 'Hi back!'
C                 eval      packed = -99999.99
C                 eval      zoned = -9999.9999
C                 eval      float = 1.1754944E-38
C                 eval      double = 2.225073858507201E-308
C                 eval      short = -32768
C                 eval      integer = -2147483648

C                 eval      *inlr = *on
```

Getting to the Java code required to call the RPG program, begin by constructing an AS400 communications object.

```
AS400 as400 = new AS400();
```

Then construct a ProgramCall object and pass it the AS400 object.

```
ProgramCall myPgm = new ProgramCall(as400);
```

So far, the tasks are simple enough, but now we begin the tedious process of composing parameters. First, create an array to hold all the parameters you will use.

```
ProgramParameter myPgmParms[] = new ProgramParameter[7];
```

Next, create individual ProgramParameter objects and place them in the array. The ProgramParameter class has constructors to help you create input parameters, output parameters, and input/output parameters. Choosing the right constructor is essential to getting the type of parameter you are after. The ProgramParameter constructors are described in Table 5.9.

TABLE 5.9
<h2 align="center">ProgramParameter Constructors</h2>

Purpose	Constructor	Parameters
Input-only	ProgramParameter (byte[] bytearray)	Passing a byte array to the constructor creates an input-only parameter.

continued

TABLE 5.9 *CONTINUED*

Purpose	Constructor	Parameters
Output-only	ProgramParameter (int length)	Passing an output length to the constructor constructor creates an output-only parameter.
Input/Output	ProgramParameter (byte[] bytearray, int length)	Passing a byte array and an output length output length to the constructor creates an input/output parameter.

Data is passed to and from AS/400 programs as AS/400 data types stored as arrays of bytes encoded in EBCDIC. Realizing that most programmers won't relish the task of translating to and from EBCDIC themselves, IBM supplies helper classes to do some of the dirty work.

In this example, we construct the first parameter, a character string, using the AS400Text helper class.

```
String i_char = "Hi there!";
AS400Text textConverter = new AS400Text(10);
myPgmParms[0] =
    new ProgramParameter(textConverter.toBytes(i_char), 10);
```

With subsequent parameters we'll move more quickly, but for this first one, let's take it a line at a time. The first statement is straightforward; a string is created.

```
String i_char = "Hi there!";
```

The next statement creates an AS400Text helper object for a character field with a length of 10 bytes.

```
AS400Text textConverter = new AS400Text(10);
```

The third statement creates a program parameter object and sets the first element of the parameter's array with this object.

```
myPgmParms[0] =
    new ProgramParameter(textConverter.toBytes(i_char), 10);
```

The input/output constructor of the ProgramParameter class is used to create the object, which is apparent because both a byte array and a return length are passed to the constructor. The **toBytes** method of the helper object converts the Java string into a byte array encoded in EBCDIC. By placing the program parameter object in the first element of the parameters array, we ensure that this data is passed to the RPG program as its first input parameter when the program is executed later.

The rest of the parameters follow the same basic pattern of creating a data object, creating a helper object, constructing a parameter object, and setting a parameter array element.

CREATING THE TESTPGM PROGRAM

To create TESTPGM, the program used by the examples in this book, follow these steps:

1. If it doesn't already exist, create a source physical file for ILE RPG members in the EXAMPLES library.

   ```
   CRTSRCPF FILE(EXAMPLES/QRPGLESRC)
   ```

2. Start SEU to create a source member.

   ```
   STRSEU SRCFILE(EXAMPLES/QRPGLESRC) SRCMBR(TESTPGM)   +
          TYPE(RPGLE) TEXT('Program call tester')
   ```

3. Type the ILE RPG source code shown in Figure 5.4.

4. Compile the source code to create an executable program object.

   ```
   CRTBNDRPG PGM(EXAMPLES/TESTPGM)                       +
             SRCFILE(EXAMPLES/QRPGLESRC)
   ```

Instructions for restoring the complete EXAMPLES library from the CD-ROM accompanying this book are included in Appendix A.

In this example, we demonstrate converting to a packed decimal format. The following code constructs an input/output parameter for a packed decimal field with a length of seven digits and two decimal positions.

```
BigDecimal i_packed = new BigDecimal("99999.99");
AS400PackedDecimal packedConverter =
    new AS400PackedDecimal(7, 2);
myPgmParms[1] =
    new ProgramParameter(packedConverter.toBytes(i_packed), 7);
```

Zoned decimal fields work in the same way, but they use a different helper class.

```
BigDecimal i_zoned = new BigDecimal("9999.9999");
AS400ZonedDecimal zonedConverter = new AS400ZonedDecimal(8, 4);
myPgmParms[2] =
    new ProgramParameter(zonedConverter.toBytes(i_zoned), 8);
```

The AS/400 supports two types of floating-point numbers. The AS/400's 4-byte, single-precision floating-point number is the equivalent of Java's Float object type, while the 8-byte, double-precision floating-point number corresponds to Java's Double object type.

```
Float i_float = new Float(3.4028235E38);
AS400Float4 float4Converter = new AS400Float4();
myPgmParms[3] =
    new ProgramParameter(float4Converter.toBytes(i_float), 4);
```

```
Double i_double = new Double(1.797693134862315E308);
AS400Float8 float8Converter = new AS400Float8();
myPgmParms[4] =
    new ProgramParameter(float8Converter.toBytes(i_double), 8);
```

The AS/400 supports the equivalent of Java's Short and Integer object types. These objects are converted as signed binary numbers of two bytes or four bytes, respectively.

```
Short i_short = new Short((short)32767);
AS400Bin2 binary2Converter = new AS400Bin2();
myPgmParms[5] =
    new ProgramParameter(binary2Converter.toBytes(i_short), 2);

Integer i_integer = new Integer(214783657);
AS400Bin4 binary4Converter = new AS400Bin4();
myPgmParms[6] =
    new ProgramParameter(binary4Converter.toBytes(i_integer), 4);
```

Although we do not show it here, you can also convert Java's Long object type as an unsigned binary number using the AS400UnsignedBin4 helper class. On the AS/400 side, the target for a Java long integer is a 10-digit unsigned integer.

Now that all the input parameters are converted and the program parameters array is established, the program to execute and the parameters can be associated with one another. The **setProgram** method of the program call object is used for this purpose.

```
myPgm.setProgram("/QSYS.LIB/EXAMPLES.LIB/TESTPGM.PGM",
    myPgmParms);
```

The **run** method of the program call object executes the program set up in the previous step.

```
myPgm.run()
```

If the program executes without errors, the **run** method returns a Boolean value of "true"; otherwise, it returns a value of "false." It's always a good idea to check for successful program execution before trying to extract output parameters.

The business of extracting output parameters is somewhat easier than constructing input parameters. Again, let's start with the first parameter, a character string, and take the code apart in some detail. Just as the Java program passes program parameters to the RPG program as byte arrays of EBCDIC encoded data, the RPG program passes back to the Java program the same type of information. The trick is to take this byte data and construct Java objects.

```
String o_character =
    (String)textConverter.toObject(myPgmParms[0].getOutputData());
```

A byte array is retrieved from the parameter list using the **getOutputData** method on the first element of the myPgmParms program parameter array. This byte array is fed directly to the AS400Text helper object's **toObject** method. These two steps are combined into this code snippet.

```
textConverter.toObject(myPgmParms[0].getOutputData())
```

Every instance of a helper class has a **toObject** method that returns a Java data type. The helper classes and the data types they operate on are shown in Table 5.10.

TABLE 5.10
Data Conversion Helper Classes

Helper Class	AS/400 Data Type	Java Data Type Returned by toObject Method
AS400Bin2	Signed integer (2-byte)	Short
AS400Bin4	Signed integer (4-byte)	Integer
AS400Float4	Floating-point (4-byte, single precision)	Float
AS400Float8	Floating-point (8-byte, double precision)	Double
AS400PackedDecimal	Packed decimal	BigDecimal
AS400Text	Character field	String
AS400UnsignedBin2	Unsigned integer (2-byte)	Integer
AS400UnsignedBin4	Unsigned integer (4-byte)	Long
AS400ZonedDecimal	Zoned Decimal	BigDecimal

As you can see, instances of the AS400Text class return Java String objects. Knowing this, you can safely cast the object returned by the **toObject** method to a string reference.

```
String o_character =
    (String)textConverter.toObject(myPgmParms[0].getOutputData());
```

With this compound statement, the output parameter from the RPG program is converted to a Java string.

The rest of the output parameters work in the same way. A Java object is constructed by passing a byte array returned from the program call to the appropriate helper object and casting the result of a **toObject** method call to a Java data type. The parameter conversions for packed and zoned decimal fields are shown below.

```
BigDecimal o_packed =
    (BigDecimal)packedConverter.toObject(
    myPgmParms[1].getOutputData());

BigDecimal o_zoned =
    (BigDecimal)zonedConverter.toObject(
    myPgmParms[2].getOutputData());
```

The parameter conversions for single-precision and double-precision floating-point numbers are shown below.

```
Float o_float =
    (Float)float4Converter.toObject(
    myPgmParms[3].getOutputData());

Double o_double =
    (Double)float8Converter.toObject(
    myPgmParms[4].getOutputData());
```

Last, here are the parameter conversions for short integer and integer values.

```
Short o_short =
    (Short)binary2Converter.toObject(
    myPgmParms[5].getOutputData());

Integer o_integer =
    (Integer)binary4Converter.toObject(
    myPgmParms[6].getOutputData());
```

NOTE: These data conversion classes are not designed exclusively for converting program parameters. Any time you receive untranslated AS/400 data in a Java program, you can convert data with these classes. For example, you might use this feature with a Java TCP/IP Sockets server that you create to handle network clients. Data coming into your Java server from the AS/400 might be in EBCDIC, representing AS/400 data types. You can take that raw data and pass it through the appropriate data conversion classes. Responses to the client go through the opposite process — conversion from Java data types to AS/400 data types encoded in EBCDIC.

FOR FURTHER STUDY

When working with the Toolbox, it is important to keep object-oriented design principles in mind. With the Toolbox, IBM provides the basic components you need to access AS/400 resources. Nothing prevents you from combining these basic components into more sophisticated components that go beyond being merely functional.

For example, with the program call feature, you could create your own classes to provide a simpler interface for setting and retrieving parameters. For example, you might create classes to represent each of the AS/400 data types (e.g., AS400ZonedParm, AS400PackedParm, or AS400FloatParm). In these classes you could provide **getXXXX** and **setXXXX** methods (e.g., **getParmData**, **setParmData**) in which you handle the conversion for the parameter's data type. This is a nice way to ensure that you get the conversion right every time, and it beats hand coding the conversion code for every program parameter on every program call.

DATA QUEUE AND PRINT FEATURES

In this section, we discuss two important components of the Toolbox: support for data queues and for printing. The data queue support offered by the Toolbox is a great way to interface your Java programs with RPG, Cobol, and even CL programs on the AS/400. Data queues have been around for a long time and including this support in the Toolbox is recognition of their power and flexibility.

The second Toolbox feature covered in this section is the Print feature. With this feature, your Java programs can access your AS/400's output queue, printer, and spooled file resources. If you've wondered how you are supposed to produce AS/400 reports using Java, this section should answer your questions.

Data Queues

For communicating between programs, it's hard to beat the AS/400 data queue. The Toolbox supports both keyed and nonkeyed data queues in your Java programs.

By their nature, data queues operate on free-format information. It is up to you to construct a data queue entry on the sending side and deconstruct it on the receiving end. If the data queue entry is character data, construction and deconstruction is not a difficult task. However, if the data queue entry is made up of more complex data types, like packed decimal and floating point numbers, parsing the data into and back out of the data queue entry can be an Herculean task.

By combining data queue support and a component of record-level access — record formats — the Toolbox helps you impose structure on your data. These features greatly simplify the chore of creating and parsing data queue entries.

Figure 5.5 shows the source code for an RPG IV program, a close cousin of the RPG program used to test program calls. This code sends a data queue entry composed of various data types to a Java program and then waits for a data queue entry to come back.

FIGURE 5.5

RPG IV Program TESTDQ

```
*...1....+....2....+....3....+....4....+....5....+....6....+....7....+....8
D DQEntry       DS           100
D  character                  10     inz('Hi there!')
D  packed                     7P 2   inz(-99999.99)
D  zoned                      8S 4   inz(-9999.9999)
D  float                      4F     inz(1.1754944E-38)
D  double                     8F     inz(2.225073858507201E-308)
D  short                      5I 0   inz(-32768)
D  integer                   10I 0   inz(-2147483648)

C                    call     'QSNDDTAQ'
C                    parm     'TESTDQ'     DQName         10
C                    parm     'EXAMPLES'   DQLib          10
C                    parm     100          DQLen           5 0
C                    parm                  DQEntry
C                    parm     10           DQKeyLen        3 0
C                    parm     'KEYDATA1'   DQKey          10
```

continued

FIGURE 5.5 *CONTINUED*

```
*...1....+....2....+....3....+....4....+....5....+....6....+....7....+....8
C                       call      'QRCVDTAQ'
C                       parm      'TESTDQ'       DQName
C                       parm      'EXAMPLES'     DQLib
C                       parm      100            DQLen
C                       parm                     DQEntry
C                       parm      -1             DQWait          5 0
C                       parm      'EQ'           DQCond          2
C                       parm      10             DQKeyLen
C                       parm      'KEYDATA2'     DQKey
C                       parm                     DQSndLen        3 0
C                       parm                     DQSndID         44

C      character        dsply
C      packed           dsply
C      zoned            dsply
C      float            dsply
C      double           dsply
C      short            dsply
C      integer          dsply
C      'wait'           dsply                    wait            1

C                       eval      *inlr = *on
```

Begin the Java program by creating an AS400 communications object.

```
AS400 as400 = new AS400();
```

Next, use an instance of the KeyedDataQueue class to create a data queue object, accepting as parameters an AS400 object and an IFS path to a data queue.

```
KeyedDataQueue keyedDQ = new KeyedDataQueue(as400,
    "/qsys.lib/examples.lib/testdq.dtaq");
```

In the real world, data queue entries are often made up of complex data. To write a data queue entry composed of various character and numeric data types, you must construct a byte array containing the data translated from Java data types to AS/400 data types. When you read a data queue entry composed of complex data types, you have to go the other way and convert the AS/400 data to something Java can recognize. The best way to convert data utilizes the support you've already seen in this chapter for record-level access and for data conversion.

The rest of this section describes the Java code necessary to read a data queue entry composed of several different data types and then to write back a data queue entry in the same format. The sample RPG program TESTDQ works with this Java code.

RECEIVING DATA QUEUE ENTRIES

The first step is to create a record format object. This record format is not linked to a database file; it is basically an empty shell waiting for you to provide it with field descriptions.

```
RecordFormat myRecFormat = new RecordFormat();
```

CREATING THE TESTDQ PROGRAM

To create the TESTDQ program used by the examples in this book, follow these steps:

1. If it doesn't already exist, create a source physical file for ILE RPG members in the EXAMPLES library.

    ```
    CRTSRCPF FILE(EXAMPLES/QRPGLESRC)
    ```

2. Start SEU to create a source member.

    ```
    STRSEU SRCFILE(EXAMPLES/QRPGLESRC) SRCMBR(TESTDQ)      +
           TYPE(RPGLE) TEXT('Data queue tester')
    ```

3. Type the ILE RPG source code shown in Figure 5.5.

4. Compile the source code to create an executable program object.

    ```
    CRTBNDRPG PGM(EXAMPLES/TESTDQ)                         +
              SRCFILE(EXAMPLES/QRPGLESRC)
    ```

5. Use the following command on an AS/400 command line to create a keyed data queue.

    ```
    CRTDTAQ DTAQ(EXAMPLES/TESTDQ) MAXLEN(100) SEQ(*KEYED) +
            KEYLEN(10)
    ```

Instructions for restoring the complete EXAMPLES library from the CD-ROM accompanying this book are included in Appendix A.

The next step is to create field description objects for each of the fields that you want in your record format. Field description objects are constructed based on AS/400 data types. The helper classes you used with the Program Call Toolbox feature reappear here and are used by the field description objects to concretely define the data type, including the field length if required. Each field description object is assigned a field name, which is used later to set and retrieve values on the field description objects.

The first field description we will create is for a 10-character text field. The constructor for the CharacterFieldDescription class is passed an AS400Text helper object with a length of 10 characters and the field name CHARACTER as a string constant.

```
CharacterFieldDescription fd_character =
    new CharacterFieldDescription(new AS400Text(10),
    "CHARACTER");
```

The next two field descriptions are for packed-decimal and zoned-decimal fields. In our example, an AS400PackedDecimal helper object creates a packed-decimal field description for a numeric field with a length of seven digits and two decimal positions. For the zoned decimal field description, an AS400ZonedDecimal helper object creates a zoned decimal field with a length of eight digits and four decimal positions. The field names PACKED and ZONED identify these two fields.

```
PackedDecimalFieldDescription fd_packed =
    new PackedDecimalFieldDescription(
    new AS400PackedDecimal(7, 2), "PACKED");

ZonedDecimalFieldDescription fd_zoned =
    new ZonedDecimalFieldDescription(
    new AS400ZonedDecimal(8, 4), "ZONED");
```

A single-precision floating-point numeric field description and a double-precision floating-point numeric field description are created below.

```
FloatFieldDescription fd_float =
    new FloatFieldDescription(new AS400Float4(), "FLOAT");
FloatFieldDescription fd_double =
    new FloatFieldDescription(new AS400Float8(), "DOUBLE");
```

The field names FLOAT and DOUBLE are assigned to these two fields.

Finally, we create the last two field descriptions, one for a short integer and the other for a regular integer. These fields are given the names SHORT and INTEGER. Notice how in every case a data conversion helper object is used to construct a field description.

```
BinaryFieldDescription fd_short =
    new BinaryFieldDescription(new AS400Bin2(), "SHORT");
BinaryFieldDescription fd_integer =
    new BinaryFieldDescription(new AS400Bin4(), "INTEGER");
```

After creating all the field description objects, you can associate them with the empty record format created earlier. Execute the **addFieldDescription** method for each field description, passing the field description object as a parameter.

```
myRecFormat.addFieldDescription(fd_character);
myRecFormat.addFieldDescription(fd_packed);
myRecFormat.addFieldDescription(fd_zoned);
myRecFormat.addFieldDescription(fd_float);
myRecFormat.addFieldDescription(fd_double);
myRecFormat.addFieldDescription(fd_short);
myRecFormat.addFieldDescription(fd_integer);
```

You now have a record format object that describes the data you plan to receive as a data queue entry.

NOTE: An alternative approach for creating a record format object is to create a physical file on the AS/400 in the format of your data queue entries. Then, instead of manually creating field descriptions, you can simply retrieve and use the record format of the physical file. See "Record-Level Access" earlier in this chapter for an example using an AS/400 file record description object to retrieve a record format object.

When using a keyed data queue, the sending program and the receiving program must both be coded to use the same key value. In this example, an RPG program is used to send a data queue entry with a key value of KEYDATA1. On the Java side, this key value must be converted to a byte array before it can be used to read data queue entries. An AS400Text helper object converts the Java string value KEYDATA1 to a byte array encoded in EBCDIC.

```
AS400Text keyText = new AS400Text(10);
byte[] key = keyText.toBytes("KEYDATA1");
```

With the byte array named "key," you can now read data queue entries written with the specified key value. When the **read** method successfully matches the specified key value to the key value on a data queue entry, it returns a KeyedDataQueueEntry object.

```
KeyedDataQueueEntry DQEntry = keyedDQ.read(key, -1, "EQ");
```

The **read** method of the KeyedDataQueue class accepts the following parameters:

- Key — A byte array containing the key used to match data queue entries.

- Wait interval — The interval, in seconds, to wait if the data queue contains no entries matching the key value specified. A wait time of –1 indicates that the method should wait indefinitely.

- Search type — A condition that applies when matching the data queue entry key value to the specified key value. Valid values for this parameter are EQ (equal), NE (not equal), LT (less than), GT (greater than), LE (less than or equal), GE (greater than or equal).

Data queue entries are nothing but byte data in EBCDIC format. The **getData** method of the keyed data queue entry object returns a byte array representing the data queue entry. This byte array is the input to the record format object previously established, and the result is a new record object.

```
Record record = myRecFormat.getNewRecord(DQEntry.getData());
```

By feeding this raw byte data into a record format, the Toolbox creates a record object with the byte data translated according to the data types in the field descriptions. The record object becomes a formatted representation of a data queue entry.

You can access fields in the record object in the same way that you access fields in record objects read through record-level access. Here, each field in the record object is extracted from the record and cast into a Java variable. The field name defined when the field description was created is used as a parameter to the **getField** method of the record object.

```
String d_character = (String) record.getField("CHARACTER");

java.math.BigDecimal d_packed =
    (java.math.BigDecimal) record.getField("PACKED");

java.math.BigDecimal d_zoned =
    (java.math.BigDecimal) record.getField("ZONED");

Float d_float = (Float) record.getField("FLOAT");
Double d_double = (Double) record.getField("DOUBLE");

Short d_short = (Short) record.getField("SHORT");
Integer d_integer = (Integer) record.getField("INTEGER");
```

As a final step, you can print each of the variables just to make sure that all the data came across and that the data type translations worked as expected.

```
System.out.println("Character = " + d_character);
System.out.println("Packed = " + d_packed);
System.out.println("Zoned = " + d_zoned);
System.out.println("Float = " + d_float);
System.out.println("Double = " + d_double);
System.out.println("Short = " + d_short);
System.out.println("Integer = " + d_integer);
```

This step wraps up the steps required to receive a data queue entry. Next we'll tackle sending data queue entries.

SENDING DATA QUEUE ENTRIES

When you send structured data queue entries, just as when you receive them, you need to construct a record format object, create one or more field descriptions, and associate the field descriptions with the record format. The rest of this example assumes that the record format you are using is the same record format created in the "Receiving Data Queue Entries" example.

With a valid record format, you can create an empty record object and then set field values into the record. The following line creates the empty record object.

```
Record sendRecord = myRecFormat.getNewRecord();
```

Now you can set field values into the record by using the field description field names. Here each field in the record is assigned a value appropriate to its data type.

```
sendRecord.setField("CHARACTER", "Hi back!");

sendRecord.setField("PACKED",
    new java.math.BigDecimal(99999.99));
sendRecord.setField("ZONED",
    new java.math.BigDecimal(9999.9999));
```

```
sendRecord.setField("FLOAT", new Float(3.4028235E38));
sendRecord.setField("DOUBLE",
    new Double(1.797693134862315E308));

sendRecord.setField("SHORT", new Short((short)32767));
sendRecord.setField("INTEGER", new Integer(214783657));
```

You are about to write a keyed data queue entry, so the next logical step is to create the key value to associate with the entry. As with the key constructed for receiving a data queue entry, this key value is a byte array constructed using an AS400Text helper object.

```
AS400Text keyText2 = new AS400Text(10);
byte[] key2 = keyText2.toBytes("KEYDATA2");
```

With a valid key constructed, you can write the data queue entry. In the following example, the **getContents** method of the record object returns a byte array to the **write** method of the keyed data queue object. The byte array contains the EBCDIC translation of the record contents, which is suitable for transportation to the AS/400 as a data queue entry.

```
keyedDQ.write(key2, sendRecord.getContents());
```

MORE DATA QUEUE FEATURES

The Toolbox's data queue support includes the ability to create and delete real data queue objects on the AS/400. To create a data queue, use the **create** method of a Toolbox data queue object. You must specify the data queue entry length and, for a keyed data queue, the key length.

```
keyedDQ.create(100, 10);
```

Deleting a data queue object on the AS/400 is as simple as executing the **delete** method of the Toolbox data queue object.

```
keyedDQ.delete();
```

Another nifty data queue feature is the ability to read and write character data in strings without explicitly translating the data from and to an AS/400 data type. It's as simple as this:

```
// Read keyed entry
KeyedDataQueueEntry simpleKeyedDQEntry =
    simpleKeyedDQ.read("KEYSTRING");
System.out.println(simpleKeyedDQEntry.getString());

// Write keyed entry
simpleKeyedDQ.write("KEYSTRING", "SOME DATA IN A STRING");
```

For those times when your data queue entries are composed of nothing but string data, these shortcut read and write methods make life a lot easier.

FOR FURTHER STUDY

In addition to keyed data queues, the Toolbox provides support for nonkeyed data queues. Using a nonkeyed data queue is essentially the same as using a keyed data queue except that the step of creating a key is omitted and the classes you use are DataQueue and DataQueueEntry instead of KeyedDataQueue and KeyedDataQueueEntry.

Print

The Print feature of the Toolbox provides a wide array of services for working with print facilities on the AS/400. You'll find everything from very high-level services, such as checking the status of a printer device, to very low-level services, such as reading and writing spooled files.

PRINT OBJECT LISTS

Functions are available in the Toolbox to retrieve lists of print objects. List functions are currently available for the following:

- AFP resources
- Output queues
- Printers
- Printer files
- Spooled files
- Writer jobs

The print objects contained in these lists can be acted upon individually. For example, an individual output queue can be held, released, or cleared using the Toolbox methods for an output queue object. The basic actions available for each type of print object are shown in Table 5.11.

TABLE 5.11
Print Object Actions

Print Object	Actions
AFPResource	Retrieve attributes for font resources, form definitions, page overlays, page definitions, and page segments.
OutputQueue	Hold, release, and clear queue.
Printer	Retrieve attributes (e.g. printer status).
PrinterFile	Retrieve and set attributes (e.g. copies, page rotation, form type).
SpooledFile	Hold, delete, change output queue, and send to remote system. Query and set attributes (e.g. copies, page rotation, form type). Read existing spooled file.
WriterJob	Start and end writer.

The next section presents an example of retrieving a list of output queues and manipulating the queue objects on the list. Although this example is specific to output queues, the techniques involved apply to all the print object lists and print object types.

OUTPUT QUEUE LIST

In this example, you retrieve a list of AS/400 output queues and then put all of them in a "hold" status.

As usual, you start with an AS400 communications object.

```
AS400 as400 = new AS400();
```

Now create a list object using the OutputQueueList class provided by the Toolbox. The constructor for this class accepts the AS400 communications object as its only parameter.

```
OutputQueueList outQList = new OutputQueueList(as400);
```

After you have an output queue list object, you can set a filter on the object to specify what you want the list to contain. This filter is an IFS path name for the QSYS.LIB file system, where all output queues reside. You might want to set a filter to create a list of output queues in a particular library or libraries, or you might decide to create a subset of the selection by using a generic output queue name.

```
outQList.setQueueFilter("/qsys.lib/%all%.lib/%all%.outq");
```

In the example above, the filter is set to select all output queues in all libraries on the system. Notice the special value %ALL% specified for both library and output queue. The values allowed in the library portion of the path name are as follows:

- Library name — A specific library name can be specified to select output queues from a single library.
- Generic name — You can specify a generic library name, such as PRODLIB*, to select output queues from all libraries meeting the generic selection criteria.
- Special value — Use one of the special values shown in Table 5.12 to select from a system-determined list of libraries.

The values allowed in the output queue portion of the IFS path name are as follows:

- Output queue name — The name of an output queue. An output queue list can contain more than one output queue if like-named output queues reside in more than one of the libraries searched.
- Generic name — A generic output queue name, such as QEZJOB*, that selects all output queues with names that meet the generic selection criteria.

TABLE 5.12
Special Library Values

Value	Library Selection
%ALL%	All libraries are searched for output queues.
%ALLUSR%	All user libraries are searched for output queues, excluding libraries that begin with Q (system libraries) but including libraries beginning with Q that contain user data (e.g., QUSRSYS, QGPL).
%CURLIB%	The host server job's current library is searched for output queues. If a current library is not set, the QGPL library is searched.
%LIBL%	The host server job's library list is searched for output queues.
%USRLIBL%	The libraries specified in the user portion of the host server job's library list are searched for output queues.

- Special value — A special value, %ALL%, which may be used to select all output queues from the library or libraries specified in the library portion of the path name.

With the filter set, create the output queue list by executing the **open-Synchronously** method of the output queue list object.

```
outQList.openSynchronously();
```

NOTE: It is possible to open and create the list using the openAsynchronously method of the output queue list object. When you open synchronously, the program does not continue past the method call until the entire list is built. When you open asynchronously, the program continues immediately and builds the output queue list in the background.

To create a print object list asynchronously, it is necessary to implement the PrintObjectListListener interface and to register as a listener for print object events. Using methods defined by the interface, a background thread notifies your program as items are added to the list. This example takes the easy way out by opening the list using the openSynchronously method.

When the list of output queue objects finishes building, you can begin interrogating the list to work with individual output queue objects. From the output queue list, execute the **getObjects** method to obtain an enumeration of the output queue objects on the list.

```
java.util.Enumeration enum = outQList.getObjects();
```

With the enumeration in hand, you can walk the list of output queue objects. The following code takes each output queue object in the enumeration, prints the name of the output queue, and places the output queue on hold.

```
for( ; enum.hasMoreElements(); )
{
   OutputQueue queue = (OutputQueue)enum.nextElement();

   System.out.println("Output queue: " + queue.getName());
   queue.hold();
}
```

WRITING REPORTS IN JAVA

You can't bake a cake without breaking eggs and you can't write business soft-ware without producing reports. The RPG language came from this inherent business need, and chances are you've already discovered Java's serious report-writing limitations.

The Toolbox simplifies matters somewhat by letting you write reports in Java as AS/400 spooled files. Through this Toolbox feature, you can control the attributes of the spooled file, such as number of copies and page rotation, and you can specify an output queue where the spooled file should go. This example walks you through creating a spooled file on the AS/400.

Start with the ubiquitous AS400 communications object.

```
AS400 as400 = new AS400();
```

Next, create an instance of the OutputQueue class. This instance is used in a later step as a target for your spooled file. The output queue object is con-structed with the AS400 communications object and an IFS path name pointing to an existing output queue.

```
OutputQueue outQ = new OutputQueue(as400,
    "/qsys.lib/examples.lib/myoutq.outq");
```

Now create a print parameters object and set the "save spooled file" and "number of copies" parameters. Use the **setParameters** method to establish spooled file characteristics based on constant values (e.g., ATTR_SAVE, ATTR_COPIES) defined by the PrintObject class.

```
PrintParameterList printParms = new PrintParameterList();
printParms.setParameter(PrintObject.ATTR_SAVE, "*YES");
printParms.setParameter(PrintObject.ATTR_COPIES, 2);
```

Next, use the SpooledFileOutputStream class to create a Java output stream and route it to an AS/400 spooled file. The constructor accepts an AS400 commu-nications object, print parameters object, printer file object, and an output queue object. The AS400 communications object is required, but the others are optional.

```
SpooledFileOutputStream output =
    new SpooledFileOutputStream(as400, printParms, null, outQ);
```

If you pass null as one of the optional parameters, a default value is used. In this example, a null value is passed for the printer file parameter. The default printer file used by the spooled file output stream is QPNPSPRTF.

With the output stream object you have just created, it is possible to begin writing ASCII data to a spooled file immediately. However, you often want to print on AS/400 system printers, and that requires SNA Character Stream (SCS) data in your spooled files. Spooled file data in SCS format is encoded in EBCDIC with embedded codes to control print formatting and font characteristics. The Toolbox has this covered too, but it adds a layer of complexity. The printer you are targeting may limit your use of an SCS feature. This example uses the SCS support with the fewest features, which means that it is likely to work properly with the majority of system printers.

To print an SCS data stream, you must wrap the spooled file output stream with an SCS writer object. All print functions are executed on the writer object so that it can make the proper character set translations and embed the right print control codes in the spooled file.

```
SCS5256Writer printWriter = new SCS5256Writer(output);
```

To print using the SCS writer, execute the **write** method, passing it the string you want to print. To start printing at a particular column, use the **absoluteHorizontalPosition** method, passing it the column number where it should begin printing. To cause a line break, execute the **newLine** method. You can force buffered data to be written by executing the **flush** method.

```
printWriter.write("hi");
printWriter.asboluteHorizontalPositioning(50);
printWriter.write("ho");

printWriter.newLine();

printWriter.write("hi");
printWriter.asboluteHorizontalPositioning(50);
printWriter.write("ho");

printWriter.flush();
```

The results of these eight lines of Java code is a spooled file on the AS/400 containing these two lines of SCS printable data:

```
hi                                                    ho
hi                                                    ho
```

As with any output stream, when you are completely finished writing to it, execute the **close** method.

```
printWriter.close();
```

Even with the Toolbox, printing an entire report of any complexity requires a great deal of manual effort in Java. This is a problem crying out for someone to create a WYSIWYG report design tool that can generate the Java code required to print sophisticated reports.

In addition to creating reports as spooled files, you can also use the Toolbox to manipulate existing spooled files. To obtain a spooled file object for the just-created "hi ho" report, execute the **getSpooledFile** method on the spooled file output stream object.

```
SpooledFile spooledFile = output.getSpooledFile();
```

With a spooled file object, you can print the characteristics of a spooled file.

```
System.out.println("Spooled file       : " +
    spooledFile.getName());
System.out.println("Spooled file number: " +
    spooledFile.getNumber());
System.out.println("Job name           : " +
    spooledFile.getJobName());
System.out.println("Job number         : " +
    spooledFile.getJobNumber());
System.out.println("Job user           : " +
    spooledFile.getJobUser());
```

This code prints information similar to the following for the "hi ho" report.

```
Spooled file       : QPNPSPRTF
Spooled file number: 15
Job name           : QPRTJOB
Job number         : 097235
Job user           : DAND
```

NOTE: You can obtain a spooled file object for any spooled file on the system by using the SpooledFileList class in much the same way that you obtained output queue objects by using the OutputQueueList class.

An even better use of a spooled file object is to send a spooled file to a remote system. The **sendTCP** method of the spooled file object uses TCP/IP to deliver a spooled file to a remote system. The first step is to create another print parameter list to set the attributes for send operation.

```
PrintParameterList sendParms = new PrintParameterList();
sendParms.setParameter(PrintObject.ATTR_RMTSYSTEM, "CHICAGO");
sendParms.setParameter(PrintObject.ATTR_RMTPRTQ, "QPRINT");
sendParms.setParameter(PrintObject.ATTR_SCS2ASCII, "*NO");
sendParms.setParameter(PrintObject.ATTR_DESTINATION, "*AS400");
```

Here, the parameter list is set to target a remote system named CHICAGO and the remote print queue is set to QPRINT. Because the destination system is another AS/400, the SCS-to-ASCII transformation option is set to *NO and the destination system type is set to *AS400.

The **sendTCP** method of the spooled file object is executed and passed the print parameter list.

```
spooledFile.sendTCP(sendParms);
```

The result of this operation is that your spooled file is sent to a remote AS/400 system while retaining the original SCS formatting.

Toolbox Features in V3R2M1

In the first update of the Toolbox, the V3R2M1 release, IBM added several capabilities to the core functionality of the Toolbox:

- Users
- Jobs
- Message Queues
- User Spaces
- Digital Certificates

Let's look at each of these features.

Users

In the V3R2M1 version of the Toolbox, a feature gives you the ability to list AS/400 system users and groups. Currently, this feature only lets you retrieve user information. Later versions of the Toolbox may provide the capability to update user information and perform functions such as creating new user profiles.

To retrieve a list of AS/400 system users, first create a UserList object, passing it an AS400 connection object.

```
UserList userList = new UserList(as400);
```

Next, retrieve the list by executing the **getUsers** method of the user list object.

```
java.util.Enumeration userEnum = userList.getUsers();
```

Loop through the resulting enumeration to access each User object on the list.

```
for( ; userEnum.hasMoreElements(); )
{
   User user = (User)userEnum.nextElement();
   System.out.println("      " + user.getName() + " " +
      user.getDescription());
}
```

Retrieving a list of AS/400 system groups is an almost identical process. After constructing a user list object, set the user information filter to indicate that only groups should be retrieved.

```
userList.setUserInfo(UserList.GROUP);
```

With the filter set, the **getUsers** method returns an enumeration of groups.

Another interesting use for user list objects is to list only the members of a particular group. Again, this procedure is nearly identical to retrieving a simple list of users. To retrieve a list of the users belonging to the PROGRAMMER group, set both the user information and the group information filters like this:

```
userList.setUserInfo(UserList.MEMBER);
userList.setGroupInfo("PROGRAMMER");
```

With the filters set, the **getUsers** method returns an enumeration of the users belonging to the specified group.

Jobs

A feature that retrieves lists of AS/400 jobs is similar to the Toolbox feature that retrieves lists of users. As with the Users feature, the Jobs feature currently supports only inquiry into the attributes of jobs. Future versions of the Toolbox may support changing job attributes.

To retrieve a list of AS/400 system jobs, first create a JobList object, passing it an AS400 communications object.

```
JobList jobList = new JobList(as400);
```

Then, to retrieve the list, execute the **getJobs** method of the job list object.

```
java.util.Enumeration enum = jobList.getJobs();
```

Loop through the resulting enumeration to access each Job object on the list.

```
for( ; enum.hasMoreElements(); )
{
    Job job = (Job)enum.nextElement();
    System.out.println("Job Name: " + job.getName());
    System.out.println("Job Number: " + job.getNumber());
    System.out.println("Job User: " + job.getUser());
    System.out.println();
}
```

In addition to retrieving the basic identifying attributes for a job (i.e., job name, job number, and user ID), you can access job information such as run priority, status, and CPU usage.

To retrieve just a subset of the jobs on a system, set a filter on the job list object before retrieving the list. To retrieve the jobs for only a single user, set the user filter like this:

```
jobList.setUser("DAND");
```

With the filter set, execute the **getJobs** method of the job list object. Using similar filters, you can create subsets of the list by job name and job number. The filters may be used alone or together.

In addition to retrieving lists of jobs and retrieving job properties, you can also list the job log messages for a specific job with the JobLog class.

Message Queues

The V3R2M1 Toolbox provides a nice set of features for working with AS/400 message queues and the individual messages on those queues. Your Java programs can easily send and receive AS/400 messages and list the messages residing on queues.

To send a message to a message queue, first construct a MessageQueue object, passing it an AS400 communications object. The second parameter to the constructor is the IFS path name pointing to an AS/400 message queue. Alternatively, you can specify the MessageQueue.CURRENT constant as a pointer to the message queue of the current user.

```
MessageQueue queue =
    new MessageQueue(as400, MessageQueue.CURRENT);
```

Next, execute either the **sendInquiry** or **sendInformational** method to send a message to the queue. Here is the method call required to send an informational message.

```
queue.sendInformational("Hi there!");
```

Inquiry messages require that you specify the IFS path to a message queue where you wish to receive a reply.

```
queue.sendInquiry("Hi there!",
    "/QSYS.LIB/EXAMPLES.LIB/REPLYQ.MSGQ");
```

To retrieve the messages on a message queue, execute the **getMessages** method on the message queue object.

```
java.util.Enumeration enum = queue.getMessages();
```

Loop through the resulting enumeration to access each message on the queue.

```
for( ; enum.hasMoreElements(); )
{
   QueuedMessage message = (QueuedMessage)enum.nextElement();
   System.out.println("From Job : " + message.getFromJobName());
   System.out.println("From User: " + message.getUser());
   System.out.println("Text      : " + message.getText());
   System.out.println();
}
```

The QueueMessage class defines messages contained on message queues. This class is an extension of the AS400Message class described in "Command Call," earlier in this chapter.

User Spaces

A user space is an AS/400 object that can contain data of any type and composition. You often find system APIs using user spaces to return information of variable length and structure. Support for user spaces enables access to system APIs and allows for more complex exchanges of data between Java and the AS/400.

Digital Certificates

Digital certificates authenticate information sent and received on the Internet and may be used for encryption. The Toolbox provides features to maintain lists of digital certificates in user profiles and in validation lists.

Graphical Access

IBM introduced a large number of "visual access" classes in the V3R2M1 release. These classes are graphical components designed to help you develop applications by reducing the coding required. For example, the ProgramCallButton is a graphical button that encapsulates the functions of a Toolbox program call. Another example is the SQLStatementMenuItem class, an extension of a graphical menu item with the added capability to execute an SQL statement when it is selected. Using the SQLStatementMenuItem eliminates the need to hand code JDBC database access into an application.

Where lists are involved, visual access classes provide graphical views to the list data. Figure 5.6 shows a user list class in an application.

FIGURE 5.6
User List Visual Access Example

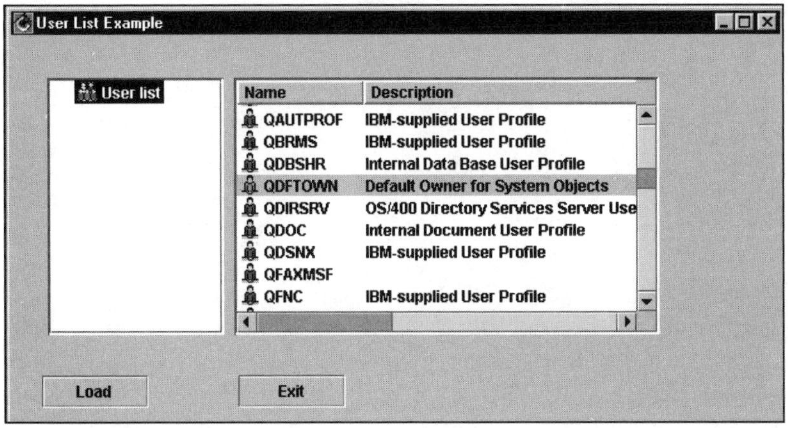

Chapter 6

A Java Sockets Server

You've had a chance to get into the nuts and bolts of the AS/400's Java support. Now it is time to bring this information together and put it to work. Rather than showing large, complex applications, the next three chapters take on small, easily digestible examples. In this chapter, you get a taste of TCP/IP sockets programming by revisiting the Customer Tracking application from the early chapters of this book and making it talk to your AS/400.

CLIENT/SERVER COMPUTING

The design model used in the next three chapters is one of client/server computing. Before you start to look at this chapter's client/server implementation, it is important to consider the pros and cons of client/server computing in general. The term *client/server* describes an application in which two or more computer systems collaborate to get the important work done. Collaborative computing has existed in various forms for quite some time. In the modern network computing models — those that take advantage of local area networks (LANs), wide area networks (WANs), or the Internet — the client/server approach to software development is standard operating procedure.

The alternatives to client/server applications — applications that reside and execute on one computer, relying on a hard-wired delivery mechanism such as dumb terminals — are inherently simpler than client/server applications. Typically, however, these server-only applications cannot deliver the features that modern users have come to expect. In addition, feature-rich server-only solutions require hefty servers. In the client/server world, some of the processing is offloaded from servers to client workstations and, as the features of a system grow, it often makes sense to use a few small servers instead of one huge server. Users get the system features they demand without having to purchase a single mega-server to keep performance at a reasonable level.

It is foolish to underestimate the complexities that client/server applications bring to the table. Instead of one server controlling all aspects of application execution and delivery, you may have multiple servers sharing the workload and any number of clients contributing as well. Instead of one potential point of failure, client/server solutions have many. Rapidly vanishing are the days when an application developer could focus on programming. Today's client/server developers must be savvy about networks, operating systems, and workstations in addition to being sharp Java coders. If a client/server application isn't working, the problem might be the application programming but it might also be the network or an incompatibility between the application and something else running on a workstation. If you aren't careful, what you save in server costs is eaten up by the costs of maintaining your network and client workstations.

Design client/server solutions with as much flexibility as possible. Well-designed solutions leave a lot of room for growth before encountering performance bottlenecks. When you implement a client/server solution, be diligent about testing your code — particularly your client code — in a variety of environments. Don't assume that all workstations running your application will be configured in the same way.

In the next three chapters, you will see a number of ways to make client/server connectivity a reality, but you must decide which technology makes sense in your environment.

SOCKETS

One mechanism for providing client/server application connectivity is TCP/IP sockets. In a nutshell, sockets let you connect a client to a server and send data back and forth. To program using sockets, you create a server to listen for and process requests from one or more clients.

To connect with your server, the client must know two pieces of information — the IP address of the server platform and the port that the server application is listening on. A port is simply an integer that you choose, ranging from 1 to 65535; at this port, your server application can listen for its clients, distinguishing them from other types of activity.

For example, Telnet terminal applications always connect to the server using port 25, and your Web browser knows that HTTP serving always takes place on port 80. The Customer Tracking application server in this chapter uses 8500, which was selected arbitrarily, as its port number. The only caveat to selecting a port is that the numbers 1 through 1023 are reserved for well-known industry standards, such as Telnet and HTTP. Normally, your applications can safely use any port number from 1024 to 65535.

A sockets connection provides you with input and output streams, which let you easily read and write data between systems in the same manner that you read and write data using stream files (i.e., files in the IFS). Going one step further, using the serialization feature of Java, you can use socket streams to exchange entire objects between systems.

Figure 6.1 illustrates a simple client/server association using sockets. In this example, client and server applications use simple input and output streams to perform byte-level read and write operations.

Figure 6.2 shows a client/server relationship where object streams are layered on top of the input and output streams. Now the client and server applications can use more sophisticated write object and read object operations to exchange entire objects.

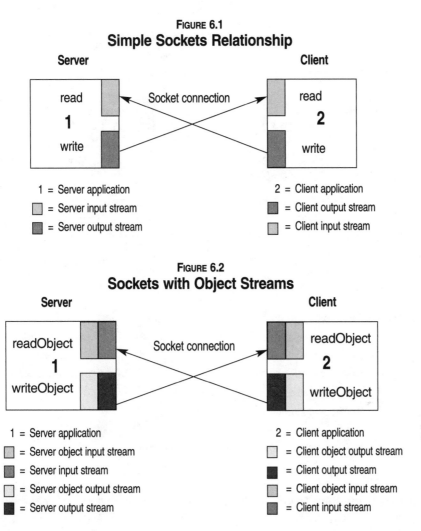

FIGURE 6.1
Simple Sockets Relationship

Server   **Client**

read	Socket connection	read
1		2
write		write

1 = Server application

⬜ = Server input stream

⬛ = Server output stream

2 = Client application

⬛ = Client output stream

⬜ = Client input stream

FIGURE 6.2
Sockets with Object Streams

Server   **Client**

readObject	Socket connection	readObject
1		2
writeObject		writeObject

1 = Server application

⬜ = Server object input stream

⬛ = Server input stream

⬜ = Server object output stream

⬛ = Server output stream

2 = Client application

⬜ = Client object output stream

⬛ = Client output stream

⬜ = Client object input stream

⬛ = Client input stream

In Java, it is easy to create a sockets server application capable of serving a single client. Unfortunately, going beyond one client requires that you get quite a bit more sophisticated with your coding. For a server to handle multiple clients, the server must be capable of spawning multiple threads, at least one thread per client, so that independent client communications can take place simultaneously.

Figure 6.3 illustrates a sockets server written so that multiple clients can attach at the same time. Still just one server listens on a single port for clients to connect, but a separate, threaded sockets communication object is spawned to handle each client.

FIGURE 6.3
Multithreaded Sockets Server

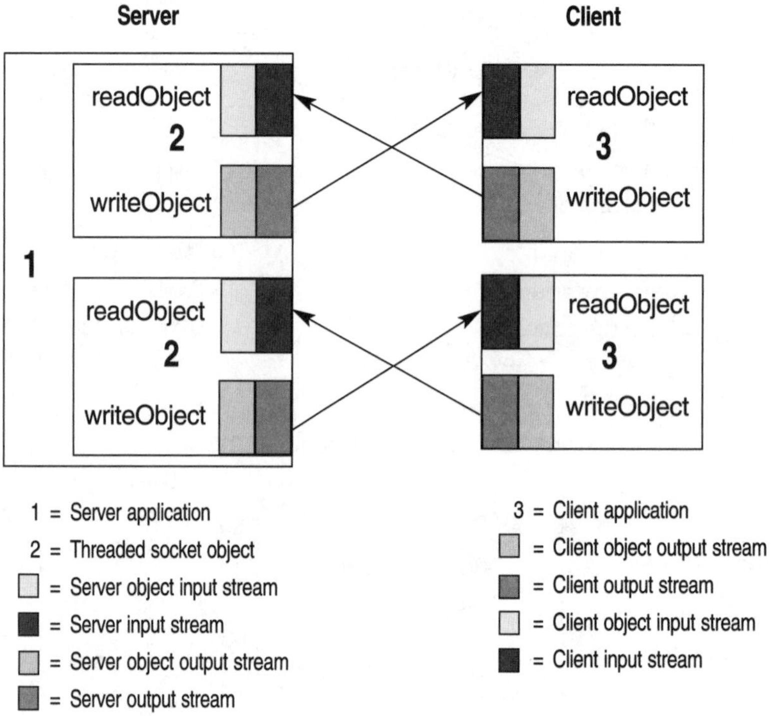

1 = Server application
2 = Threaded socket object
□ = Server object input stream
■ = Server input stream
□ = Server object output stream
■ = Server output stream

3 = Client application
□ = Client object output stream
■ = Client output stream
□ = Client object input stream
■ = Client input stream

THE CUSTOMER TRACKING APPLICATION REVISITED

When you left the Customer Tracking application in Chapter 2, it was a functioning client application without any connection to an AS/400 server. Chief among the features lacking in that application was the ability to save the list of customers you created. Each time you ran the Customer Tracking application, you started with an empty list of customers. Obviously, in the real world, that just wouldn't do.

Figure 6.4 shows an updated version of the Customer Tracking application running on a PC with customer data retrieved from the CUSTMAST database table on the AS/400. The new Customer Tracking application includes a button to refresh the list of customers in addition to buttons for adding, changing, and deleting customers.

The server side of this application is shown in Figure 6.5. A message is displayed each time a client establishes a connection.

FIGURE 6.4

Customer Tracking Application — Client

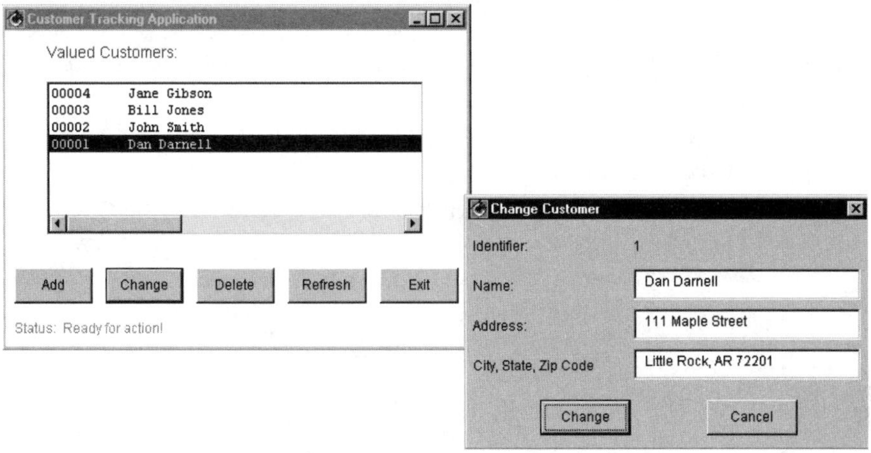

FIGURE 6.5

Customer Tracking Application — Server

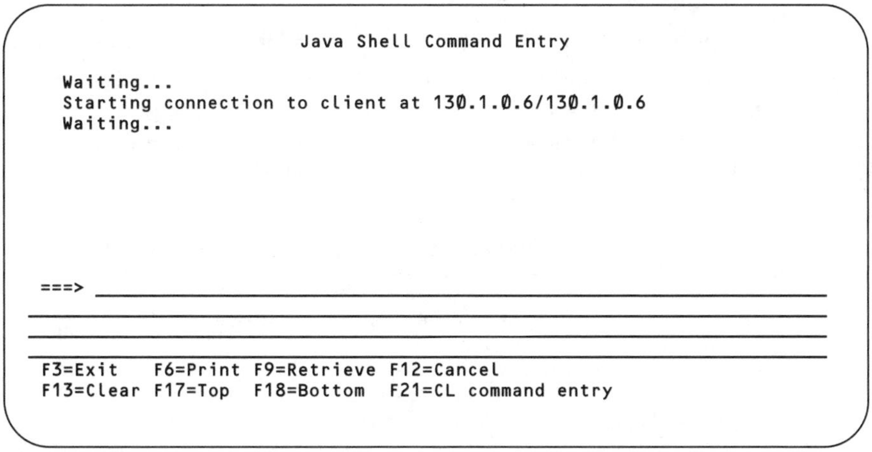

```
                    Java Shell Command Entry

    Waiting...
    Starting connection to client at 130.1.0.6/130.1.0.6
    Waiting...




    ===>  _____
          _____
          _____
    _____
    F3=Exit   F6=Print F9=Retrieve F12=Cancel
    F13=Clear F17=Top  F18=Bottom  F21=CL command entry
```

This version of the Customer Tracking application is more robust than the early version, but you should still avoid thinking of it as production-quality application software. In the interests of clarity and simplicity, sacrifices had to be made. For example, error handling is still minimal. Also, a component such as the AWT's List box is a very poor substitute for a true multicolumn list box, such as one you might obtain from IBM's Web Runner group or another JavaBean vendor.

Running the Application

On the server side, the CustomerHostServer class is executable and it is intended to run on your AS/400. On the client side, the CustomerTracking class is executable — it can run on a PC or any other Java-capable graphical workstation. To run the Customer Tracking application using VisualAge for Java, follow these step-by-step instructions:

1. On your AS/400, create the CUSTMAST database table from Chapter 5 in a library named EXAMPLES.

2. Change the SYSTEM, USERID, and PASSWORD constants in the Customer-HostSocket class. These pieces of information are used to connect with your AS/400 database.

   ```
   private static final String SYSTEM = "SYSTEM";
   private static final String USERID = "USERID";
   private static final String PASSWORD = "PASSWORD";
   ```

3. Change the HOST constant in the CustomerListKeeper class to the TCP/IP address of your AS/400. This information is used to connect the client to the server. Depending on your network configuration, you can use either the IP address

   ```
   private static final String HOST = "198.0.0.10";
   ```

   or the system name of your AS/400

   ```
   private static final String HOST = "SYSTEM";
   ```

4. Create a /myjava/examples/sockets directory in the IFS on your AS/400. Place the CustomerHostServer and CustomerHostSocket classes into this directory. Placing these classes in this exact directory structure is crucial. See "On Classpath and Packages" for information about the package structure used in this example.

5. Start the server portion of the application from an OS/400 command line with this Run Java command.

   ```
   JAVA CLASS(examples.sockets.CustomerHostServer)          +
        CLASSPATH('/myjava')
   ```

   When the server is ready to accept client connections, the message "Waiting..." is displayed.

6. Start the client portion of the application from a VisualAge for Java project or package view. Select the CustomerTracking class and then right-click on the class. Choose the Run, Run main option from the pop-up menu.

   When the client application starts, it connects with the server automatically. Wait for a successful connection and the status message "Connected. Press Refresh button to build list" in the client window. When you press the Refresh button, the list of customers is constructed and the status message changes to "Ready for action!" If an error occurs at any point, the status message in the client window reflects it. For example, if you try to start the client before starting the server, you see the status message "Connection refused."

Each time a client connects with the server, the server displays the client's address in a message, such as "Starting connection to client at 130.1.0.16/130.1.0.16." Use these messages to determine whether clients are successfully connecting with the server.

The rest of this chapter looks at the programming involved in the TCP/IP sockets-based Customer Tracking application. You will explore the important concepts and learn the coding behind a sockets-based client/server application using serialized objects and multithreaded communications. First, though, you get a brief look at how the Customer Tracking application uses the native DB2/400 JDBC driver.

NATIVE DATABASE DRIVER

One advantage of a client/server design is that you can place the database access portion of your application on the AS/400 server, where there is an optimized JDBC driver. Besides providing potential performance gains, moving the data access portion of your applications to the server can also improve your application's security. A proprietary sockets-based server of your own creation very effectively limits potentially harmful actions on the part of a client application. A client application using the Toolbox JDBC driver can access and update almost any file on the system, subject to the AS/400's own object-level security. In contrast, a client application communicating with a sockets server can only touch files using the protocol that your server application defines.

As an example of using the native DB2/400 JDBC driver, the code contained in the Customer Tracking server's CustomerHostSocket class is shown below. In the **run** method of this class, a database connection is established.

```
Class.forName("com.ibm.db2.jdbc.app.DB2Driver");
dbConn = DriverManager.getConnection("jdbc:DB2://" +
    SYSTEM, USERID, PASSWORD);
```

The **forName** method of the Class class is executed to register the native JDBC driver. A string with the package-qualified name of the driver class is passed to the **forName** method. Use this technique when you want the driver class to be located at runtime instead of at compile-time.

For the Customer Tracking application, we use the forName technique because the application is maintained in VisualAge for Java, where the AS/400's DB2Driver class is not normally available. If you run the server portion of the application in VisualAge for Java, you receive the "Class not found" exception when the runtime attempts to locate the DB2Driver class.

The **getConnection** method of the DriverManager class establishes a connection with the DB2/400 database. The Uniform Resource Locator (URL) required to locate the database access protocol is jdbc:DB2. Contrast this with

---

ON CLASSPATH AND PACKAGES

Packages are used in Chapters 6, 7, and 8 to keep the example applications segregated. For instance, the example classes in this chapter reside in the examples.sockets package. To execute the example applications on the AS/400, you should have a basic understanding of directory structure and the role that the classpath plays when classes reside within packages.

On the Run Java command, you specify a package-qualified class name in this way:

```
JAVA CLASS(examples.sockets.CustomerHostServer)
```

Java runtime environments assume that your package structure mirrors your directory structure, with each piece of a package name representing a directory. In our example, the package name calls for the CustomerHostServer class to reside in the examples/sockets directory off the root directory of the IFS. The role of the classpath is to tell the runtime to start looking for package directories somewhere other than in the root directory.

Consider this modified Run Java command:

```
JAVA CLASS(examples.sockets.CustomerHostServer)    +
    CLASSPATH('/myjava')
```

With the classpath specified on this command, the runtime is told to look for the examples/sockets directory structure beginning with the /myjava directory. In other words, the runtime appends the classpath directory to the package directories (e.g., /myjava/examples/sockets) before it attempts to load any classes.

---

the AS/400 Toolbox for Java driver which uses the URL jdbc:as400. The native driver's URL is meant to aid you in keeping your Java code portable between DB2 database servers.

After you register the driver and obtain a connection, the rest of the database code is just plain JDBC. Snippets of JDBC code and SQL are sprinkled throughout the rest of this chapter.

CUSTOMER TRACKING — DESIGN AND IMPLEMENTATION

The Customer Tracking application is composed of two server classes — CustomerHostServer and CustomerHostSocket — and four client classes — CustomerTracking, CustomerListKeeper, CustomerList, and CustomerItem. The location and function of each class is shown in Table 6.1.

TABLE 6.1
Customer Tracking Application Classes

Class	Location	Description
CustomerHostServer	Server (executable)	Sockets server. The entry point for client connections.
CustomerHostSocket	Server	Server-side multithreaded sockets communications.
CustomerTracking	Client (executable)	User interface for the Customer Tracking application.
CustomerListKeeper	Client	Client-side sockets communications.
CustomerList	Client	Graphical component extended from the AWT's List component. Provides list handling capabilities specific to the application.
CustomerItem	Client	Customer object. Holds information about a single customer.

On the surface, the client design has changed very little since you first saw it in Chapter 2. The CustomerTracking class still presents the graphical user interface, and the CustomerListKeeper class keeps up with CustomerItem objects using a hash table. The major design differences in this client are below the surface, where the CustomerListKeeper class exchanges information with the AS/400 through sockets.

On the server side, an object of the CustomerHostSocket class (a socket object), is instantiated by the CustomerHostServer class each time a client connection is established. The socket object is a kind of server helper where the bulk of the communication with a client takes place. The relationship between client and server application components is illustrated in Figure 6.6.

When you develop a client/server application, you face a chicken-and-egg scenario, except the pertinent question here is "Which comes first, the client or the server?" Typically, the server functions are developed first, and then the client is written to use the server functions. However, to describe both the client and the server coherently, we approach them as if they were developed in unison, usually describing the client side first.

FIGURE 6.6
Customer Tracking Application Design

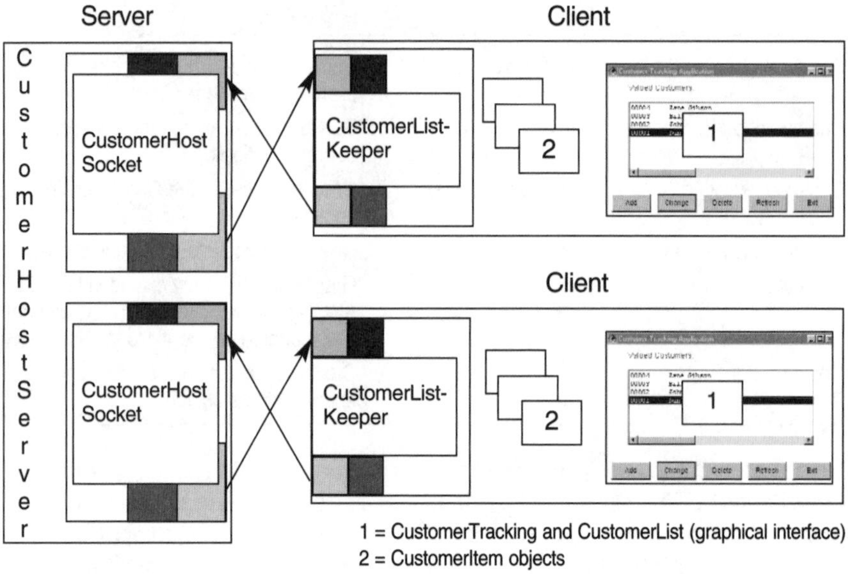

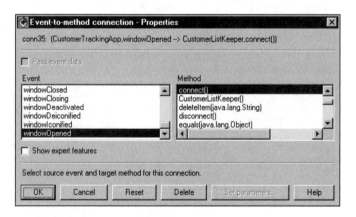

Server | Client

1 = CustomerTracking and CustomerList (graphical interface)
2 = CustomerItem objects

Getting Connected — Client Side

The first logical action for the client to perform is to connect with the server. Look at the connection properties in the Visual Composition Editor (VCE) design screen shown in Figure 6.7.

FIGURE 6.7
Connect to Server

On the windowOpened event, the client executes the CustomerListKeeper class's **connect** method. Here is the code from the **connect** method that connects the client with the server.

```
connection = new Socket(HOST, 8500);
```

The constant HOST is defined as an instance variable in the CustomerList-Keeper class. It provides the IP address of the server system. The second parameter to the Socket class's constructor is the port number on which to connect — the CustomerHostServer is hardcoded to listen on port 8500. The "connection" instance variable refers to the Socket object constructed here.

Immediately after creating the new socket object, we construct an instance of the DataOutputStream over the socket's simple output stream.

```
d_output =
    new DataOutputStream(connection.getOutputStream());
```

The DataOutputStream class supplies methods for writing Java data types, such as integers, to the socket stream. Later, the client will use this data output stream as it sends requests to the server.

Getting Connected — Server Side

The CustomerHostServer class extends Java's ServerSocket class, which makes the CustomerHostServer class itself a sockets server. Extending the ServerSocket class makes coding the server application a breeze. In the **main** method of the CustomerHostServer class, a new CustomerHostServer object is instantiated, listening on port 8500.

```
server = new CustomerHostServer(8500);
```

Next, we begin an endless while loop. Inside the loop, the newly created server object is set to wait for client connections by calling the **accept** method.

```
while(true) {
    CustomerHostSocket socket =
        (CustomerHostSocket)server.accept();
    socket.start();
}
```

The result of a successful client connection is an object of type Customer-HostSocket returned by the **accept** method. Socket communications take place through this object, a subclass of Java's Socket class. As soon as a client contacts the server, the CustomerHostSocket object is started. The Customer-HostSocket class is multithreaded so that the next iteration of the while loop can take place immediately and the server can begin waiting on the **accept** method again for another client. If 100 clients connect to the server, then 100 CustomerHostSocket objects are created and started, each running in its own thread. In case you are wondering, the number of threads supported by the operating system determines the overall limit on client connections in this application. A single AS/400 job, such as our sockets server, can contain as many as 32,767 separate threads.

For the **accept** method to return an instance of the customized socket class CustomerHostSocket, the CustomerHostServer class must override the base ServerSocket class's **accept** method. The details of the overridden **accept** method are fundamental to this design, which extends Java's ServerSocket and Socket classes. Here is the complete code for the overridden **accept** method:

```
public Socket accept() throws IOException {
    CustomerHostSocket s = new CustomerHostSocket();
    implAccept(s);
    return s;
}
```

The overridden **accept** method contains code to instantiate a new Customer-HostSocket. Don't let the call to the **implAccept** method confuse you. The architecture of Java's socket support offers the **implAccept** method as an easy way to execute the platform implementation's socket binding mechanism. The **implAccept** method takes as a parameter an instance of the Socket class. Recall that the **accept** method normally blocks until a client connection is made. When you pass the **implAccept** method an instance of the Socket class or, as in this case, a subclass of the Socket class, the **implAccept** method is where the server waits for a client connection. This wait point is down deep in the implementation of sockets and is unique to the platform. All you need to know is that when the **implAccept** method returns, the socket object you passed it is connected to a client.

Basic Requests — List Customers, Client Side

After connecting to the server, the client can begin two-way communications with the host through its socket object. The server, in the form of a Customer-HostSocket object, provides the client with five functions:

- List all customers
- Add a customer
- Change a customer
- Delete a customer
- Disconnect

The Customer Tracking application is structured so that user input, normally communicated by clicking a button, causes the client's CustomerListKeeper class to request one of these five functions.

Table 6.2 shows the essential communications-related methods defined for the CustomerListKeeper class.

TABLE 6.2
CustomerListKeeper Class Methods

Method	Description
connect	Establishes sockets communications with the server.
disconnect	Disconnects from the server.
refresh	Requests a list of customers from the server. The server returns a hash table of customer objects.
addItem	Sends customer information to the server so that it can be added to the database. The server returns a customer object.
fetchItem	Returns a requested customer object from an internal hash table of all customers. Used with the changeItem method for customer changes.
changeItem	Sends a customer object to the server so that the server can update the appropriate customer record in the database.
deleteItem	Sends a customer object to the server so that the server can delete the appropriate customer record from the database.

The first part of each client-originated communication with the server is a request type that corresponds to one of the five basic functions. Some request types tell the server to read and process additional information from the socket stream. Other request types ask the server to send information back to the client. The request types are defined as integer constants in both the CustomerListKeeper and CustomerHostSocket classes. The request types and associated actions are summarized in Table 6.3.

TABLE 6.3
Request Type Constants

Request Type Constant	Action
RQS_LIST	Requests list of customers.
RQS_ADD	Requests addition of a new customer.
RQS_CHANGE	Requests changes to an existing customer.
RQS_DELETE	Requests deletion of an existing customer.
RQS_QUIT	Requests disconnection of the sockets.

To illustrate the relationship between client activities and request types, let's consider the **refresh** method and the RQS_LIST action. Figure 6.8 shows the Visual Composition Editor connections necessary to refresh the list of customers.

FIGURE 6.8
Refresh Action Connection

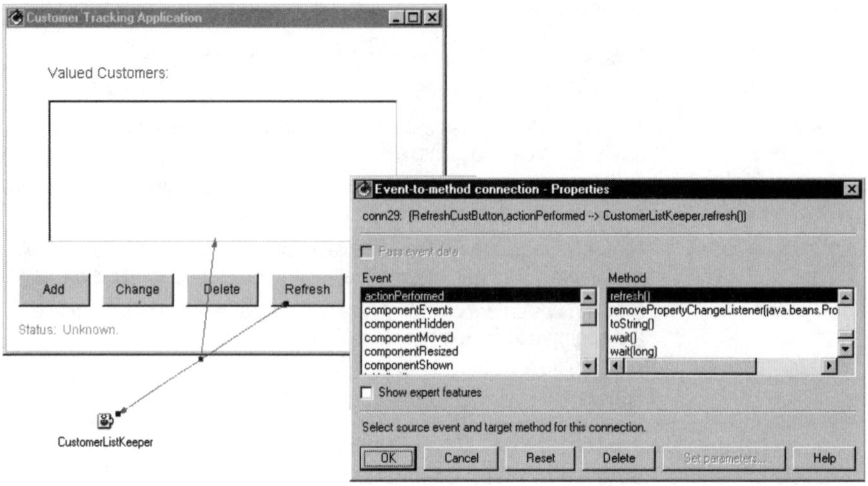

When the Refresh button is clicked (actionPerformed event), the **refresh** method of the CustomerListKeeper class is executed. The **refresh** method communicates with the server to obtain a hash table of all customers:

```
d_output.writeInt(RQS_LIST);
ObjectInputStream input =
    new ObjectInputStream(connection.getInputStream());
custList = (Hashtable)input.readObject();
```

First, the RQS_LIST constant is written to the socket data output stream. On the server side, the request type is read and a hash table created. Back on the client side, an ObjectInputStream is constructed over the socket's simple input stream. The ObjectInputStream class provides a **readObject** method which, in this case, reads the hash table object created by the server. The client uses this hash table to keep track of customers and as a cross-reference between Customer IDs and customer objects. The hash table is also used to build the visual list of customers.

Basic Requests — List Customers, Server Side
On the server, each CustomerHostSocket object created in the CustomerHostServer class's main loop is responsible for communicating with a single client and acting on specific requests from that client. Table 6.4 shows the methods defined for the CustomerHostSocket class.

TABLE 6.4

CustomerHostSocket Class Methods

Method	Description
start	Starts a thread to begin socket communications.
run	The target method of the thread. The request-processing loop is executed here.
list	Processes a list request. Reads all CUSTMAST table rows and constructs CustomerItem objects to match each one. Inserts the customer objects into a hash table and sends the hash table to the client.
add	Processes an add request. Reads raw customer information from the client. Sends a customer object back to the client and writes a database record.
change	Processes a change request. Reads a customer object from the stream. Extracts the customer ID from the object and updates the associated database record with new customer information.
delete	Processes a delete request. Reads a customer object from the stream. Extracts the customer ID from the object and deletes the associated database record.
quit	Performs database connection cleanup activities and closes down the socket connection.

Request types are processed in the CustomerHostSocket class's **run** method. Some initial housekeeping establishes a database connection and prepares several SQL statements for later execution. Next, an instance of the DataInputStream class is constructed over the socket's simple input stream. This object lets the server read the integer requests written to the stream by the client.

```
d_input = new DataInputStream(getInputStream());
```

Next is a while loop. In this loop, client requests are received and processed until the client explicitly asks to disconnect from the server. This request code stops on the **readInt** method until the client sends a request.

```
while(true)
{
    int requestType = d_input.readInt();

    if(requestType == RQS_LIST)
        list();
    else if(requestType == RQS_ADD)
        add();
    else if(requestType == RQS_CHANGE)
        change();
    else if(requestType == RQS_DELETE)
        delete();
    else if(requestType == RQS_QUIT)
    {
        quit();
        break;
    }
}
```

In the list request example, when the client sends the RQS_LIST request type, the server executes its **list** method. Here is the code that makes up this method:

```
Hashtable h = new Hashtable(100);
ResultSet rs = pSelect.executeQuery();

while(rs.next())
{
    CustomerItem tempItem =
        new CustomerItem(
        (rs.getBigDecimal("CUSTID", 0)).intValue(),
            rs.getString("CUSTNAME"),
            rs.getString("CUSTSTREET"),
            rs.getString("CUSTCITY"));
    h.put(new Integer(tempItem.getID()), tempItem);
}

ObjectOutputStream output =
    new ObjectOutputStream(getOutputStream());
output.writeObject(h);
```

NOTE: The prepared SQL statement pSelect looks like this:

```
pSelect = dbConn.prepareStatement("SELECT * FROM " +
    "EXAMPLES.CUSTMAST ORDER BY CUSTID");
```

The server queries the CUSTMAST table and creates a hash table containing one CustomerItem object for each database record. Then the server sends the hash table to the client through an object output stream.

The mechanism by which objects can be written to and read from streams is called *serialization*. Serialization is Java's term for the translation of an object's contents to a standardized stream of bytes. Once an object is serialized, it can be written intact to a stream file or, as in this application, exchanged with another system through a socket stream.

The act of serialization is complex. Instead of considering just a single class, the serialization process walks the class hierarchy to save information from superclasses of the class being serialized. Fortunately, the Java language hides the complexities of serialization, supplying a very simple mechanism for application programmers to use.

In the Customer Tracking application, the CustomerItem class must be capable of serialization so that customer objects can be exchanged between client and server. To make the CustomerItem class capable of serialization, it must implement the Serializable interface from the java.io package:

```
public class CustomerItem implements java.io.Serializable
```

Unlike most interfaces, the Serializable interface contains no method signatures. The empty Serializable interface is only a signal to the world that we want the CustomerItem class to participate in serialization.

Java's ObjectInputStream and ObjectOutputStream classes provide an implementation of serialization that you can use in your applications. In the case of an input stream, the ObjectInputStream class supplies a **readObject** method. For the ObjectOutputStream, the method supplied is **writeObject**.

Let's look again at the last two statements in the **list** method:

```
ObjectOutputStream output =
    new ObjectOutputStream(getOutputStream());
output.writeObject(h);
```

You can see that an instance of the ObjectOutputStream class is created over the server socket's simple output stream and then the entire hash table is serialized and sent to the client by the **writeObject** method.

Add Customer — Client Side

With the connection mechanism and the protocol for client/server communications defined, let's look at the remaining client requests and server functions. To add a new customer, individual data items such as customer name and customer address are passed through the data output stream to the server. The server accepts this information and creates a CustomerItem object from the data, returning this object to the client. The server then inserts a row into the CUSTMAST database table. The client receives the new customer object and adds the object to its hash table. As a final step, the client updates the visual list of customers. The Add action, from the perspective of the Visual Composition Editor, is shown in Figure 6.9.

When the Add button on the Add Customer dialog box is clicked, the **addItem** method of the CustomerListKeeper class is executed. Customer information is passed into the **addItem** method as parameter-from-property connections. Following is the code from the **addItem** method that is responsible for sending information about a new customer to the server.

```
d_output.writeInt(RQS_ADD);
d_output.writeUTF(name);
d_output.writeUTF(street);
d_output.writeUTF(cityStateZip);
```

As with all requests coming from the client, the first piece of data sent through the socket data output stream is an integer constant that represents the request type. Following the request type is the customer information. The **writeUTF** method, also supplied by the DataOutputStream class, is an easy and effective way to write string data to a socket stream.

FIGURE 6.9

Add Action Connections

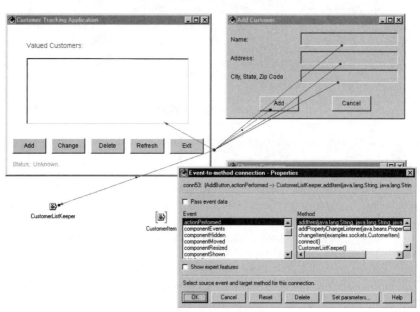

The server accepts the new customer information and sends a CustomerItem object back to the client. Still in the **addItem** method of the CustomerListKeeper class, the client reads the CustomerItem object from the stream and adds it to its hash table of customers.

```
ObjectInputStream input =
    new ObjectInputStream(connection.getInputStream());
ci = (CustomerItem)input.readObject();
custList.put(new Integer(ci.getID()), ci);
```

Add Customer — Server Side

On the server side of a customer addition, a new customer ID number is calculated by taking the highest customer ID number in use and incrementing it by one. The following code retrieves and increments the customer ID:

```
int custID = 0;
ResultSet rs = pMaxID.executeQuery();
if(rs.next())
    custID = rs.getInt(1);
custID++;
```

NOTE: The prepared SQL statement pMaxID uses the Max(CUSTID) operator to return the highest numbered customer ID in the CUSTMAST table.

```
pMaxID = dbConn.prepareStatement("SELECT " +
    "Max(CUSTID) FROM EXAMPLES.CUSTMAST");
```

Information identifying the new customer is read from the socket data input stream using the **readUTF** method. Naturally, the server and client must agree on the order of the information. If the client writes the customer information as name, street, and city/state/zip, then the server must read it in the same order.

```
String name = d_input.readUTF();
String street = d_input.readUTF();
String cityState Zip = d_input.readUTF();
```

Next, the server instantiates a CustomerItem object to represent the new customer. A constructor has been added to the CustomerItem class to accept all customer information, including the customer ID. The newly constructed customer object is written to the socket stream so that the client can pick it up.

```
CustomerItem ci =
    new CustomerItem(custID, name, street, cityStateZip);
ObjectOutputStream output =
    new ObjectOutputStream(getOutputStream());
output.writeObject(ci);
```

As a final step, the server inserts a record into the CUSTMAST table to keep a permanent record of the new customer.

```
pInsert.setBigDecimal(1, new BigDecimal(ci.getID()));
pInsert.setString(2, ci.getName());
pInsert.setString(3, ci.getStreet());
pInsert.setString(4, ci.getCityStateZip());
pInsert.executeUpdate();
```

NOTE: The prepared SQL statement pInsert looks like this:

```
pInsert = dbConn.prepareStatement("INSERT " +
    "INTO EXAMPLES.CUSTMAST (CUSTID, " +
    "CUSTNAME, CUSTSTREET, CUSTCITY) " +
    "VALUES(?, ?, ?, ?)");
```

Change Customer — Client Side

In the case of a customer change, a CustomerItem object is sent from the client to the server, where the server then updates the database. On the client side, the visual list of customers is updated to reflect the new customer information.

Making a customer change is a two-step process on the client side. A CustomerItem object must be retrieved from the client's internal hash table and then sent to the server for processing. The Visual Composition Editor connections for the first step are shown in Figure 6.10.

When the Change button is clicked on the main application frame, the **fetchItem** method of the CustomerListKeeper class is executed. The **fetchItem** method returns a CustomerItem object from the internal hash table; this object

FIGURE 6.10
Change Action Connections — Step 1

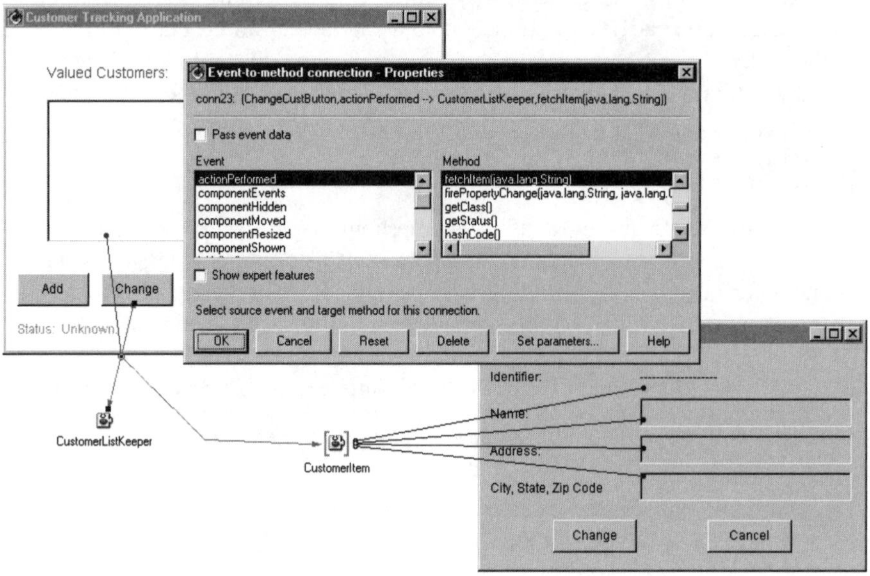

corresponds to the customer selected on the visual list. The Change Customer dialog box allows changes to all customer information except the customer ID, which acts as a key to the server database.

Step 2 of the client-side customer change is shown in Figure 6.11.

When the Change button is clicked on the Change Customer dialog box, the **changeItem** method of the CustomerListKeeper class communicates with the server to make the change permanent. As always, the first piece of information sent to the server is the request type.

```
d_output.writeInt(RQS_CHANGE);
```

Following the request type, the **changeItem** method sends the server a CustomerItem object with the updated customer information.

```
ObjectOutputStream output =
    new ObjectOutputStream(connection.getOutputStream());
output.writeObject(ci);
```

As a part of the second step, the visual list is updated to reflect changed customer information.

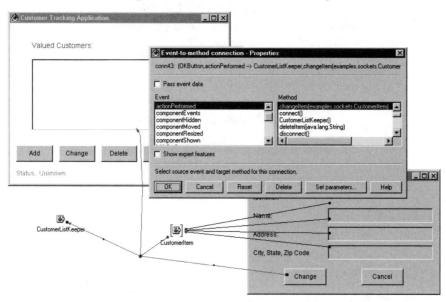

Figure 6.11
Change Action Connections — Step 2

Change Customer — Server Side

The request type RQS_CHANGE is picked up by the CustomerHostSocket object that is servicing the client and the **change** method is executed. An ObjectInput-Stream is constructed over the socket's input stream and the **readObject** method of the ObjectOutputStream class provides the deserialization function that reconstructs the CustomerItem object sent by the CustomerListKeeper.

```
ObjectInputStream input =
    new ObjectInputStream(getInputStream());
CustomerItem ci = (CustomerItem)input.readObject();
```

Then it's just a matter of a little JDBC code to update the appropriate database table row with the new customer information.

```
pUpdate.setString(1, ci.getName());
pUpdate.setString(2, ci.getStreet());
pUpdate.setString(3, ci.getCityStateZip());
pUpdate.setBigDecimal(4, new BigDecimal(ci.getID()));
pUpdate.executeUpdate();
```

NOTE: The prepared SQL statement pUpdate looks like this:

```
pUpdate = dbConn.prepareStatement("UPDATE " +
    "EXAMPLES.CUSTMAST SET CUSTNAME = ?, " +
    "CUSTSTREET = ?, CUSTCITY = ? " +
    "WHERE CUSTID = ?");
```

Delete Customer — Client Side

To delete a customer, a CustomerItem object is sent from the client to the server, with the server taking responsibility for deleting the customer record from the database table. The client's visual list of customers is updated to remove the customer item selected for deletion.

The Visual Composition Editor connections for a customer deletion are shown in Figure 6.12.

FIGURE 6.12
Delete Action Connections

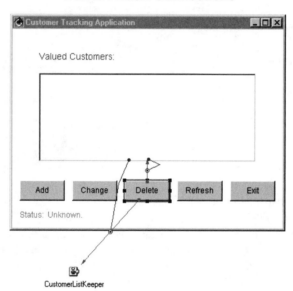

When the Delete button is clicked, the **deleteItem** method of the CustomerListKeeper class communicates with the server to delete a customer.

First, the CustomerItem object representing the customer selected for deletion is retrieved from the internal hash table.

```
CustomerItem ci = (CustomerItem)custList.get(i_ID);
```

The communication with the server is nearly identical to a change action, except that the RQS_DELETE constant is sent as the request type. Following the request type, the **deleteItem** method sends the server a CustomerItem object representing the customer to delete from the database.

```
d_output.writeInt(RQS_DELETE);
ObjectOutputStream output =
    new ObjectOutputStream(connection.getOutputStream());
output.writeObject(ci);
```

Delete Customer — Server Side

The coding required on the server side of a customer deletion is very similar to the coding required for a customer change. The **delete** method of the CustomerHostSocket class is executed when the server receives the RQS_DELETE request type constant. An ObjectInputStream is constructed over the socket's input stream and the **readObject** method is executed to obtain the CustomerItem object sent by the client.

```
ObjectInputStream input =
    new ObjectInputStream(getInputStream());
CustomerItem ci = (CustomerItem)input.readObject();
```

Using information from the CustomerItem object, the customer record is deleted from the database table.

```
pDelete.setBigDecimal(1, new BigDecimal(ci.getID()));
pDelete.executeUpdate();
```

NOTE: The prepared SQL statement pDelete looks like this:

```
pDelete = dbConn.prepareStatement("DELETE " +
    "FROM EXAMPLES.CUSTMAST " +
    "WHERE CUSTID = ?");
```

Disconnect — Client and Server

Gracefully disconnecting the client from the server is an important step in an application using sockets. If the client application ends before the socket connection is closed, it can take the server some time to determine that the client has gone away and then to terminate the connection abnormally. Disconnecting abnormally most often results in a Java exception in the CustomerHostSocket object that was servicing the client.

In the Customer Tracking application, a normal disconnect is triggered when the Exit button is clicked. Figure 6.13 shows the Visual Composition Editor connection between the Exit button and the **disconnect** method of the CustomerListKeeper class.

The Java code for the client's **disconnect** method sends the RQS_QUIT request type to the server and then closes the client side of the socket connection.

```
d_output.writeInt(RQS_QUIT);
connection.close();
```

On the server side, the **quit** method of the CustomerHostSocket class cleans up the database resources and then closes the server side of the socket connection.

```
pSelect.close();
pInsert.close();
pUpdate.close();
pDelete.close();
dbConn.close();
close();
```

FIGURE 6.13
Disconnect Action Connections

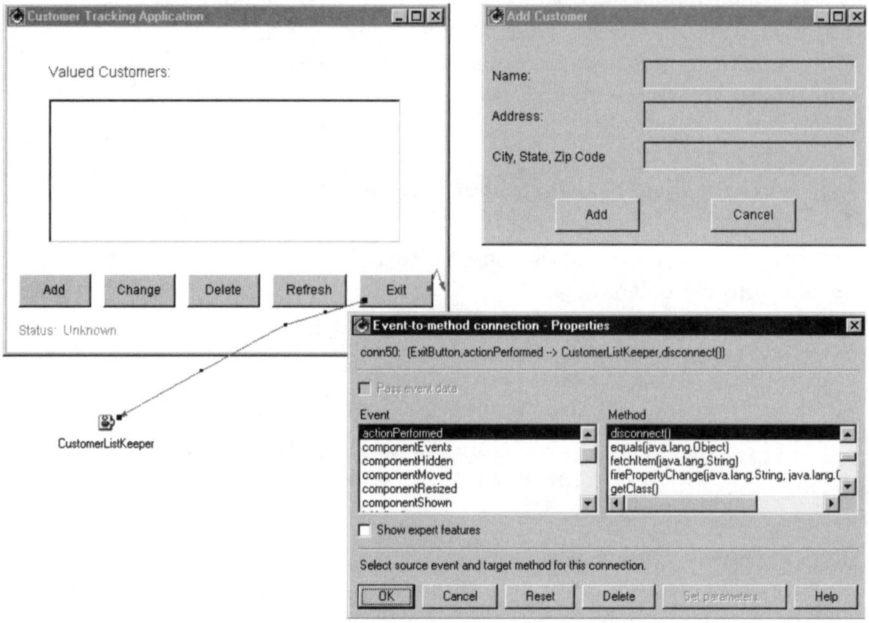

After the socket connection is closed, the server classes' processing loop is exited and the **run** method ends. When the **run** method ends, the thread dedicated to handling the socket connection automatically ends and the object instance of the CustomerHostSocket class is garbage collected.

MULTIPLE CLIENT CONNECTIONS

The sockets server example in this chapter is capable of supporting any number of clients. The OS/400 Network Status (NETSTAT) command may be used as a diagnostic tool when programming with sockets. Let's look at an example.

Connect at least two clients to the server — you can either start the client on multiple PCs or run multiple instances of the client on one PC. Type the NETSTAT command at an OS/400 command line and you are prompted with these menu options:

1. Work with TCP/IP interface status

2. Display TCP/IP route information

3. Work with TCP/IP connection status

Choose the "Work with TCP/IP connection status" option to see the screen shown in Figure 6.14.

FIGURE 6.14
Network Status Display — 1

```
                    Work with TCP/IP Connection Status
                                               System:   SYSTEM
Local internet address . . . . . . . . . . . :    *ALL

Type options, press Enter.
  4=End    5=Display details

    Remote          Remote     Local
Opt Address         Port       Port      Idle Time  State
 _  130.1.0.6       1116       8500      000:01:39  Established
 _  130.1.0.7       1117       8500      000:01:36  Established
 _  130.1.0.8       1118       8500      000:01:24  Established




                                                            Bottom
F5=Refresh   F11=Display byte counts   F13=Sort by column
F14=Display port numbers   F22=Display entire field   F24=More keys
```

Press Page down on this display until you encounter the connections to local port 8500. Anything connected to port 8500 is a Customer Tracking application client connected to the server. From this screen, you can determine the IP address of each connected client.

Press the F11 (Display byte counts) key to see the display shown in Figure 6.15.

FIGURE 6.15
Network Status Display — 2

```
                    Work with TCP/IP Connection Status
                                               System:   SYSTEM
Local internet address . . . . . . . . . . . :    *ALL

Type options, press Enter.
  4=End    5=Display details

    Remote          Remote     Local
Opt Address         Port       Port     User      Bytes Out   Bytes In
 _  130.1.0.6       1116       8500     DAND           2706        314
 _  130.1.0.7       1117       8500     DAND            902        306
 _  130.1.0.8       1118       8500     DAND           1804        612




                                                            Bottom
F5=Refresh    F11=Display connection type   F13=Sort by column
F14=Display port numbers   F22=Display entire field   F24=More keys
```

Here you can determine the user ID that the server job is running under and see basic information about the amount of data exchanged between client and server. Use option 5 (Display details) to see detailed connection information that you can use to diagnose potential network and/or application problems. You can use option 4 (end) to disconnect a troublesome client from the server immediately.

In Chapter 8, you will see another way to make this application work in a multiple client environment. Using Remote Method Invocation (RMI), a feature of Java, the example in Chapter 8 eliminates the need to hand code socket communications, simplifying the application logic and making it easier to code. What RMI takes away from you is the control that you have with hand-coded sockets to define your own communications protocols. As you go about the business of writing serious Java applications, there will likely be times when a hand-coded socket server is the most expedient and reliable means of achieving your ends. It is also worth remembering that you can code socket-based clients to take advantage of existing host servers providing features such as e-mail (POP3), Telnet, and File Transfer Protocol (FTP).

Chapter 7

Toolbox Examples

In Chapter 5, you took a guided tour through the AS/400 Toolbox for Java and learned the basics of using each of its major features. In this chapter, you will see the Toolbox features used in simple graphical applications. These examples should give you a better idea of how to use the Toolbox in client-side applications that access AS/400 data and other resources.

DESIGN OVERVIEW

The examples in this chapter are based on the coding techniques presented in Chapter 5. The difference is that we have added a graphical user interface to make each Toolbox feature interactive.

All the examples in this chapter are structured in a similar way. Java Frame classes comprise the user interface, and Toolbox functions are encapsulated in helper classes. This structure is very basic, but standard, object-oriented design. Whenever possible in object-oriented programming, the user interface of an application should be separate from the business logic or database access.

In the Visual Composition Editor (VCE), user interface components and helper classes are connected. All helper classes contain a **connect** method and a **quit** method. In the **connect** method, a helper class creates an AS400 connection object and connects to a service. For example, the **connect** method of the IFSHelper class looks like this:

```
as400 = new AS400();
as400.connectService(AS400.FILE);
```

NOTE: All the helper classes used here, such as the IFSHelper class, are custom classes written for the examples in this chapter; they are not a part of IBM's AS/400 Toolbox for Java.

In the **quit** method, a helper class executes Java's system **exit** method to end the program and shut down the Java Virtual Machine (JVM).

```
System.exit(0);
```

Helper classes also define methods beyond the **connect** and **quit** methods that are specific to their functionality. For example, the IFSHelper class contains a **getFileContents** method, while the ProgramHelper supplies a **callProgram** method.

In addition to showing you Toolbox functions in action, this chapter serves as a lesson in using the VCE feature of VisualAge for Java to build applications. As with most examples in this book, the VCE links visual components with other, nonvisual "worker" components, effectively eliminating hand coding of the user interface.

INTEGRATED FILE SYSTEM (IFS)

The Integrated File System (IFS) Toolbox feature gives you direct access to IFS resources such as directories and files. Our IFS example application consists of two classes, IFSHelper and IFSExampleGUI. The IFSHelper class uses the Toolbox to access IFS resources. The IFSExampleGUI class is executable — it presents the user interface and utilizes functions of the helper class. This example application is seen in operation in Figure 7.1.

FIGURE 7.1
IFS Access Example

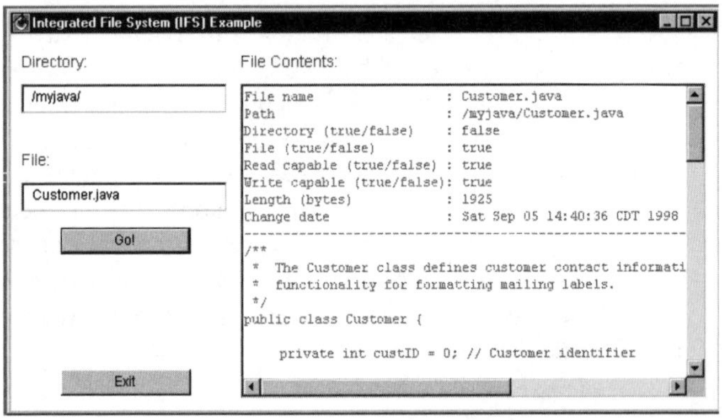

Start the IFS example application from a VisualAge for Java project or package view. Select the IFSExampleGUI class in the examples.toolbox package and right-click the class. Choose Run, Run from the pop-up menu. When the application initializes, the AS/400 sign-on prompt shown in Figure 7.2 appears. Type the system name of your AS/400, your user ID, and your password, and click OK.

NOTE: When prompted to sign on to the AS/400, it is normally a good idea to check the Default user ID and Save password boxes. These switches tell the Toolbox to retain the user ID and password. If another service is used in the same application, the default user ID and password are reused. If you don't check these boxes, you will be prompted repeatedly for sign-on information as your application connects to additional Toolbox services.

FIGURE 7.2
AS/400 Sign-On Prompt

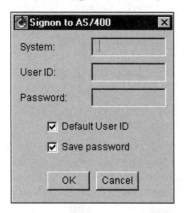

After the application has established a connection with your AS/400, type an IFS directory and file name and click Go! to view the attributes and contents of the file. Type a directory name and leave the file name blank to view the attributes of the directory alone. Default values — the /myjava directory and Customer.java file — are supplied by the application. Be aware that viewing the contents of an IFS file other than a text file may produce unpredictable results.

The VCE design screen for the IFS example application is shown in Figure 7.3.

FIGURE 7.3
IFS Access Example VCE Screen

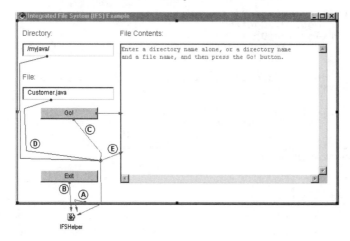

When the application is started and the main window is opened, the event-to-method connection at A executes the **connect** method of the helper class. At B, another event-to-method connection marries a click on Exit to the **quit** method of the helper class.

Clicking Go! executes the **getFileContents** method of the IFSHelper class, an action represented by the event-to-method connection between the button and the helper class at C. The **getFileContents** method requires two string parameters — a directory name and a file name — as shown in this method signature:

```
public String getFileContents(String directory, String file)
```

The parameter-from-property connections at D supply parameter values from the two text fields to the button's event-to-method connection. The **getFileContents** method returns a string value containing the IFS directory/file attributes and file contents. The connection at E shows that this return value sets the text in the File Contents text area. The string that sets the text contains embedded line feeds so that lines are properly formatted for display in the text area.

The **getFileContents** method uses the techniques described in Chapter 5 to access directory and file information. An IFSFile object is created using the directory and file names provided as string parameters.

```
IFSFile myFile = new IFSFile(as400, directory.trim() +
    file.trim());
```

Then, if the object points to a directory, the **list** method is executed to retrieve the directory contents. If the object points to a file, an IFSTextFileInputStream object is created and the file's contents are retrieved. In either case, a string buffer is used to compose the string returned by the method.

```
// If object is a directory, list directory contents
if(myFile.isDirectory())
{
    buffer.append("Directory contents      :\n");
    String[] dirContents = myFile.list();
    for(int i = 0; i < dirContents.length; i++)
        buffer.append("      /" + dirContents[i] + "\n");
}

// If object is a file, read and print file contents
if(myFile.isFile())
{
    IFSTextFileInputStream st =
        new IFSTextFileInputStream(as400, myFile,
        IFSTextFileInput Stream.SHARE_ALL);
    buffer.append(st.read(st.available()));
    buffer.append("\n");
}
```

COMMAND EXECUTION

With the Toolbox, you can execute any OS/400 command capable of running in a batch mode. This feature is the easiest of the Toolbox features to implement. Let's look at an example application using command execution.

Using VisualAge for Java, select the CommandExampleGUI class in the examples.toolbox package and then right-click to display the options menu. Choose Run, Run from the pop-up menu and, when prompted, supply an AS/400 system name, user ID, and password.

The window shown in Figure 7.4 appears. A default command is provided in the Command to Execute text field; you can also type your own command request. Click Execute to run the command.

FIGURE 7.4
Command Execution Example

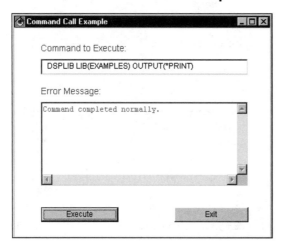

If all goes well, the message "Command executed normally" appears in the Error Message text area. If not, an exception or host error message is displayed in the message area.

The VCE design screen for the command execution example is shown in Figure 7.5.

When the windowOpened event occurs, the **connect** method of the CommandHelper is executed to connect with the command service of the Toolbox. Clicking Exit executes the **quit** method of the helper class, which ends the application and shuts down the JVM.

When Execute is clicked, the event-to-method connection shown at A calls the **executeCommand** method. The signature of this method is shown below.

```
public String executeCommand(String command)
```

The text field connection supplying the command parameter is shown at B and the resulting text area message is set by the connection at C.

Command Execution Call Example VCE Screen

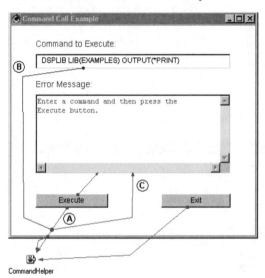

Internally, the CommandHelper class uses a Toolbox CommandCall object to execute the command you give.

```
// Create a CommandCall object
CommandCall commandCall = new CommandCall(as400);

if(commandCall.run(command))
    buffer.append("Command completed normally.\n");
else
{
    buffer.append("Command did not complete normally:\n");
    . . .
}
```

If the command does not complete successfully, the **getMessageList** method on the CommandCall object retrieves host system messages.

```
/* If a host error occurred, construct a string listing
 * the error message details.
 */
AS400Message[] messages = commandCall.getMessageList();
if(messages != null)
{
    for(int i = 0; i < messages.length; i++)
    {
        buffer.append(messages[i].getID() + "   " +
        messages[i].getText() + "\n");
    }
}
```

PROGRAM CALL

The program call feature of the Toolbox lets you take advantage of your investment in AS/400 programs written in languages such as RPG and Cobol. In this section, the ProgramHelper class uses the Toolbox to call RPG program TESTPGM first used in Chapter 5. The ProgramExampleGUI class is executable and provides the user interface for the application.

To run the program call example application, make sure that TESTPGM is in the EXAMPLES library. With the RPG program in place, select the ProgramExampleGUI class in the examples.toolbox package and right-click to display the Options menu. Choose Run I Run from the menu to run the application shown in Figure 7.6. When prompted, supply an AS/400 system name, user ID, and password.

FIGURE 7.6
Program Call Example

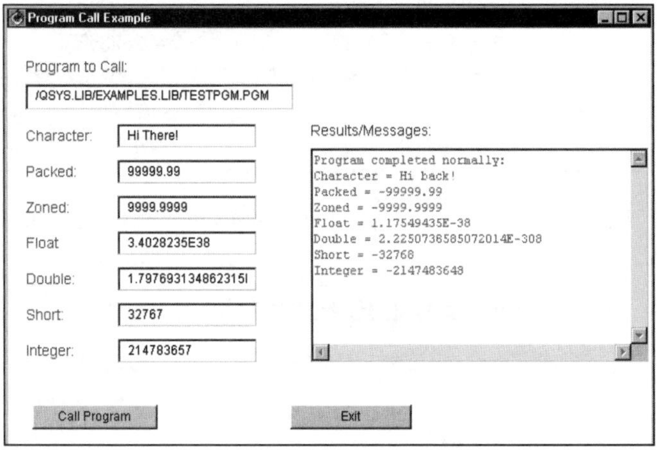

NOTE: **The process of running a class should be familiar to you by now from this and previous examples. Future examples in this chapter will shortcut these instructions by assuming you know how to run the executable class using VisualAge for Java.**

The application supplies a default path for TESTPGM. Changing the program name to anything other than TESTPGM is not a good idea — this application is written to pass specific parameters to the program it calls.

Type values for the program parameters (e.g., Character, Packed, Zoned) in the fields and click Call Program to call the program. The values you supply must conform to the data types that the called program is expecting. For example, the length of the zoned decimal field is defined to be seven, with two decimal positions; the length of the packed decimal field is eight with four decimal positions. You will receive an error message in the text area if you fail to provide the right type of data in a parameter. In a more robust application, you would want to perform data type and reasonability checking before letting the application use data entered by a user.

Table 7.1 shows the minimum and maximum values allowed for each input parameter.

TABLE 7.1
Min/Max Parameter Values

Parameter	Min Value	Max Value
Character	1 character	10 characters
Zoned decimal	-99999.99	99999.99
Packed decimal	-9999.9999	9999.9999
Float	1.17549435E-38	3.4028235E38
Double	2.2250738585072014E-308	1.797693134862315E308
Short	-32768	32767
Integer	-2147483648	214783657

The VCE design screen for the program call example is shown in Figure 7.7.

FIGURE 7.7
Program Call Example VCE Screen

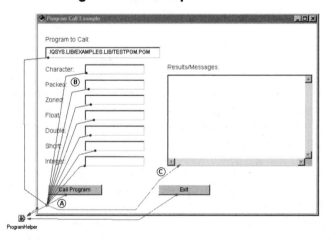

As in previous examples, the **connect** method of the ProgramHelper class is executed when the windowOpened event occurs and the **quit** method is executed when Exit is clicked.

Clicking Call Program executes the **callProgram** method of the helper class, as is shown by the event-to-method connection at A. The **callProgram** method has the following signature:

```
public String callProgram(String program, String i_char,
    java.math.BigDecimal i_packed,
    java.math.BigDecimal i_zoned, Float i_float,
    Double i_double, Short i_short, Integer i_integer)
```

The text fields at B supply parameter values, including the name of the program to call and individual data elements, in parameter-from-property connections. The event-to-method connection at C sets the text area with the return value from the **callProgram** method, a string containing the formatted results of the TESTPGM program call.

The **callProgram** method of the ProgramHelper class converts the input parameters to AS/400 data types and executes the host RPG program.

```
// Create a new program call object.
ProgramCall myPgm = new ProgramCall(as400);

// Construct program parameters.
ProgramParameter myPgmParms[] = new ProgramParameter[7];

// Convert to character
AS400Text textConverter = new AS400Text(10);
myPgmParms[0] =
    new ProgramParameter(textConverter.toBytes(i_char), 10);

// Convert to packed
AS400PackedDecimal packedConverter =
    new AS400PackedDecimal(7, 2);
myPgmParms[1] =
    new ProgramParameter(packedConverter.toBytes(i_packed), 7);

. . .

// Set program name and parameters for the program call.
myPgm.setProgram(program, myPgmParms);

// Execute program call.
if(myPgm.run())
{
    . . .
}
```

With a successful program call, values returned from the host program are converted from AS/400 data types back to Java data types and formatted for display in the Results/Messages text area.

```
// Execute program call.
if(myPgm.run())
{
    buffer.append("Program completed normally:\n");

    // Retrieve result parameters.
    String o_character =
        (String)textConverter.toObject(
        myPgmParms[0].getOutputData());
    BigDecimal o_packed =
        (BigDecimal)packedConverter.toObject(
        myPgmParms[1].getOutputData());

    . . .

    // Construct a string from the result parameters.
    buffer.append("Character = " + o_character + "\n");
    buffer.append("Packed = " + o_packed + "\n");

    . . .

}
```

If the program call is not successful, exception and host error messages are returned and displayed in the Results/Messages text area in the same way as they are with a command call.

DATABASE ACCESS

So far, Toolbox features have been implemented one at a time in standalone examples. By now you get the idea that it is easy to put Toolbox classes to work in graphical applications. In this section, two Toolbox features are combined for an example of database access.

The Toolbox JDBC driver accesses the CUSTMAST table using an SQL statement, and the Record Level Access Toolbox feature accesses the same table at a record level. Seeing the Toolbox database features together in one application lets you better judge performance and other usability issues.

The database example application comprises two classes. The DatabaseExampleGUI class is executable, while the DatabaseHelper class contains the database access logic used for JDBC and record-level access.

Running the Application

This example requires that you create the CUSTMAST table from Chapter 5 in the EXAMPLES library. Make sure that the table contains at least a few records before running the application so that you have data to work with. If you invest the time to populate the table with a large number of records, you can use this example application to effectively compare the performance and features of your two primary means of database access using Java.

Run the DatabaseExampleGUI class to see the application shown in Figure 7.8.

FIGURE 7.8
Database Example

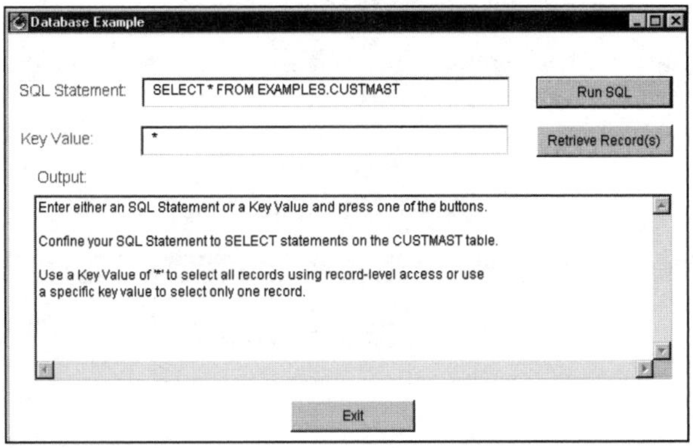

The way this application performs its duties depends on the information you give it and the buttons you click. If you provide an SQL statement and click Run SQL, the application uses JDBC to produce a list of customers in the Output text area. However, if you supply a key value and click Retrieve Record(s), the application uses record-level access to produce the list of records.

For example, using the following default SQL statement, the list builds with all customers found in the CUSTMAST table.

```
SELECT * FROM EXAMPLES.CUSTMAST
```

Click Run SQL with the default SQL statement to produce results similar to those shown in Figure 7.9.

FIGURE 7.9
List of All Customers

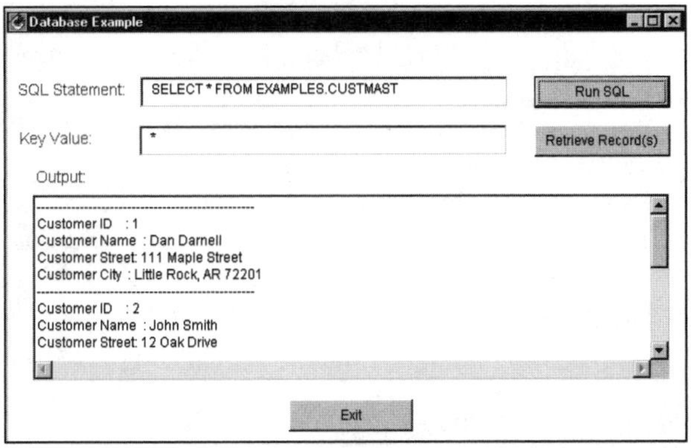

Another way to use the JDBC mode of access is to retrieve a single customer. Type an SQL statement such as

```
SELECT * FROM EXAMPLES.CUSTMAST WHERE CUSTID = 4
```

Click Run SQL to retrieve only the customer with a customer identifier of 4. The results of this query are shown in Figure 7.10.

FIGURE 7.10
Retrieve One Customer

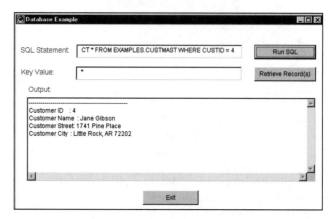

It is possible to retrieve the same type of information using record-level access. To retrieve all records in the CUSTMAST table, type a key value consisting of a single asterisk (*) and click Retrieve Record(s). The * value means nothing special to the Toolbox; it is a feature specific to this application. When the helper class sees the asterisk, it performs a loop, retrieving all records in the table instead of retrieving just a single record.

To retrieve just one record, type a numeric key value and click Retrieve Record(s).

The VCE design screen for the database access example application is shown in Figure 7.11.

Again, the **connect** method of the helper class is executed when the window is opened and the **quit** method is executed when Exit is clicked.

The **connect** method in this example does more than just establish an AS/400 connection; it also establishes a JDBC connection and a keyed file object for record-level access. Here is the code added to the method to set the stage for database access:

```
// Create database connection and keyed file access object
DriverManager.registerDriver(
    new com.ibm.as400.access.AS400JDBCDriver());
conn = DriverManager.getConnection("jdbc:as400://" +
    as400.getSystemName());
```

FIGURE 7.11
FIGURE 7.11
Database Example VCE Screen

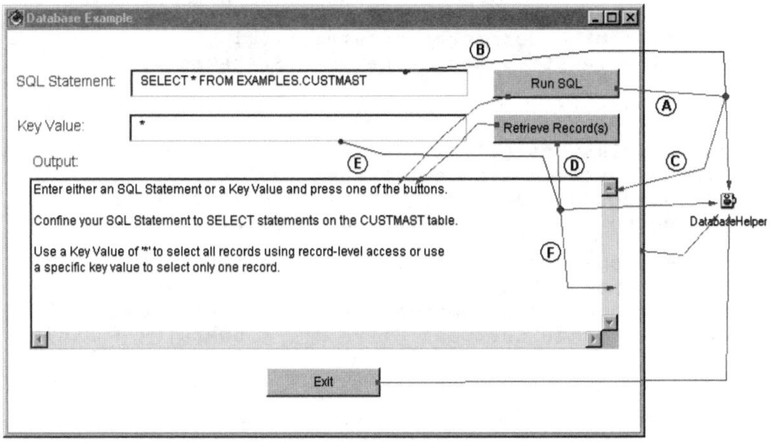

```
// Create a keyed file object and open it
myFile = new KeyedFile(as400,
    "/qsys.lib/examples.lib/custmast.file");

// Create a file record description object
AS400FileRecordDescription myFileDesc =
    new AS400FileRecordDescription(as400,
    "/qsys.lib/examples.lib/custmast.file");

// Get the record format(s) from the record description
RecordFormat recFormats[] =
    myFileDesc.retrieveRecordFormat();

// Associate the record format with the file
myFile.setRecordFormat(recFormats[0]);

// Open the file
myFile.open(AS400File.READ_ONLY, 0,
    AS400File.COMMIT_LOCK_LEVEL_NONE);
```

SQL

Clicking Run SQL executes the **runSQL** method of the helper class, as shown by the event-to-method connection at A in Figure 7.11. The method signature for the **runSQL** method is

```
public String runSQL(String sqlStatement)
```

The method accepts as a parameter the SQL statement supplied in the text field at B. The event-to-method connection at C sets the Results text area with data passed back as a string return value from the **runSQL** method call.

Internally, the **runSQL** method executes a simple JDBC query and processes the results. As customer data is parsed from the result set, it is added to a string buffer that, in the end, is returned as a string to set the text area.

```
Statement stmt = conn.createStatement();
ResultSet rs = stmt.executeQuery(sqlStatement);

while(rs.next())
{
    int custID = rs.getInt("CUSTID");
    String custName = rs.getString("CUSTNAME");
    String custStreet = rs.getString("CUSTSTREET");
    String custCity = rs.getString("CUSTCITY");

    buffer.append("Customer ID     : " + custID + "\n");
    buffer.append("Customer Name   : " + custName + "\n");
    buffer.append("Customer Street: " + custStreet + "\n");
    buffer.append("Customer City   : " + custCity + "\n");
}
```

Record-Level

The event-to-method connection at D shows the relationship between clicking the Retrieve Record(s) button and the **retrieveRecords** method of the helper class. The key value at E is passed to the **retrieveRecords** method as a parameter and, as with the SQL process, the method's return value fills the text area with customer information.

The method signature for the **retrieveRecords** method is

```
public String retrieveRecords(String keyValue )
```

As noted previously, a key value parameter of * reads all records, while a specific numeric key value reads only one record. The Java programming behind these actions follows.

```
// Read all records
if(keyValue.equals("*"))
{
    myFile.positionCursorBeforeFirst();

    while(true) // Loop until all records are read
    {
        Record record = myFile.readNext();

        if(record == null) // Break out of the loop
            break;

        printRecord(record, buffer);

    }
}
else // Read one record by key value
{
    // Create a key array and set the key value
    Object[] key = new Object[] {
        new java.math.BigDecimal(keyValue)};
```

```
// Read a record by key
Record record = myFile.read(key);

if (record != null)
    printRecord(record, buffer);
}
```

The **printRecord** method called out of both the multiple record and single record routines parses data from records retrieved and adds it to a string buffer as a means of constructing a return value to set the Results text area.

```
buffer.append("Customer ID     : " +
    record.getField("CUSTID") + "\n");
buffer.append("Customer Name   : " +
    record.getField("CUSTNAME") + "\n");
buffer.append("Customer Street: " +
    record.getField("CUSTSTREET") + "\n");
buffer.append("Customer City  : " +
    record.getField("CUSTCITY") + "\n");
```

Performance

In most cases, JDBC and record-level access appear to perform equally well. This is good news — it means that you can use the one that best suits your application design.

The primary advantage of JDBC access continues to be its cross-platform capability and simplicity. A disadvantage of JDBC is that it's not usually suitable for retrieving a small number of records from a large table.

The advantage of record-level access is its suitability to single-record retrieval and random record access. The trade-off to record-level access is a higher degree of coding complexity.

DATA QUEUE

This example uses the data queue feature of the Toolbox to exchange structured data between client and server applications. On the server side, RPG IV program DQINTF provides a screen where you can enter data queue data. This program, shown in Figure 7.12, is based closely on the TESTDQ program that you saw in Chapter 5.

FIGURE 7.12

RPG IV Program DQINTF

```
*...1....+....2....+....3....+....4....+....5....+....6....+....7....+....8

FDQINTF    cf   e           workstn

D DQEntry          DS           100    INZ
D  char                         10
D  packed                       7P 2
D  zoned                        8S 4
D  float                        4F
D  double                       8F
```

continued

FIGURE 7.12 CONTINUED

```
*...1....+....2....+....3....+....4....+....5....+....6....+....7....+....8
C                      dow        *inkc = *off

C                      eval       message = 'Type field values ' +
C                                 'and press the Enter key to send ' +
C                                 'a data queue entry.'

C                      exfmt      dq01

* F3=Exit
C                      if         *inkc
C                      leave
C                      endif

* Send a data queue entry
C                      call       'QSNDDTAQ'
C                      parm       'TESTDQ'      DQName         10
C                      parm       'EXAMPLES'    DQLib          10
C                      parm       100           DQLen           5 0
C                      parm                     DQEntry
C                      parm       10            DQKeyLen        3 0
C                      parm       'KEYDATA1'    DQKey          10

C                      eval       message = 'Waiting to receive a ' +
C                                 'reply from the client.  Input ' +
C                                 'is inhibited.'
C                      write      dq01

* Receive a data queue entry
C                      call       'QRCVDTAQ'
C                      parm       'TESTDQ'      DQName
C                      parm       'EXAMPLES'    DQLib
C                      parm       100           DQLen
C                      parm                     DQEntry
C                      parm       -1            DQWait          5 0
C                      parm       'EQ'          DQCond          2
C                      parm       10            DQKeyLen
C                      parm       'KEYDATA2'    DQKey
C                      parm                     DQSndLen        3 0
C                      parm                     DQSndID        44

C                      enddo

C                      eval       *inlr = *on
```

The Data Description Specifications (DDS) required for the RPG program are shown in Figure 7.13. For more information about creating the display file, the RPG program, and the data queue used in this section, see "Creating DQ Interface Program."

To run this example, add the EXAMPLES library to your library list and then call DQINTF.

```
ADDLIBLE LIB(EXAMPLES)
CALL PGM(EXAMPLES/DQINTF)
```

FIGURE **7.13**

DQ Interface DDS Source

```
*...1....+....2....+....3....+....4....+....5....+....6....+....7....+....8
A                              DSPSIZ(24 80 *DS3)
A       R DQ01
A                              CA03
A                              FRCDTA
A                            2 2DATE
A                              EDTCDE(Y)
A                            2 31'Data Queue Tester'
A                              COLOR(WHT)
A                              DSPATR(HI)
A                            2 72TIME
A         MESSAGE    78A  0  5 2COLOR(BLU)
A                            7 6'Character'
A         CHAR       10A  B  7 21
A                            9 6'Packed'
A         PACKED     7Y 2B  9 21EDTWRD('    .  ')
A                           11 6'Zoned'
A         ZONED      8Y 4B 11 21EDTWRD('    .   ')
A                           13 6'Float'
A         FLOAT      9F 4B 13 21FLTPCN(*SINGLE)
A                           15 6'Double'
A         DOUBLE     15F 5B 15 21FLTPCN(*DOUBLE)
A                           23 2'F3=Exit'
A                              COLOR(BLU)
```

Next, run the executable DataQueueExampleGUI class to see the window shown in Figure 7.14.

FIGURE **7.14**

Data Queue Example

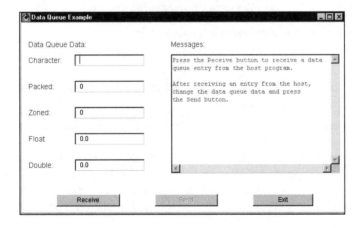

CREATING THE DQ INTERFACE PROGRAM

To create the display file, the RPG program, and the data queue used by the examples in this book, follow these steps:

1. If they don't already exist, create source physical files to hold DDS and ILE RPG source members in the EXAMPLES library.

```
CRTSRCPF FILE(EXAMPLES/QDDSSRC)
CRTSRCPF FILE(EXAMPLES/QRPGLESRC)
```

2. Start SEU to create a display file DDS source member.

```
STRSEU SRCFILE(EXAMPLES/QDDSSRC) SRCMBR(DQINTF)       +
       TYPE(DSPF)                                     +
       TEXT('Data queue interface-display file')
```

Type the source code shown in Figure 7.13 and compile the source code to create a Display File object.

```
CRTDSPF FILE(EXAMPLES/DQINTF) SRCFILE(EXAMPLES/QDDSSRC)
```

3. Start SEU to create an ILE RPG source member.

```
STRSEU SRCFILE(EXAMPLES/QRPGLESRC) SRCMBR(DQINTF)     +
       TYPE(RPGLE) TEXT('Data queue interface')
```

Type the source code shown in Figure 7.12 and compile the source code to create an executable program object.

```
CRTBNDRPG PGM(EXAMPLES/DQINTF)                        +
          SRCFILE(EXAMPLES/QRPGLESRC)
```

4. Create a data queue for the interface program to use.

```
CRTDTAQ DTAQ(EXAMPLES/DQINTF) MAXLEN(100)             +
        SEQ(*KEYED) KEYLEN(10)
```

For instructions on restoring the complete EXAMPLES library from the CD-ROM accompanying this book, see Appendix A.

The AS/400 screen displayed by the DQINTF program appears as shown in Figure 7.15. Type values for each field and press Enter to send a data queue entry to the Java client. At this point, the RPG program automatically waits for a response from the client. While the program is waiting, screen fields can no longer accept input.

On the Java client, click Receive to receive the data queue entry sent by the server program. Each of the Data Queue Data text fields should populate with the data that you keyed in on the AS/400 screen. If an error occurs, the Messages text area reflects the error condition.

FIGURE 7.15
DQINTF Input Screen

```
┌─────────────────────────────────────────────────────────────────────┐
│                                                                       │
│  12/13/99                  Data Queue Tester              14:38:11     │
│                                                                       │
│  Type field values and press the Enter key to send a data queue entry.│
│       Character      HI THERE!                                        │
│       Packed         12345.67                                         │
│       Zoned          1234.5678                                        │
│       Float                 1.0000E+000                               │
│       Double                    2.00000E+000                          │
│                                                                       │
│                                                                       │
│                                                                       │
│  F3=Exit                                                              │
│                                                                       │
└─────────────────────────────────────────────────────────────────────┘
```

After receiving data queue data on the client, you can change the information in the text fields and click Send to return a data queue entry to the server. The minimum and maximum values that you can specify for the text fields are the same as those listed in the program call example.

This example is structured in a way that requires you to coordinate your actions between the AS/400 screen and the Java client, alternating on the client between Receive and Send actions and doing the opposite on the AS/400 screen. When the Receive button is enabled, the Send button is disabled and vice versa. If either the Java program or the RPG program is cancelled prematurely or ends abnormally, it is possible to leave orphaned entries on the data queue. If you notice strange behavior in the application, simply delete and re-create the data queue and restart both sides of the application.

You may be tired of seeing the same application design pattern used in this chapter's examples — if so, you'll be glad that this one is a little different. Instead of setting up the helper class's **send** and **receive** methods to accept a slew of parameter-from-property connections, the DataQueueHelper class implements its data as properties. In the VCE, the text fields are connected directly to the helper's properties using property-to-property connections. This structure makes the worker methods easier to implement (they accept no parameters) but requires a little extra code in the class to manage the properties. The VCE design screen for the data queue example application is shown in Figure 7.16.

As values are changed in the text fields, property-to-property connections such as the one shown at A update properties in the helper class. A property is defined in the helper class for each data type (e.g., Character, Packed, Zoned) exchanged through the data queue. These properties are called bound properties, which means that modifying a property initiates a property change event.

FIGURE 7.16
Data Queue Example VCE Screen

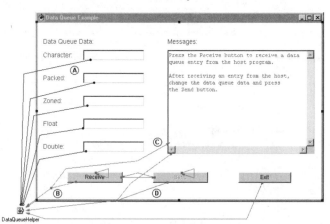

Wiring two-way property-to-property connections in the VCE makes the text fields listen for property change events coming from the helper class properties. When helper class properties change as the result of receiving a data queue entry, the displayed text fields change also.

In the other direction, the helper class properties are updated by *focus lost* events on the individual text fields. In a focus lost event, the helper class properties are changed as you change text field values, then move from one text field to another. The details of one property-to-property connection are shown in Figure 7.17.

An instance variable in a class becomes an official property by adhering to naming conventions set forth in Sun Microsystems' JavaBeans standard. For example, the Character property is considered readable when the DataQueue-Helper class contains an accessor (get*Property*) method.

```
public String getCharacter() {
    return d_character;
}
```

Including a mutator (set*Property*) method in the class makes the property writeable as well as readable. A property change is fired in the mutator method, making it a bound property.

```
public void setCharacter(String newValue) {
    String oldValue = d_character;
    d_character = newValue;
    firePropertyChange("character", oldValue, newValue);
}
```

When the window is opened, the **connect** method of the DataQueueHelper class sets up the objects required for sending and receiving data queue entries.

FIGURE 7.17

Property-to-Property Connection Details

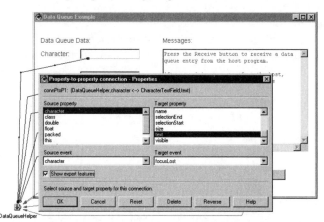

These objects include a keyed data queue, record format, and multiple field descriptions — the field descriptions being associated with the record format.

```
// Create data queue object
keyedDQ = new KeyedDataQueue(as400,
    "/qsys.lib/examples.lib/testdq.dtaq");

// Create record format
myRecFormat = new RecordFormat();

// Create field descriptions
CharacterFieldDescription fd_character =
    new CharacterFieldDescription(new AS400Text(10),
    "CHARACTER");
PackedDecimalFieldDescription fd_packed =
    new PackedDecimalFieldDescription(
    new AS400PackedDecimal(7, 2),
    "PACKED");
ZonedDecimalFieldDescription fd_zoned =
    new ZonedDecimalFieldDescription(
    new AS400ZonedDecimal(8, 4),
    "ZONED");
FloatFieldDescription fd_float =
    new FloatFieldDescription(new AS400Float4(),
    "FLOAT");
FloatFieldDescription fd_double =
    new FloatFieldDescription(new AS400Float8(),
    "DOUBLE");

// Associate field descriptions with record format
myRecFormat.addFieldDescription(fd_character);
myRecFormat.addFieldDescription(fd_packed);
myRecFormat.addFieldDescription(fd_zoned);
myRecFormat.addFieldDescription(fd_float);
myRecFormat.addFieldDescription(fd_double);
```

The application uses two buttons to control the data queue activities. The Receive button at B in Figure 7.16 is connected to the **receive** method of the helper class with an event-to-method connection. In the method, a data queue entry is read from the keyed data queue. From the data queue entry, a record object is parsed, conforming to the record format established in the **connect** method. Properties of the helper class are set by extracting the individual data elements from the record object.

```
// Create key
AS400Text keyText = new AS400Text(10);
byte[] key = keyText.toBytes("KEYDATA1");

// Wait on data queue read
KeyedDataQueueEntry DQEntry = keyedDQ.read(key, -1, "EQ");

// Parse data from data queue entry
Record record = myRecFormat.getNewRecord(DQEntry.getData());
setCharacter((String) record.getField("CHARACTER"));
setPacked((java.math.BigDecimal) record.getField("PACKED"));
setZoned((java.math.BigDecimal) record.getField("ZONED"));
setFloat((Float) record.getField("FLOAT"));
setDouble((Double) record.getField("DOUBLE"));
```

Any errors returned by the **receive** method call are set in the Messages text area using a string return value. This action is represented by the connection at C.

When Send is clicked, the **send** method of the helper class is executed. The event-to-method connection for this is shown at D. With property-to-property connections to take care of setting data values, the signature of the **send** method is very simple.

```
public String send()
```

Internally, the **send** method creates a new record object by using the record format established in the **connect** method. Next, helper class properties set the individual data elements in the record. Last, a key value is established and a data queue entry written to the keyed data queue.

```
// Create data queue entry
Record sendRecord = myRecFormat.getNewRecord();
sendRecord.setField("CHARACTER", getCharacter());
sendRecord.setField("PACKED", getPacked());
sendRecord.setField("ZONED", getZoned());
sendRecord.setField("FLOAT", getFloat());
sendRecord.setField("DOUBLE", getDouble());

// Construct key
AS400Text keyText2 = new AS400Text(10);
byte[] key2 = keyText2.toBytes("KEYDATA2");

// Write data queue record
keyedDQ.write(key2, sendRecord.getContents());
```

As with the **receive** method, errors occurring during the process are set in the Messages text area using the string return value.

Spooled File

By combining the spooled file feature of the Toolbox with a graphical interface, you can create a simple report designer in Java. A more robust report design tool with access to data fields, variable line spacing, and multiple formats would be a hefty project and is beyond the scope of this chapter. You can, however, use the example presented here as a basis for creating your own more full-featured report designer.

Run the executable SpooledFileExampleGUI class to see the window shown in Figure 7.18.

FIGURE 7.18
Spooled File Example

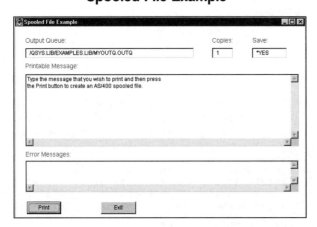

In the Output Queue text field, you can specify the name of an AS/400 output queue to hold your spooled files. You can accept the default value or override it with the name and location of another output queue. Besides specifying the output queue, you can also specify the number of copies and save status for the spooled files you create. In the Printable Message text area you can type any amount of constant data that you would like to print on the AS/400. Clicking Print causes the helper class to take your printable message and write it to an AS/400 spooled file. Errors that occur during this process are displayed in the Error Messages text area.

The VCE design screen for this example application is shown in Figure 7.19 At A, you can see an event-to-method connection between the Print button on the graphical user interface and the **print** method of the SpooledFileHelper class. The **print** method accepts parameters of the output queue, number of copies, save status, and printable message text.

```
public String print(String printData, String outputQueue,
    int copies, String save)
```

The parameters are provided by parameter-from-property connections such as the one at B.

FIGURE 7.19
Spooled File Example VCE Screen

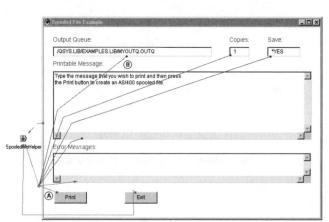

In a fashion similar to that demonstrated in Chapter 5, print parameters are constructed from the **print** method's input parameters. A spooled file output stream is constructed with the print parameters and the parameter-supplied output queue name and the output stream is then encapsulated in a writer object.

```
// Create parameters for new spooled file
PrintParameterList printParms = new PrintParameterList();
printParms.setParameter(PrintObject.ATTR_COPIES, copies);
printParms.setParameter(PrintObject.ATTR_SAVE, save);

// Construct an output queue object
OutputQueue outQ = new OutputQueue(as400, outputQueue);

// Open a spooled file
SpooledFileOutputStream output =
    new SpooledFileOutput Stream(as400,
    printParms, null, outQ);

// Wrapper the spooled file with a writer
SCS5256Writer printWriter = new SCS5256Writer(output);
```

The entire printable message is written to an AS/400 spooled file with one simple statement.

```
// Output to spooled file
printWriter.write(printData);
```

Embedded line feeds, spaces, and tabs are properly translated to produce printed AS/400 output that mirrors the data keyed into the text area.

This example is a simple but powerful example of Toolbox functionality. With very little effort, you can put together Java applications using substantial features of the AS/400. VAJ and the VCE let you create an application that requires very little or no hand coding to define the relationship between user interface and application logic.

Chapter 8

Remote Method Invocation

In this chapter, you are introduced to the concepts and coding involved in creating an application using Remote Method Invocation (RMI) support. RMI is a Java technology for creating client/server applications. You will learn how IBM's VisualAge for Java (VAJ) helps you develop RMI-based applications. You will also learn more about ways a client/server approach gives you more control over aspects of an application such as performance.

NOTE: The example presented in this chapter uses features found only in VAJ Enterprise Edition.

BEYOND SOCKETS

Sockets are a flexible and powerful way to create client/server applications, but you pay a price — coding a custom protocol to exchange data is complicated. Java offers an alternative to coding your own sockets protocol, a feature called Remote Method Invocation (RMI). With RMI, the Java language lets you distribute objects and execute methods on the remote objects as though they were local. The underlying technology for RMI is still TCP/IP sockets, but your applications are effectively insulated from the network communications aspects of sockets programming.

Workload Distribution

Designing a well-performing and secure Java application requires that you think about where your application code will run. Most client/server applications are made up of components for a graphical user interface (GUI), database access, and business logic.

Business logic is defined as the programming unique to the business purpose of the application. For example, in an order entry application you would likely need a business logic component to calculate shipping and handling charges. Sometimes database access and business logic components are combined into composite components, but very often these components remain distinct.

With an AS/400, business logic and database access components are likely to perform the best, and be the most secure, on the server. The GUI almost certainly belongs on the client.

At a minimum, workload distribution planning is simply deciding before you write an application where you will place the components of an application. For example, with the Customer Tracking application in Chapter 6, we decided up front that the database access would reside on the server; then a customized server application was written to fit this design. This approach allows for very little flexibility. What if database access on the server does not perform up to expectations? Or what if your user base increases ten-fold and you have to move some business logic components to a separate server? With a customized socket server approach, solving these kinds of problems requires rewriting the application.

At its best, workload distribution lets you make new decisions about the partitioning of application components after the application is written and even after the application is in use. In the best designs, an application component can run on any platform — wherever you decide that it makes the most sense in terms of maintenance, performance, security, and network load balancing. When you code with RMI, your applications are enabled for exactly this kind of robust workload distribution.

Theory

When you code for RMI, you intend for one or more application objects to reside on a server platform instead of on each client. When a client executes a method on a server object, the Java Virtual Machine (JVM) on the server is doing the work. The client can execute server object methods, even those requiring parameters, and receive a return value, just as with any other method call. In fact, you can't distinguish by sight an RMI method call from a regular method call.

RMI works by allowing you to create an object on the client to act on behalf of the real object, which resides on the server. This client object is called a *stub*. The stub object looks to the client just like the real server application object, but it is actually a communications component.

On the server side, another object, the *skeleton*, is set up to communicate with the stub on the client. The skeleton object's job is to receive requests from the client stub and pass them to the real application object. Because methods return values, the communications between stub and skeleton are two-way. The skeleton accepts method calls, with or without parameters, and passes back a method's return value to the stub. This basic RMI mechanism is illustrated in Figure 8.1.

The stub and skeleton are Java classes that are usually generated by a tool in the Java Development Kit, the RMI Compiler. The RMI Compiler command, rmic, is available on the AS/400 through the QShell Interpreter. Specify the name of a class that you want to enable for remote execution, and the utility automatically creates both the stub and skeleton classes.

Some innovative technology in Java handles RMI, particularly the passing of parameters and return values. For a parameter (or return value) to go out over the network, it must be translated to a format suitable for transportation. For primitive values this translation is no big deal — creating a suitable binary representation is easy — but what about complex objects?

FIGURE 8.1
Elements of RMI

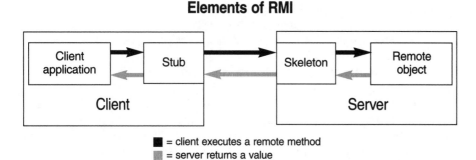

■ = client executes a remote method
▨ = server returns a value

The serialization mechanism discussed in Chapter 6 turns objects into streams of bytes, which are then easily exchanged between systems. The process by which RMI translates parameters and return values is called *marshalling*. As with the low-level sockets communications between stub and skeleton, parameter marshalling is almost an automatic process as far as you, the application developer, are concerned.

Almost, but not entirely, automatic. Any object that you intend to pass via RMI must be capable of serialization, and this requirement may demand work on your part. As described in Chapter 6, a class must implement the Serializeable interface to support serialization. Normally, implementing this simple, no-method interface is enough, but sometimes you must do quite a bit more. Instance variables that are system dependent cannot be serialized effectively.

For example, a reference to a thread inside an object on one system makes sense only in the context of that system. If the object is sent to a remote system, the thread reference is no longer valid and might even crash the application. Use the transient modifier on the instance variable declaration to keep the variable out of the serialization byte stream.

```
private transient Thread myThread = null;
```

Before you automatically mark a class as Serializable and try to use it with RMI, be sure that you have a thorough understanding of the class's inner workings and take the time to handle system-dependent references.

Practice

When it comes to invoking methods on remote objects and passing parameters, RMI handles a lot of work for you. Where RMI begins to become a burden is in coding classes that you want to enable as server objects. To work as an RMI remote object, your server class must extend UnicastRemoteObject. Methods in the class that you want to make accessible to the client must be defined in an interface that extends the Remote interface. Furthermore, each of the methods defined by your interface must declare that they can throw a RemoteException

exception. Then, to add one more degree of complexity, the server object must register itself with a special RMI naming service.

Your client isn't completely exempt from RMI-specific coding either. It must access the naming service to locate the server object before it can begin making remote method calls.

Most books on advanced Java programming teach you the coding skills necessary to write your own applications using RMI. While RMI coding skills are useful, hand coding RMI-based applications doesn't get you much further than hand coding sockets-based applications. When you hand code sockets, you write more communications code than an application developer should be forced to write. When you hand code RMI, you write more support code than should be necessary to take advantage of a built-in language feature. The way to avoid the complexities of RMI coding is with the RMI Access Builder tool included with VAJ Enterprise Edition.

With VAJ, instead of hand coding RMI support into your server classes, you let the tool generate support classes for you to use. Using the RMI Access Builder, you literally write an application as though it will run entirely on the client. Only when you decide to deploy your application do you choose which components to enable under RMI.

IBM's tool is extremely robust, providing services that would be difficult at best to code for yourself. The RMI Access Builder generates support for all the functions provided by the VCE, not just for simple method calls. For example, you can make property-to-property connections in the VCE between local and remote objects and even link remote object events to actions in other remote objects! Not only does the RMI Access Builder lift the coding burden for basic RMI support, it also provides extraordinary functionality cloaked by the simplicity of the VCE.

To work with the RMI Access Builder in VAJ, the IBM-supplied project called IBM Enterprise RMI Access Builder must be present in your workspace. To add the IBM Enterprise RMI Access Builder to your workspace, follow these steps:

1. From the File menu, select Quick Start or press the F2 function key. The Quick Start dialog box is displayed.

2. Select Features from the box on the left and then Add Feature from the box on the right. Click OK. A list of available features is displayed.

3. From the list of features, select the IBM Enterprise RMI Access Builder and click OK. The appropriate project is added to your workspace. If the project is already in your workspace, it will not appear on the list of features.

Using any tool to avoid the intricacies of RMI has a down side. If you haven't coded a down-and-dirty RMI application by hand, you won't have a complete understanding of the inner workings of RMI. This lack of knowledge can make debugging and troubleshooting more problematic. Also, in the case of VAJ's RMI tool, you are tying your applications to an IBM library of supporting Java classes. This adds a wrinkle to your application development and deployment because you are relying on IBM's continued support for their tool.

The benefits of the RMI Access Builder in VAJ make this trade-off easier to stomach, but it is a trade-off nonetheless. In this chapter's examples, the trade-off is deemed acceptable, and we use the RMI Access Builder to generate everything required to support RMI.

Registry

A service called the RMI registry is provided on the server platform. Any server object that wants to make itself visible to the outside world as a remote object must register itself with this service. Once registered, client applications can locate and use the remote server object.

Start the RMI registry on the AS/400 using the rmiregistry tool in the QShell Interpreter. The registry is designed to listen on a TCP/IP port for clients in search of remote objects. By default, the port used by the registry is 1099. You can specify an alternative port to listen on by supplying the port number as a parameter to the rmiregistry command.

You should need only a single instance of the registry to serve remote objects unless you have clients coded to look for registries on different ports. For example, you might have clients coded for the default port of 1099 and clients coded for some other unique port number. In practice, it simplifies matters to ensure that all clients attach to a single registry.

Because many clients may attach to the registry, it makes sense to run the registry as an AS/400 batch job instead of in an interactive session. Following is a Submit Job (SBMJOB) command that starts a QShell session as a batch job and automatically starts the rmiregistry tool. The registry uses 1099, the default port number.

```
SBMJOB CMD(STRQSH CMD('rmiregistry'))
```

To start the RMI registry listening on a port other than the default, specify the port number as the first parameter to the rmiregistry command. For example, to start the registry using port number 8000, use the following command:

```
SBMJOB CMD(STRQSH CMD('rmiregistry 8000'))
```

The RMI registry uses the classpath environment variable to locate server objects. It is essential that you set the classpath for the RMI registry job in a fashion appropriate to your application before you invoke the rmiregistry tool. You can copy the classpath from an interactive session to a submitted batch job by using the Copy Environment Variables (CPYENVVAR) parameter on the SBMJOB command. With the classpath environment variable set, the following command submits the rmiregistry tool to run in batch using the same classpath as the submitting job.

```
SBMJOB CMD(STRQSH CMD('rmiregistry')) CPYENVVAR(*YES)
```

The RMI registry allows a client class to look up a remote object using a unique name given to the object when it was registered. Once located, the RMI registry returns a stub to the client. As you read in the "Theory" section earlier in this chapter, the client uses the stub to communicate with the server object. The process of registering a server object is called *binding* the object. As long as you use the RMI Access Builder to generate RMI classes for you, the mechanics of this process are somewhat irrelevant.

On the server side, the VAJ-generated classes take care of the binding step and, on the client, the registry lookup is automated as well. You must start the registry to enable RMI, and that is really all you need to do. Once started, the RMI registry works like other TCP/IP host services such as Telnet.

To provide a complete understanding of the role of RMI and the VAJ RMI Access Builder tool in application development, the rest of this chapter is devoted to an example.

CUSTOMER TRACKING APPLICATION

One last time, the Customer Tracking application makes an appearance. This time around, RMI is used to distribute the database access to the server. On the client side, this version of the application includes the same buttons and other features as the example in Chapter 6, but the server side of the application is generated almost entirely by VAJ. As with the application example in Chapter 6, this version of the client uses the CUSTMAST database table on the AS/400 to make customer information persistent, and you can still run as many instances of the client as you wish.

Running the Application

It is slightly more problematic to run the RMI-enabled Customer Tracking application than it was to run the sockets version. You must put quite a few classes in the right place and activate two server applications before a client can connect. However, if you follow these step-by-step instructions, you shouldn't have any problems.

1. On your AS/400, make sure that the CUSTMAST database table from Chapter 5 is created and in a library called EXAMPLES.

2. Change the SYSTEM, USERID, and PASSWORD constants in the Customer-ListKeeper class. These pieces of information are used to connect with your AS/400 database.

```
private static final String SYSTEM = "SYSTEM";
private static final String USERID = "USERID";
private static final String PASSWORD = "PASSWORD";
```

3. Change the Server Host IP Name property of the CustomerListKeeper
   proxy bean. This information is used to connect the client to the server.
   Figure 8.2 shows a Properties dialog box in the VCE. You can type either
   the IP address or the system name of your AS/400.

FIGURE 8.2
Proxy Bean Host Property

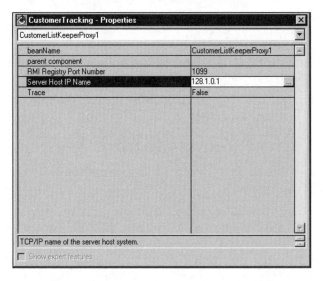

4. Create a /myjava/examples/rmi directory in the IFS on your AS/400 and
   export the following classes from the VAJ examples.rmi package into this
   directory:

   - CustomerHostServer
   - CustomerItem
   - CustomerListKeeper
   - CustomerListKeeperProxyIf
   - CustomerListKeeperProxy_Stub
   - CustomerListKeeperProxyS
   - CustomerListKeeperProxyS_Skel
   - CustomerListKeeperProxyS_Stub
   - CustomerListKeeperProxyPropertyChangeListenerRmiIf

5. Start the RMI registry on the server. To start the RMI registry, you must first
   set the classpath to include any resources that your remote objects require.
   In the case of the Customer Tracking application, these resources include

not only the classes in the /myjava directory but also the VAJ file ivjeab.zip containing RMI Access Builder support classes. Find this file in the IBMVJava\eab\runtime directory and copy it to the /myjava directory in the IFS on your AS/400. Set the classpath with the following command:

```
ADDENVVAR ENVVAR(CLASSPATH)                          +
          VALUE('/myjava:/myjava/ivjeab.zip')
```

After setting the classpath, submit the following Start QShell (STRQSH) command to start the RMI registry.

```
SBMJOB CMD(STRQSH CMD('rmiregistry')) CPYENVVAR(*YES)
```

The CPYENVVAR parameter is specified so that the submitted job inherits the submitting session's classpath.

6. Start the server portion of the application from an OS/400 command line with this Run Java command:

```
JAVA CLASS(examples.rmi.CustomerHostServer)          +
     CLASSPATH('/myjava:/myjava/ivjeab.zip')
```

When the server is ready to accept client connections, the message "Server prepared" is displayed.

7. Start the client portion of the application from a VAJ project or package view. Select the CustomerTracking class in the examples.rmi package and right-click the class. From the pop-up menu, choose Run, Run.

   When the client application starts, it connects with the server automatically. Wait for a successful connection and the status message "Connected. Press Refresh button to build list" in the client window. When you click Refresh, the list of customers is constructed and the status message changes to "Ready for action!" No messages are issued on the server side to indicate that a client has connected.

Design and Implementation

Communication between the client-side user interface and the server-side database access component is handled entirely by RMI. You can use the same RMI model and tools in situations where you also have business logic components. The features of RMI allow you to place your remote objects wherever you wish. You can easily distribute database and business logic among multiple servers, if that is what your situation demands. Also, because RMI support is used, multiple clients are enabled by default; it is not necessary to write a customized server to spawn threaded communications objects.

CLIENT

The client side of the Customer Tracking application consists of three hand-written classes, CustomerTracking, CustomerList, and CustomerItem. As shown in Table 8.1, the functionality of each class remains the same as in Chapter 6.

TABLE 8.1
Client-Side Application Classes

Class	Description
CustomerTracking	User interface for the Customer Tracking application (executable).
CustomerList	Graphical component extended from the AWT's List component. Provides list handling capabilities specific to the application.
CustomerItem	Customer object. Holds information about a single customer.

NOTE: Further into the example, you will see that VAJ generates a multitude of additional classes to support RMI on the client. These are detailed in "Using the RMI Access Builder," later in this chapter.

The CustomerListKeeper class has undergone the most changes in this application. This class now handles all the database access and it is coded to execute on either the client or the server. It doesn't start out on the server side, however. As the Customer Tracking application is developed, the CustomerListKeeper class resides on the client. When development is complete and application functionality is tested, the RMI Access Builder enables the CustomerListKeeper class for remote execution.

Let's look at the new features of the CustomerListKeeper class and then examine the RMI Access Builder process in detail.

Figure 8.3 shows the VCE design screen for the Customer Tracking application before running the RMI Access Builder against the CustomerListKeeper class.

At this stage, the application consists only of the classes shown in Table 8.1 and the CustomerListKeeper class; all these classes reside and execute on the client. The functionality of the application is exactly the same as it will be after it is enabled for RMI. At this stage, the primary benefit you derive is simpler coding. The only consideration given to RMI is making the CustomerItem class support serialization by having it implement the Serializable interface.

The methods defined to the CustomerListKeeper class haven't changed much since the example in Chapter 6, but the internal workings of the methods are radically different. Recall that in Chapter 6 a server class named CustomerHostSocket was responsible for accessing the database. Here, the CustomerListKeeper takes care of this work itself. To give you a better idea of the role that the CustomerListKeeper now plays, take a look at the latest version of the **connect** method, shown in Figure 8.4.

FIGURE 8.3
Pre-RMI Design Screen

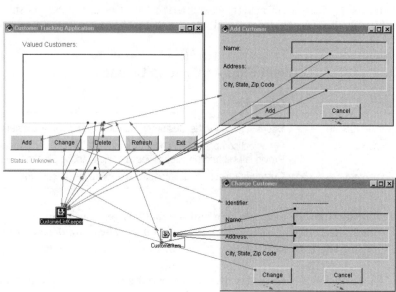

FIGURE 8.4
CustomerListKeeper Connect Method

```java
public void connect() {

    setStatus("Status:  Connecting...");

    try
    {
        Class.forName(JDBC_Driver_DB2);
        dbConn = DriverManager.getConnection(JDBC_URL_DB2 +
            "://" + SYSTEM, USERID, PASSWORD);
    }
    catch(Exception e1)
    {
        try
        {
            Class.forName(JDBC_Driver_Toolbox);
            dbConn = DriverManager.getConnection(JDBC_URL_Toolbox +
                "://" + SYSTEM, USERID, PASSWORD);
        }
        catch(Exception e2)
        {
            e2.printStackTrace();
            setStatus("Error:  " + e2.getMessage());
        }
    }

    try
    {
        pSelect = dbConn.prepareStatement("SELECT * FROM " +
            "EXAMPLES.CUSTMAST ORDER BY CUSTID");
```

continued

FIGURE 8.4 *CONTINUED*

```
pMaxID = dbConn.prepareStatement("SELECT Max(CUSTID) FROM " +
    "EXAMPLES.CUSTMAST");
pInsert = dbConn.prepareStatement("INSERT INTO " +
    "EXAMPLES.CUSTMAST (CUSTID, CUSTNAME, CUSTSTREET, " +
    "CUSTCITY) VALUES(?, ?, ?, ?)");
pUpdate = dbConn.prepareStatement("UPDATE EXAMPLES.CUSTMAST " +
    "SET CUSTNAME = ?, CUSTSTREET = ?, CUSTCITY = ? " +
    "WHERE CUSTID = ?");
pDelete = dbConn.prepareStatement("DELETE FROM " +
    "EXAMPLES.CUSTMAST WHERE CUSTID = ?");
}
catch(SQLException e3)
{
    e3.printStackTrace();
    setStatus("Error:  " + e3.getMessage());
}

setStatus(
    "Status:  Connected.  Press Refresh button to build list.");
}
```

Where before this method connected the client to the server, now the only connecting going on is to the database. Instead of coding just for the server's native DB2/400 driver, this method is now capable of connecting to the AS/400 database using either the AS/400 Toolbox for Java driver or the native driver. If it doesn't find one, it uses the other. This technique allows the CustomerListKeeper class to work in the design mode, where all classes reside on the client, and under RMI, where it is distributed to the server.

Another example of the new CustomerListKeeper class can be found in the **changeItem** method, shown in Figure 8.5. Here you see that the database access is contained entirely within the CustomerListKeeper class, with no messy sockets connectivity or object streams to juggle.

FIGURE 8.5

CustomerListKeeper ChangeItem Method

```
public String changeItem(CustomerItem ci) throws Exception {
    try
    {
        pUpdate.setString(1, ci.getName());
        pUpdate.setString(2, ci.getStreet());
        pUpdate.setString(3, ci.getCityStateZip());
        pUpdate.setBigDecimal(4, new BigDecimal(ci.getID()));

        pUpdate.executeUpdate();
    }
    catch(Exception e)
    {
        setStatus("Error:  " + e.getMessage());
        throw e;
    }

    setStatus("Status:  Customer information changed.");

    String formatID = "00000" + ci.getID();
    int formatIDLength = formatID.length();
    return formatID.substring(formatIDLength - 5, formatIDLength) +
        "    " + ci.getName();
}
```

USING THE RMI ACCESS BUILDER

Taking the CustomerListKeeper class remote in VAJ is accomplished with the RMI Access Builder tool. This tool generates several classes, including two so-called proxy classes. One proxy class resides on the client and the other is on the server. The proxy classes provide an application layer between a remote server object and a client using the server object. In this layer, IBM has implemented additional features, such as event handling, that aren't supported by standard RMI.

Using RMI Access Builder generated classes, the RMI model is enhanced beyond the way it was described in "Theory," earlier in this chapter. Specifically, the client application now interfaces directly with the generated client-side proxy class; this proxy class, in turn, uses RMI to communicate with the generated server-side proxy class. Between the two proxy classes are standard RMI stub and skeleton classes to handle the proxy-to-proxy communications. Note that the remote server object itself (CustomerListKeeper) no longer requires stub and skeleton classes to support it because the server-side proxy acts on its behalf.

To use the RMI Access Builder, select the CustomerListKeeper class in the examples.rmi package and select Tools, Remote Bean Access, Create Proxy Beans from the pop-up menu as shown in Figure 8.6.

FIGURE 8.6
Remote Bean Generation

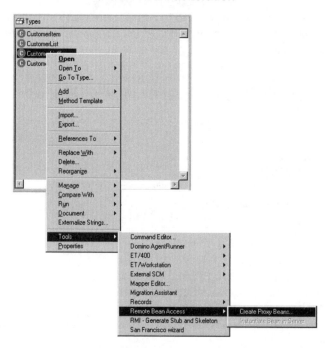

The Create Proxy Bean SmartGuide, shown in Figure 8.7, appears and asks you to provide a base name. This name is the prefix for a slew of beans the tool generates.

FIGURE 8.7
Create Proxy Bean SmartGuide

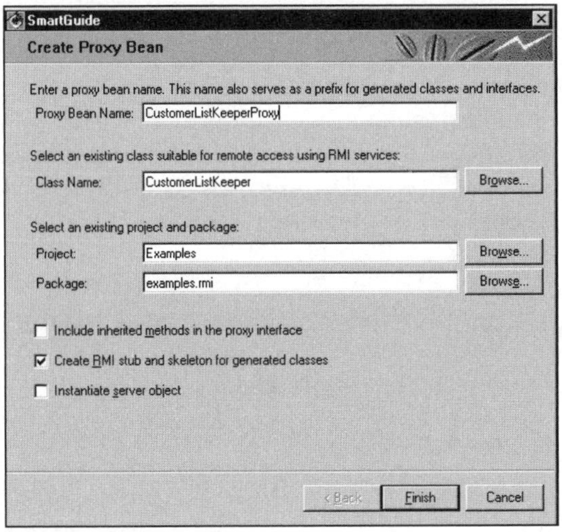

In this example, the name CustomerListKeeperProxy is the proxy bean name. In the Class Name field, type the name of the class that you wish to enable for remote access (in this case, CustomerListKeeper). You can specify a target project and package for the generated classes or accept the default values. Using the checkboxes, you can set processing options. In this example, we selected the "Create RMI stub and skeleton for generated classes" option, which allows the tool to invoke the RMI compiler (rmic) over the generated classes. This option saves the step of creating Java's stub and skeleton classes separately for the generated proxy classes.

When the RMI Access Builder tool is invoked on the CustomerListKeeper class, it generates the proxy classes and interfaces shown in Table 8.2.

TABLE 8.2
Common Generated Proxy Classes and Interfaces

Class or Interface	Description
CustomerListKeeperProxy	Class generated to act as the client-side proxy
CustomerListKeeperProxyBeanInfo	Class generated to define the bean properties of the CustomerListKeeperProxy class

continued

TABLE 8.2 *CONTINUED*

Class or Interface	Description
CustomerListKeeperProxyIf	Interface generated to define the remote methods available in the CustomerListKeeperProxy class
CustomerListKeeperProxyS	Class generated to act as the server-side proxy

In addition, for each event that a remote server object can trigger, the RMI Access Builder generates one additional class and one additional interface. Recall that event handling is not a standard feature of RMI. Rather, this support is provided by IBM's generated code and the RMI Access Builder. Table 8.3 shows the class and interface generated by the RMI Access Builder to support the CustomerListKeeper classes' property change event.

TABLE 8.3
Additional Generated Classes and Interfaces

Class or Interface	Description
CustomerListKeeperProxyjava_beans_PropertyChangeEvent	Class generated to encapsulate a server object event, making it capable of remote access
CustomerListKeeperProxyProperty-ChangeListenerRmiIf	Interface generated to define the remote methods of the event class available to the client

When the RMI Access Builder invokes the RMI Compiler (rmic) command, the stub and skeleton classes shown in Table 8.4 are generated. These classes are the link between the RMI Access Builder's generated code and the standard RMI mechanism.

TABLE 8.4
RMI Compiler-Generated Classes

Class or Interface	Description
CustomerListKeeperProxy_Skel	The skeleton class for the generated client-side proxy
CustomerListKeeperProxy _Stub	The stub class for the generated client-side proxy
CustomerListKeeperProxyS_Skel	The skeleton class for the generated server-side proxy
CustomerListKeeperProxyS_Stub	The stub class for the generated server-side proxy

You should never modify the Java code in any of the classes that the RMI Access Builder generates. Each time this tool is executed for an application class, all the generated classes are re-created. If you modify a generated class, your changes will be lost.

CLIENT REVISITED

With the generated RMI classes in hand, it is time to revisit the VCE design screen for the Customer Tracking application. At this point, we must replace the CustomerListKeeper class used throughout application development with the generated CustomerListKeeperProxy class. At first glance, this appears to be a daunting task. The CustomerListKeeper bean has at least seven direct connections, and at least that many more connections supply parameters to those direct connections or act on a return value. As you are well aware, the VCE design screen represents a lot of user-interface code, and retaining the connections is paramount to keeping the application in working order.

Fortunately, VAJ and the VCE come to the rescue. You can drag a connection from one bean and drop it on another, as long as the target bean has a feature exactly like the source bean's feature. Drop the CustomerListKeeperProxy class on the VCE design screen by selecting the "Choose bean" icon on the palette. In the Choose Bean dialog box that appears, specify the fully qualified class name, examples.rmi.CustomerListKeeperProxy. Click OK and then drop the bean next to the existing CustomerListKeeper bean.

Next, transfer connections one at a time from the CustomerListKeeper bean to the CustomerListKeeperProxy bean. To transfer a connection from one bean to another, first click on the connection. Next, click on the end of the connection. As you move the mouse pointer, the connection detaches. Drop the connection on the target bean and it reattaches automatically.

Figure 8.8 shows the VCE design screen midway through the process of transferring connections from the CustomerListKeeper bean to the CustomerListKeeperProxy bean.

You can see the dashed line and the spider pointer as the connection for the delete action is transferred from one bean to the other. (See "Morphing" for an alternative method of relocating bean connections.)

After all the connections are moved from the CustomerListKeeper bean to the CustomerListKeeperProxy bean, you can delete the CustomerListKeeper bean from the VCE design screen. The finished product appears as shown in Figure 8.9.

From this point, the Customer Tracking application uses RMI to communicate with the remote server object through the CustomerListKeeperProxy bean. It is worth emphasizing that not one line of RMI code was written by hand to make this setup work.

FIGURE 8.8
VCE Design Screen — Transferring Connections

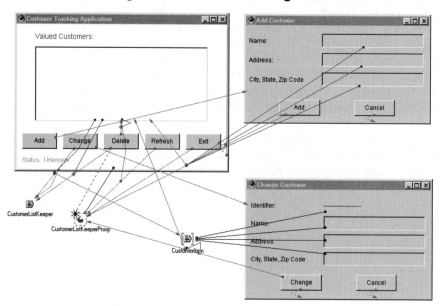

FIGURE 8.9
VCE with Proxy Connections

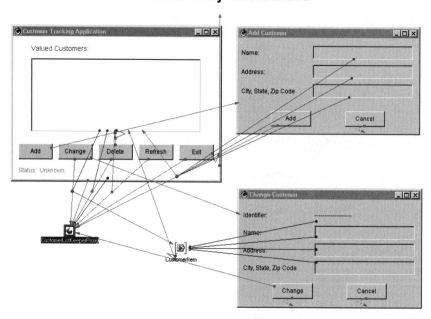

MORPHING

The VCE provides an alternative to relocating connections from the CustomerListKeeper bean to the CustomerListKeeperProxy bean. The technique, called *morphing*, involves using the VCE to automatically transform one bean type into another. Instead of moving the bean connections one at a time, follow these steps to morph the beans:

1. Right-click on the CustomerListKeeper bean on the VCE display. Select the Morph into option from the pop-up menu.

2. In the Morph Into dialog box, replace the default class name with the package-qualified name of the CustomerListKeeperProxy class (e.g., examples.rmi.CustomerListKeeperProxy).

3. Click OK, and the CustomerListKeeper bean is transformed into a CustomerListKeeperProxy bean automatically. All of the pre-existing connections are maintained.

An advantage of morphing is that it lets you quickly change to and from the RMI-enabled design. It is just as easy to morph this application back to the local implementation as it is to morph it into an RMI-enabled application.

SERVER

To use the server classes that VAJ generates, you must create your own "jump start" class. This class simply kicks off the show by creating an instance of the CustomerListKeeperProxyS class. In the Customer Tracking application, the CustomerHostServer contains a **main** method with the following code:

```
CustomerListKeeperProxyS server =
    new CustomerListKeeperProxyS();
```

This code is the only line of handwritten Java code required to implement the server side of the RMI-enabled Customer Tracking application.

DEPLOYMENT

By this point, you've used the RMI-enabled Customer Tracking application and you've learned about the multitude of classes that VAJ generates for you to support RMI. One of RMI's obvious benefits is that remote classes can reside on the server instead of on the client. In the Customer Tracking application, the CustomerListKeeper class, formerly a client-only class, is relocated to the server. It is less obvious where to locate all the proxy classes, interfaces, stubs, and skeletons.

The following application classes are deployed on the client side.

- CustomerItem
- CustomerList
- CustomerTracking

The RMI support classes on the client are listed below.

- CustomerListKeeperProxy
- CustomerListKeeperProxyBeanInfo
- CustomerListKeeperProxy_Skel
- CustomerListKeeperProxy_Stub
- CustomerListKeeperProxyIf
- CustomerListKeeperProxyS_Stub
- CustomerListKeeperProxyjava_beans_PropertyChangeEvent
- CustomerListKeeperProxyPropertyChangeListenerRmiIf

The following application classes reside on the server side.

- CustomerHostServer
- CustomerItem
- CustomerListKeeper

The following supporting RMI classes are on the server side.

- CustomerListKeeperProxyIf
- CustomerListKeeperProxy_Stub
- CustomerListKeeperProxyS
- CustomerListKeeperProxyS_Skel
- CustomerListKeeperProxyS_Stub
- CustomerListKeeperProxyPropertyChangeListenerRmiIf

The RMI model as it is enhanced by VAJ is complicated, but that's the price you pay for ease of programming. In truth, it isn't as baffling as it might first appear, and you can follow some handy guidelines, listed in Table 8.5, that can help you determine where a class or interface should be located in an RMI scenario such as this one.

TABLE 8.5
Guidelines for Class/Interface Deployment

Class/Interface	Location
Server application classes (e.g., CustomerListKeeper)	Reside only on the server.
Client application classes (e.g., CustomerTracking, CustomerList)	Reside only on the client.
Shared application classes	Reside on both client and server. An example of this setup is the CustomerItem class. The CustomerListKeeper class creates customer objects and uses them extensively, but elements of the GUI also use these objects.
The server jump-start class (e.g., CustomerHostServer)	Resides only on the server, as does the class it instantiates, the server-side proxy (e.g., CustomerListKeeperProxyS).
The client-side proxy class	Resides only on the client, along with the associated BeanInfo class. The BeanInfo class is used only at design time.
Interfaces generated by the RMI Access Builder	Reside on both client and server.
Event classes generated by the RMI Access Builder	Reside on the client.
The stub and skeleton for a server class	Reside on the server, with a copy of the stub on the client side.

As with the sockets server example in Chapter 6, you can use the OS/400 Network Status (NETSTAT) command to diagnose connection problems. Using the Network Status display, look for connections on the port where you have the RMI registry listening. You should find client connections on this port as well as the RMI registry "listener."

Appendix A

Installing Example Code

The example code presented in this book is available for you to install from the companion CD-ROM. On a Windows 95/98/NT system, insert the CD-ROM into your reader; an installation screen should appear automatically. Click the Download Example Code label on the installation screen to create directories and files on your local hard drive. Two directories are created for you — c:\book\as400 and c:\book\vaj. Follow the instructions in this appendix to install files from these directories as an AS/400 library and a VisualAge for Java (VAJ) project.

In addition to the book's example code, the CD-ROM contains copies of VAJ Professional Edition and the AS/400 Toolbox for Java. IBM has graciously provided both of these software products in their full versions — these are not limited trial editions. From the installation screen, click the Download IBM VisualAge for Java 2.0 label to install VisualAge for Java Professional Edition on your hard drive. Click the Download IBM AS/400 Toolbox for Java label to install the Toolbox. Review the readme.txt file located in the root directory of the CD-ROM for instructions on adding the Toolbox to your VisualAge for Java workspace.

AS/400 EXAMPLES LIBRARY

By following these instructions, you will create a library called EXAMPLES on your AS/400. In this library, you will find source code and compiled programs representing the server side of the client/server examples found in this book. To successfully complete this installation using these instructions, your Windows 95/98/NT PC must be attached through a TCP/IP connection to your AS/400. To ensure success, perform the installation steps in this section under a user profile with *ALLOBJ (all object) authority.

CAUTION: The programs contained in the EXAMPLES library were compiled to OS/400 version V4R1M0, and the library was saved to this same release. If you are using an earlier version of OS/400, please check the book's software site on the Web at www.29thstreetpress.com/ java400. Watch this same Web site for corrections and additions to the examples.

To install the EXAMPLES library, follow these steps:

1. Locate the examples.lib file in c:\book\as400 on your local hard drive. This file contains a binary representation of the AS/400 library EXAMPLES.

2. From an OS/400 command line, create an empty save file in the QGPL library on your AS/400:

   ```
   CRTSAVF FILE(QGPL/EXAMPLES)
   ```

3. Using Windows FTP file transfer software, send the binary file examples.lib to your AS/400. The following detailed instructions place the contents of the binary file into the save file.

   a. Open a Windows 95/98/NT DOS Prompt. Change your current directory to the c:\book\as400 directory on your local hard drive. (e.g., type *cd\book\as400*). Type *ftp* and press Enter.

   b. Open a connection with your host AS/400 by typing *open 128.1.1.1*, where *128.1.1.1* is the IP address of your AS/400. (Alternatively, you may be able to use your host system name, as in *open MYSYSTEM*.)

   c. Log on to your AS/400 when prompted.

   d. Type *binary* to change the transfer mode to binary.

   e. Type *cd qgpl* to change the remote current directory to the QGPL library.

   f. Type *put examples.lib examples.file* and press Enter. You should see status messages indicating the successful transfer of the file to the host.

   g. Type *quit* and press Enter to end the FTP session. The save file in library QGPL should now be populated with the binary data representing the EXAMPLES library.

4. Restore the EXAMPLES library from the save file:

   ```
   RSTLIB SAVLIB(EXAMPLES) DEV(*SAVF) SAVF(QGPL/EXAMPLES)
   ```

   The full contents of the EXAMPLES library are now restored on your AS/400 and available for your use.

VAJ EXAMPLES PROJECT (PROFESSIONAL EDITION)

These instructions are for users of the VAJ Professional Edition software installed from the CD-ROM accompanying this book. By following these instructions, you will create a project called Examples in your VAJ Workspace. The Examples project contains the example Java applications presented in this book.

CAUTION: Because the Professional Edition of VAJ does not include support for the RMI Access Builder, you will not find the examples.rmi package in the Examples project packaged for VAJ Professional Edition. If you are using VAJ Enterprise Edition, do not follow these installation instructions; instead, refer to the instructions in "VAJ Examples Project (Enterprise Edition)" later in this appendix.

To install the Examples project, follow these steps:

1. Locate the file examples_pro.dat in c:\book\vaj on your local hard drive. This file contains a VAJ project in the Repository format.

2. Import the Examples project into your VAJ repository. The following detailed instructions lead you through the import process:

   a. From the VAJ Workbench menu bar, select File, Import.

   b. On the Import SmartGuide dialog box, choose the Repository format and click Next.

   c. On the "Import from another Repository" dialog box, type the repository name (e.g., c:\book\vaj\examples_pro.dat) and make sure the Projects box is selected.

   d. Click Details to display the available versions of the Examples project. When you select the Examples project from the list, the only available version is selected for you automatically. Click OK to complete the version selection; you are returned to the "Import from another Repository" dialog box.

   e. Click Finish to complete the import.

3. At this point, the Examples project is imported into the VAJ repository. A few more steps are required to make it accessible as an active VAJ project:

   a. From the VAJ Workbench menu bar, select Selected, Add, Project.

   b. On the Add Project SmartGuide dialog box, select the "add projects from the repository" option to display a list of available projects in the repository.

   c. From the list of repository projects, select the Examples project. The only available version of the project is selected for you automatically. Click Finish to add the project to your Workspace.

VAJ Examples Project (Enterprise Edition)

To create the Examples project, users of VAJ Enterprise Edition should import a different repository file than Professional Edition users. The Enterprise Edition version of the Examples project contains the additional package examples.rmi with the complete RMI code from Chapter 8. Also, the Enterprise Edition version of the Examples project is configured to use the Enterprise Toolkit for AS/400, which contains the AS/400 Toolbox for Java.

Before you begin installation, please ensure that the Enterprise Toolkit for AS/400 and Enterprise RMI Access Builder Library projects are in your Workspace. If you install the book's examples without them, your All Problems page will contain a multitude of Java compile errors. If you receive such errors, you can resolve them by adding the Enterprise Toolkit for AS/400 and RMI Access Builder to your workspace after the fact.

To install the Examples project, follow these steps:

1. Locate the file examples_ee.dat in c:\book\vaj on your local hard drive. This file contains a VAJ project in the Repository format.

2. Import the Examples project into your VAJ repository. The following detailed instructions lead you through the import process:

   a. From the VAJ Workbench menu bar, select File, Import.

   b. On the Import SmartGuide dialog box, choose the Repository format and click Next.

   c. On the "Import from another Repository" dialog box, select the Local repository option and type the repository name (e.g., c:\book\vaj\ examples_ee.dat) and make sure the Projects box is selected.

   d. Click Details to display the available versions of the Examples project. When you select the Examples project from the list, the only available version is selected for you automatically. Click OK to complete the version selection; you are returned to the "Import from another Repository" dialog box.

   e. Click Finish to complete the import.

3. At this point the Examples project is imported into the VAJ repository. A few more steps are required to make it accessible as an active VAJ project:

   a. From the VAJ Workbench menu bar, select Selected, Add, Project.

   b. On the Add Project SmartGuide dialog box, select the "add projects from the repository" option. A list of projects available in the repository is displayed for you.

   c. From the list of repository projects, select the Examples project. The only available version of the project is selected for you automatically. Click Finish to add the project to your Workspace.

Appendix B

AS/400 Toolbox for Java PTF Requirements

Before using the AS/400 Toolbox for Java with your AS/400, install the latest cumulative PTF package available for your system. Additionally, insure that the following PTFs are applied.

TABLE B.1
Version 4 Release 3

Licensed Program Product	PTF Number	Description
5769-SS1	SF48498	Support for the Print feature.

TABLE B.2
Version 4 Release 2

Licensed Program Product	PTF Number	Description
5769-SS1	SF46476	Support for the Print feature.
5769-SS1	SF46460	Database server support for the JDBC driver.

TABLE B.3
Version 4 Release 1

Licensed Program Product	PTF Number	Description
5769-SS1	SF42813	Fixes to the Data Queue feature.
5769-SS1	SF41926 SF42518 SF46470	Support for the Print feature.
5769-SS1	SF46499	Database server support for the JDBC driver.
5769-SS1	SF42498	Support for the Record-Level Access feature.

TABLE B.4

Version 3 Release 7

Licensed Program Product	PTF Number	Description
5716-SS1	SF42398	Fixes to the Data Queue feature.
5716-SS1	SF42316 SF42516	Support for the Print feature.
5716-SS1	SF42338	Support for the Record-Level Access feature.

TABLE B.5

Version 3 Release 2

Licensed Program Product	PTF Number	Description
5763-SS1	SF43295	Fixes to the Data Queue feature.
5763-SS1	SF42344 SF42515	Support for the Print feature.
5763-SS1	SF42337	Support for the Record-Level Access feature.

Appendix C

Recommended Reading

Conte, Paul. *Database Design and Programming for DB2/400.* Loveland, Colorado: 29th Street Press, 1997.

Although not overtly targeted to a Java audience, this definitive guide to the AS/400 database is as useful to Java programmers as it is to RPG and Cobol programmers. The author's complete coverage of database features such as SQL/400, commitment control, triggers, and constraints is invaluable when creating robust business applications with Java.

Coulthard, Phil and George Farr. *Java for RPG Programmers.* Palo Alto, California: Advice Press, 1998.

This guide to the Java programming language is aimed at programmers who use the AS/400 and the RPG language today.

Horstmann, Cay S. and Gary Cornell. *Core Java, Volumes I and II.* Upper Saddle River, New Jersey: Prentice-Hall, 1997 (Volume I), 1998 (Volume II).

This is a good guide to the Java programming language, especially for those who already have some experience with a "visual" language, such as Visual Basic or Delphi.

Index

A

Abstract Windowing Toolkit (AWT), 18–19
  defined, 18
  Remote, 18–19, 88
Accessor methods, 27
Add Customer dialog box, 33–34
ADDENVVAR (Add Environment Variable) command, 76, 98
ADDLNK (Add Link) command, 77
ADDRDBDIRE (Add RDB Directory Entry) command, 78–79
Aliases, 97–98
  creating, 97
  list of, 98
  precedence over built-in commands, 106
  removing, 98
Appletviewer command, 88
AS/400 Developer Kit for Java (ADK), 13–20
  AWT, 18–19, 88
  classes, 49
  defined, 13
  JDBC driver, 17
  JNI, 17–18
  JVM, 14–17
  Operations Navigator, 19–20
  overview, 20
  QShell, 17, 81–87
  System Debugger, 18
AS/400 sign-on, 181
AS/400 Toolbox for Java, 20–21, 107–151
  classes, 112
  command call feature, 127–128
  command execution example, 182–184
  data queue example, 193–200
  data queues, 135–142
  database access, 114–127
  database access example, 188–193
  defined, 20
  digital certificates, 151
  examples, 179–202
  getting connected and, 108
  graphical access, 151
  IFS example, 180–182
  IFS feature, 108–114
  JDBC driver, 114–119
  job lists, 149
  message queues, 149–150
  Print feature, 135, 142–147

program call example, 185–188
program call feature, 128–134
record-level access, 119–127
sign-on prompt, 109
spooled file example, 201–202
support, 20
user lists, 148–149
user spaces, 150
user/group list, 148–149
uses, 107
V3R2M0 release features, 20
V3R2M1 release features, 21, 148–151
ZIP/JAR formats, 50

B

Batch immediate (BCI) jobs, 83, 84
Beans
  lookalike, 32
  nonvisual, 30, 32
  properties, 29
  visual, 28–29, 32
Binding, 208
Blocking factor, 121
BREAK command, 70, 71
Breakpoints, 70–71
  deleting, 71
  setting, 70–71
  See also Debugging
Byte arrays, 132–133
  conversion to, 139
  defined, 132
  key value, 141
  retrieving, 132
Bytecode verification, 15

C

CallableStatement class, 119
CD, this book, 2, 26
CD (Current Directory) command, 86
Change Customer dialog box, 34–37
CHGCURDIR (Change Current Directory) command, 51, 51–52
CHKPATH (Classpath Security Level Check) parameter, 64–65
CLASS (Class) parameter, 63–64
Class variables, 9
Class/interface deployment, 221
Classes
  ADK, 49
  CallableStatement, 119
  CommandCall, 127
  CommandExampleGUI, 183
  CommandHelper, 183

Customer, 1–8, 58
CustomerHostServer, 158, 160, 161, 163
CustomerHostSocket, 160, 161, 163, 164
CustomerItem, 26, 27, 35, 160, 161
CustomerList, 160, 161
CustomerListKeeper, 27, 34, 160, 161, 164–166, 211
CustomerListKeeperProxy, 217
CustomerTracking, 28–29, 160, 161, 210
DatabaseExampleGUI, 188
DatabaseHelper, 188
DatabaseMetaData, 119
DataOutputStream, 163
DataQueue, 142
DataQueueEntry, 142
DataQueueExampleGUI, 195
DataQueueHelper, 197, 198
defined, 8
DriverManager, 116–117
execution options, 68
IFSExampleGUI, 180
IFSFile, 109, 110
IFSHelper, 179, 180
IFSInputStream, 114
IFSOutputStream, 114
IFSRandomAccessFile, 114
IFSTextFileInputStream, 110
interpretation, 65–66
KeyedDataQueue, 139
KeyedFile, 120, 125
non-public, 9
ObjectInputStream, 166
ObjectOutputStream, 169, 173
OutputQueue, 145
OutputQueueList, 143
package, 9
PrintObject, 145
ProgramHelper, 187
ProgramParameter, 129–130
proxy, 214
QueueMessage, 150
remote, 219
ResultSetMetaData, 119
running, 185
SimpleIFSExample, 111
specifying, to run, 63–64
SpooledFileExampleGUI, 201
SpooledFileHelper, 201
SpooledFileOutputStream, 145
Toolbox, 112
UnicastRemoteObject, 205
See also Helper classes
CLASSPATH (Classpath) parameter, 64
Classpaths, 64–65
  environment variable, 75–77
  packages and, 160
  security level, 64–65